Franco

African Cinema

ALSO BY K. MARTIAL FRINDÉTHIÉ
AND FROM MCFARLAND

The Black Renaissance in Francophone
African and Caribbean Literatures (2008)

Francophone African Cinema

History, Culture, Politics and Theory

K. Martial Frindéthié

McFarland & Company, Inc., Publishers

Jefferson, North Carolina, and London

Library of Congress Cataloguing-in-Publication Data

Frindéthié, Martial K. (Martial Kokroa), 1961–
   Francophone African cinema : history, culture, politics and
theory / K. Martial Frindéthié.
     p.   cm.
   Includes bibliographical references and index.

   ISBN 978-0-7864-3962-1
   softcover : 50# alkaline paper ∞

   1. Motion pictures — Africa, French-speaking.   2. Motion
pictures — Social aspects — Africa, French-speaking.   3. Motion
pictures — Political aspects — Africa, French-speaking.   4. Culture
conflict in motion pictures.   5. Africa — In motion pictures.
I. Title.
PN1993.5.A35F75   2009
791.43096'0917541 — dc22   2009010119

British Library cataloguing data are available

On the cover: Ivorian filmmaker Sidiki Bakaba during the making
of *La Victoire aux mains nues/Bare Hands Victory* (Abidjan: Kepri
Production, 2005) (Photo by Ayala Bakaba)

Manufactured in the United States of America

McFarland & Company, Inc., Publishers
  Box 611, Jefferson, North Carolina 28640
  www.mcfarlandpub.com

Acknowledgments

This book is the product of a long parturition started years ago, at various sites, in the form of conversations with some of my former professors, of discussions with colleagues, of negotiations with students, and of presentations at expert gatherings. Each one of these engagements has been highly productive in framing, adjusting or improving the arguments of the book. For that I am for ever grateful to all the people who, in one way or another, have contributed to the completion of this work. The ingratitude of fading memory will certainly cause me to fail to remember some of those who have helped me write this book; and many of those whom I recognize here have undoubtedly forgotten the invaluable help they have offered me, as it is their practice to inspire disinterestedly. I particularly would like to acknowledge the contributions of Anthony Appiah, Réda Bensmaïa, Daniel Brewer, Tom Conley, John Mowitt, Jochen Schulte-Sasse, Carla Peterson, and Orrin Wang who, by their rigorous queries, have pushed me to define my own epistemological positioning. I am grateful to Ken Arrow, Aliko Songolo, and Ngugi Wa Thiongo for inspiring me to investigate subject matters in African cinema that are not necessarily evident. Irène Assiba d'Almeïda, Lynn Bolles, Carole Boyce Davies, and Deborah Rosenfelt kept reminded me that *devenir-féminin* is the first cry of the line of flight. Merle Collin encouraged me to seek poetic flows in treatises. I thank them all for their precious insights. Bruce Dick made very useful comments on an early manuscript of this book, and I am extremely thankful to him. I am grateful to Julia Dreesen-Coulibaly for her photos. I am grateful to *Dalhousie French Studies* for allowing chapter 4 of this book, which had been published in vol. 58 of spring 2002 of the journal, to be used again here. Finally, to Mireille Dreesen-Frindéthié and to my students at the University of Maryland and at Appalachian State University who have been so patient as to test all the arguments of this book, though its flaws should be mine alone to assume, you are creators of this book as much as I am.

Contents

Preface

This book makes two fundamental contributions to the field of cultural studies. First, it demonstrates that the subjects of African cinema are existential ones. Consequently, the African filmmaker is a theoretician — a philosopher that creates new concepts (images of thought) or unveils new components of existing concepts. From this perspective, African cinema's contribution to cultural studies and contemporary literary theories deserves more attention. The critic of African cinema ought to be able to set the stage for a conversation between African filmmakers, theoreticians in their own right, and more conventional theorists, such as Hegel, Fanon, Freud, Lacan or Deleuze, whose works are well read in academia. Secondly, the book models an integrative analytical approach for the critic of African cinema. Since African films, rather than allowing viewers to escape the reality of their lives, actually shake viewers up and leave them with deep existential questions to reflect upon, African cinema inevitably ought to be "read" against the backdrop of schools of thoughts, such as structuralism, psychoanalysis, Marxism, postmodernism, feminism, postcolonial theories, but also across disciplines, such as history, archeology, sociology, and the like. Thus, whenever the "reader" of (African) cinema stumbles across ideas, he or she ought to identify them, show how these ideas have reappeared through the tortuous record of the concept, what links they have with other concepts, what new realities they name, and what problems they resolve or pose.

This book comprises nine chapters. The first chapter uses Bassek Ba Kobhio's *The Great White Man of Lambaréné* as a pretext for revisiting Fanon's untimely debate with Hegel in the context of the theory of recognition. The second chapter shows how Saussure's analogy between *chess game* and language reappears in Balufu Kanyinda's *Le damier* and Cheick Oumar Sissoko's *Guimba the Tyrant* for the purpose of assessing the foundational narratives that sustain the countless autocratic regimes of West Africa in particular, and Africa in general. Chapters 3 and 4 argue that there is an *anti-genealogical* inclination in humans; which paradoxically manifests itself as desire for geneal-

1

ogy. Through Karim Dridi's *Bye Bye* and Merzak Allouache's *Bab-El-Oued City*, the third chapter complicates — with a wink of complicity toward Deleuze, Guattari, and Derrida — Lacan's notion of desire, contending that what is expressed at the specular (linguistic) level as *desire of the object* is actually unveiled at the nomadological level (level of movement) as *desire of the opposite object*. Using Cheick Oumar Sissoko's *Finzan* and Amadou Seck's *Saaraba,* chapter 4 further elucidates this enigma by showing the central role of the Ideological State Apparatus in writing *desire of the opposite object* as *desire of the object*. In the fifth chapter, I argue that Ousmane Sembène's and Ngangura Mweze's attempts to speak for woman, respectively in *Faat Kiné* and *La vie est belle,* amount to writing a *soxual order,* that is, a gendered organization of sex and society that consolidates the hold of patriarchy. In chapter 6, Nouri Bouzid's *Bent Familia* and Mufida Tlatli's *The Silences of the Palace* permit me to make the case that the *soxual order* designed by man for the confinement of woman has turned against the former as the machinery of his own incarceration. In chapter 7, Dani Kouyaté's *Keita: The Heritage of the Griot* is a starting block for exploring the cultures and civilizations of pre-colonial Africa, its technological inventiveness, its commercial, political, labor, and social organizations, its population movements, sexual symbolisms, religious/ritualistic practices, all against the backdrop of prevalent Eurocentric claims of pre-colonial Africa as a barren land on all fronts of human ingenuity. Chapters 8 and 9 tackle the subject of globalization, a much heralded theme of the twenty-first century. After showing that globalization is no novel occurrence, these two chapters examine the fallouts for Côte d'Ivoire and for the Congo of the phenomenon, respectively through Sidiki Bakaba's *Bare Hands Victory* and Raoul Peck's *Lumumba*. Students and teachers of culture studies, history, political science, literatures, and sociology will find this book extremely useful. They will find in it, not just sporadic references to their fields of study, but rather, profound discussions of topics relevant to their practices.

Introduction

Engaging African Cinema

The aim of the present book is twofold. First, the book sets a stage for a critical encounter between Francophone African cinema and Continental European critical theory. This meeting, I hope, will allow for a greater appreciation of the often implicit — and, perhaps, untimely — conversations that take place between African filmmakers, unorthodox theoreticians, and the more conventional (Western) theorists whose works are very much part of the American university curricula. Second, the book puts together an understanding of African civilizations, cultures, and political imagination by working with interdisciplinary tools. By cross analyzing Francophone cinematic metaphors with other filmic, literary, historical, ethnographic, archeological, and scientific evidence, the second part of this book elucidates for teachers and students of cultures some tangible aspects of Sub-Saharan Africa.

Thanks to the great archeological and historical insights of such precursory studies as written by Soumanou Vieyra, Manthia Diawara, and Nwachukwu Ukadike — to cite only these few — an excellent body of literature is now available to researchers concerned with understanding the long and meandering evolution of African cinema. Nevertheless, there remains a demonstrable paucity of African film studies whose primary concern is less about periodizing than about exploring the conceptual connections between African cinema and contemporary literary theory and political imagination. Furthermore, within cultural studies as a discipline, African cinema has generally not known the academic fervor that has examined the various links between African written literatures and Continental European critical theory. Still owing to a traditional partition of written texts and visual arts, many instructors persist in restricting films, especially African films, to departments of history and anthropology, where they are usually analyzed as artifacts for comprehending "strange" communities, their births, and their social institutions. Such a museumification of African cinema, one could also argue, has

3

been partly encouraged by African filmmakers themselves, as they have sometimes contributed to the prevailing Firstworldist, exoticist conception of their
works.

By and large, African filmmakers have a tendency to perceive the body
their works as an *art engagé* whose ambition, like the purpose of the kind of
protest literature that emerged in the late 1930s in the black quarters of Paris
(Negritude), is to avert the generalized Eurocentric depiction of human experiences propagated by what Keyan G. Tomaselli has named "the dream factory," that is, Western movies.[1] African filmmakers have generally insisted that
their works should be both nationally and globally committed to addressing
African peoples' specific ontological, economic, political and social concerns.
Thus in "What is Cinema for Us?" Med Hondo argues that African cinema
should be a tool of defiance and of ontological *re-memorying:* it should help
Africans break the cloak of imperialism and Western cultural hegemony by
recapturing an African personality, collective and private way of life, cultural
code, specific art, way of communicating, and history and civilization.[2]
Hondo's conception of cinema falls within the dictates of the FEPACI (*Fédéra-
tion Panafricaine des Cinéastes*), which stipulated, in its 1975 Algiers Convention, that through their art, African filmmakers should be active in the
anti-imperialist and Pan-Africanist struggle rather than "indulge themselves
in manufacturing films for purely commercial values"—as it is often the case
in Hollywood.[3] Even non-members of the FEPACI seem to agree on the
archeological function assigned to African cinema by African filmmakers.
Thus, for the prolific Nigerian filmmaker, Chief Eddie Ugbomah, for instance,
African films, as part of the general media, should aim at valorizing African
cultures and promoting the consumption of local goods and the appreciation
of local governments' programs. "The media has enormous educational and
propaganda potential. The government can use the media to tell the people
to buy Nigerian, to be proud of Nigeria. It can communicate that it is cheaper
to grow their own rice rather than importing it. Through movies, we can start
eliminating those canker worms, tribalism and religion."[4] Similarly, Martin
Mhando and Tomaselli, have maintained that African films are unique aes-
thetically and stylistically; that unlike their Hollywood counterparts, they are
"stories that tell rather than products that sell," and should therefore be
approached from a unique African perspective, an outlook that focuses less
on contents and takes more into account the essential underlying formal structures of African films.

> [T]he combination of idealism and pedagogy found in the African film neces-
> sitates a re-questioning of aesthetics and praxis of African cinema narration
> ... "conventional theories" are insufficient and inadequate to explain [the
> African] materialist aesthetics of reality.... Even African film critics [and

filmmakers] continue to look at cinema in Africa from a continental perspective ... [which] often undermines their very conceptual positions: the iconog-
raphy, grammar and metaphors of colonial "education" already unwittingly
taint their perspective.[5]

The role of the African film critic, Mhando contends, is to unearth that formal structure. Mhando's recommendations are not only intended for the film
critic. They also concern the African filmmaker, as he suggests that the latter should always seek to work from within a cultural center, a "localised
global view" as the "focus of the highest loyalty."[6]

Beyond these prescriptive attempts, which for a long time have justified
a Firstworldist exoticist approach to African films, I contend that cultural
studies, as a discipline, must engage African cinema. It must do so no longer
through some exoticizing prism but rather through cross-fertilizing analytical lenses, that is to say, against the backdrop of such schools of thoughts as
structuralism, psychoanalysis, Marxism, postmodernism, feminism, postcolonial theories, and queer theories. I believe that such a reading of African cinema will be advantageous in two ways. Firstly, it will allow a de-stigmatization,
a de-exoticization of African cinema and a better understanding of its thematic and theoretical richness. Secondly, the growing pool of African films
will indubitably provide teachers and students of cultural studies alike an
invaluable collection of variegated reading resources upon which to draw.
Cultural studies has much to gain by *reading* African films against — or in the
tradition of— contemporary theory. I am aware of the controversy that the
notions of "theory" and "reading cinema" are likely to bring about.[7] As regards
the metaphor of reading cinema some critics may take issue with it, arguing
that such imagery disguises an overvaluation of literacy over orality/aurality.
Others might argue that film is not an idiom similar to spoken and written
languages are; therefore, to suggest that film can be read as easily as any spoken or written text obliterates its singular and complex syntax.[8]

I do not believe this to be an issue, especially in an era where the image
is increasingly becoming print and vice versa. Furthermore, one has to see
how much space is allocated to print on a television screen to understand that
screening has become reading. Viewing — especially viewing a foreign movie —
means more and more straining one's eyes on the fleeting letters at the bottom of the screen; which is even more factual for most of the movies that I
set about to discuss in this work, as they are subtitled from African languages
or Arabic into Anglo-Saxon languages. Nonetheless, my metaphor of reading
films is less to suggest the foreign viewer's activity of chasing the inevitable
subtitles of a Senegalese, Tunisian or an Ivorian film than closely analyzing
it, that is, in the tradition of literary criticism. The kind of cinema reading
that I propose in the present study is one that involves two simultaneous oper-

ations that I see as equally important: on the one hand, a traditional plot summary, which is intended to introduce the readers, many of whom may not have seen the movies in question, with the important protagonists and the chain of events that together make up the skeleton of the films and, on the other hand, a theoretical interpretation, the purpose of which is to explicate particular events in the light of larger theoretical questions confronting thinkers of all horizons and times. I hope to show through my analyses of specific African films that there exists an underlying conversation between the African filmmaker and the conventional theorist; a dialogue that is not always recognized because of the minor importance that is accorded to (black) visual art (often regarded in academia as belonging to the realm of low culture). Thus this work is an interpretative one, in the tradition of Noël Carroll; that is, interpretation as "countenancing all sorts of explanations, including also functional and causal ones."[9] It is from this perspective, one which is less concerned with classification of African cinema than with an exploration at the interface of a limited number of black French films and contemporary literary theories, an exploration that will also indicate my own reflection about the films I deal with, that I hope to add a novel contribution to the growing field of African cinema studies.

1

"There Is No Conversation Here, My Boy"

Spectral Returns of Fanon and Hegel in Bassek Ba Kobhio's The Great White Man of Lambaréné

All we can do is to allow others to discover us, as we discover them.
— Albert Schweitzer

Five decades ago, Frantz Fanon reframed the African and Caribbean liberation discourses by engaging Georg Wilhelm Friedrich Hegel, the father of the theory of phenomenology, more than a century after the latter's death. Taking to task Hegel's ethics of mutual recognition in the master/slave dialectic, Fanon argued that Hegel's theory contained a denial of the notion of racial difference; and Fanon emphasized the necessity for blacks to take into account their unique historical and biological attributes as they fight for freedom.[1] Today, globalization has become a buzzword that is often used with the assumption that industrialized and underdeveloped countries are engaged in sincere and mutual exchanges. The reality is that developed countries have often betrayed this idea of reciprocity by undermining the independence of Third World nations and by setting off instability and chaos in these nations in order to better exploit their resources. The euphoria about globalization risks leaving unquestioned the long history of Western powers' ideological duplicity and its ensuing cost of economic and social disparities between industrialized and Third World countries. For Fanon, the equation is simple: Industrialized countries and Third World countries represent, respectively, the world of the whites and that of the blacks. Whites can be sincere about goals and objectives when they talk among themselves. However, when they speak with blacks about the same issues, they talk *to* or *at* the latter, instead,

7

in a posture that leaves no doubt as to their sense of superiority and disingenuousness and makes no room for empathy.

As if he wanted to warn that any complacent optimism about the relationships between industrialized and Third World countries should be tempered with a dose of historical reality, the Cameroonian filmmaker Bassek Ba Kobhio restates Fanon's position in a filmic gesture that pits the colonizer against the soon-to-be decolonized. In his film, *The Great White Man of Lambaréné*, Ba Kobhio objects to the iconic representation of Dr. Albert Schweitzer, who is regarded throughout Europe as a benefactor of the wretched people of Africa.[2] From the filmmaker's standpoint, Schweitzer is less the much admired white philanthropist immortalized in *History* as written by the West than he is the symptom of Europe's failure to understand otherness. For Ba Kobhio, Schweitzer represents a metaphor of white Europe's hope to gain paradise by sharing the hell of the non-white other. In a sense, from the filmmaker's point of view, Schweitzer's work in Africa was prompted more by his yearning for expiation than by a sincere desire to help an equal other.

On the surface, Ba Kobhio's choice of Albert Schweitzer for his treatment of the colonial mentality seems unfair. By most accounts, Dr. Schweitzer was a flawless individual who sacrificed his life for the wretched people of Gabon; therefore, he could only draw praise for his actions. Born on January 14, 1875, in German-occupied Alsace, Albert Schweitzer grew up under the rigid religious discipline of his father, Charles Schweitzer, a reverend and a teacher; later, when came time for Young Albert to go to grammar school, his parents placed him under the regimented watch of his uncle, Louis Schweitzer. At the age of fifteen, the young Albert, who had studied music with Eugene Münch, could master the organ well enough to play it in the church of Saint-Étienne. He gave his first public concert at the age of sixteen. Determined to pursue his knowledge in music and religion, Albert Schweitzer registered as a student in music, philosophy, and religion at the Universities of Strasbourg and Berlin. In 1899 and 1900, respectively, he obtained his doctorate degrees in philosophy and theology. From 1902 to 1912, he taught the New Testament in the Department of Protestant Theology of Strasbourg. In 1913, at the age of thirty, Albert Schweitzer answered the call of the *Société des missions évangéliques de Paris* in search of volunteer doctors. He then went back to school to become a medical doctor. Eight years later, he obtained his doctorate degree in medicine and chose to serve in Africa. On April 16, 1913, the young Doctor Schweitzer arrived in Lambaréné, Gabon, with his Jewish-German wife, Hélène Bresslau, whom he had married almost a year earlier, on June 18, 1912. Albert Schweitzer's dedication to fighting malaria, leprosy and other tropical diseases in Gabon won him the recognition of the Nobel institution, which awarded him the Nobel Peace Prize in 1952. In 1957, he was inducted into the French Academy. Assisted by his wife, one young Swiss doctor, and two other nurses, Schweitzer continued to care for the people of Gabon, and he kept publishing and playing at concerts to fund his hospital until his death in 1965. Today, Doctor Schweitzer's legacy still stands in Lambaréné, four-hour drive from Libreville, Gabon. It is a hospital of about 200 beds, where approximately 650 infants are delivered each year.[3]

For the filmmaker to have made Schweitzer the scapegoat of European racism would therefore seem inexcusable. Yet, Schweitzer's professed discovery of alterity has much to teach us about the colonial idea of discovery of the other. Within the colonial racial logic, the "discovered" other figures as a soulless and shapeless object of experimentation to be manipulated and transformed at will. Albert Schweitzer is a metaphor of the gaze that the Western Scientific communities direct at Africans when Africa becomes a blank canvas of experimentation. In this sense, Schweitzer is no saint; and if Ba Kobhio is able to dig up evil in the apparently most irreproachable of men, what is there to say about the ordinary lot?

"There is no conversation here my boy"

At the beginning of Ba Kobhio's *The Great White Man of Lambaréné*, the white doctor, Schweitzer (André Wilms), and Koumba (Christophe Kpomassi as yound Koumba), a child from the village of Lambaréné, are standing on the bank of a river, scrutinizing the horizon, as if they were both expecting the same event. Then Koumba looks at the doctor and observes, disappointed, "There is no medicine, Doctor!" The doctor makes no reply. He does not even look at the boy. His eyes remain set on the horizon until the scene changes. The white doctor's lack of interest in the African boy so eager to speak with him, his posture that seems to say, "there is no conversation here, my boy," is characteristic of the racial tensions visible throughout the movie and anticipated by the failed dialogue that takes place between Koumba and the doctor a few moments later. In fact, as the two protagonists are returning to the village, the doctor, who is leading the way, casting intermittent glances at the child walking in his footsteps, suddenly stops; he turns around and looks down at the boy behind him. As if this were an invitation to speak, Koumba announces:

> When I grow up, I'm going to practice medicine like you."
> "As a nurse, like your father?" the doctor asks.
> "A nurse? No! I want to be a doctor," the child replies.
> "A doctor!" the man interjects, with a snicker, resuming his walk.

"What's so funny?" the boy inquires.

"Africa needs farmers, carpenters and nurses, not doctors."

Visibly saddened, the child stops and watches the doctor move down the path alone. The doctor lures a baby chimpanzee with a piece of candy and very affectionately picks up the animal, which climbs up his shoulders. Then, calling Koumba over, he reaches into his pocket and hands the child the same treat. These opening scenes of *The Great White Man of Lambaréné* illustrate what Fanon had decried in *Black Skin, White Masks* (1967) as the lack of reciprocity in Hegel's theory of recognition; especially as that theory is applied to the East/West relationships.[4]

Hegel on Trial at Lambaréné

In describing what happens when two or more individuals meet, Hegel hypothesizes that their encounters are necessarily structured around as many consciousnesses as these individuals represent. Each meeting between individuals, he argues, is the meeting of the consciousnesses of these individuals battling to the death for self-affirmation. For instance, in dialogical situations, the process of self-affirmation implies the clashing of the consciousness of one interlocutor against the consciousness of another interlocutor. However, Hegel insists that in a situation where several consciousnesses are vying for recognition, there is also a certain reciprocity, whereby any consciousness can only be fully recognized if, and only if, it first recognizes the consciousness that is its opposite. Nevertheless, this conditionality — the fact that for their own recognition consciousnesses have to first recognize the consciousness that opposes them — does not preclude individual consciousnesses from remaining distinct from the ones they are competing against. This is a complex relationship, as consciousnesses are discreet or disconnected, and, at the same time, mutually dependent upon one another. This complexity is, however, essential for the *subjective integrity* of individual consciousnesses throughout the process of recognition. Hegel cautions that the arena for the life-and-death struggle, which brings the subjects' "certainty of themselves, the certainty of being for themselves, to the level of objective truth," should remain purely *metaphysical*, rather than *physical*, that is, philosophical rather than material. The struggle for recognition by which one consciousness has to die in order for its opposite to be acknowledged takes place at the level of imagination and not at the level of reality.[5] How can it be explained that one can kill one's opposite without really killing it, and why is it crucial for an individual that what is killed as his or her opposite should, at the same time, be let to survive?

German philosopher Georg Wilhelm Friedrich Hegel (1770-1831) posited in *The Phenomenology of Spirit* that any intersubjective relationship entails two or more consciousnesses vying for recognition; consciousnesses which ultimately recognize one another as equal.

For Hegel, subjects attain recognition through three stages; which are consecutively, *being-in-itself*, *being-for-itself*, and finally, *being-in-and-for-itself*. The first phase, or being-in-itself, is a subjective consciousness. It is a moment that lacks truth. The stage of being-in-itself concerns the subject who has not yet understood the necessity of engaging his or her other, and thus fails to acknowledge his or her connection with that other to whom he or she belongs as a part. This first consciousness, the consciousness of being-in-itself, is narcissistic and desire-driven. According to Hegel, any individual that has not yet engaged his or her other, that is, any individual that "has not staked [his or her] life, may no doubt be recognized as a person; but [he or she] has not attained the truth of this recognition as an independent self-consciousness."[6] However, if that first consciousness, being-in-itself, comes to the realization of its imaginary nature and acknowledges the need to gain objectivity through the other, by engaging the other, by staking its life in a struggle against the other, by fighting the other to death, then it has attained the second level of recognition; which is being-for-itself.[7] The third and final moment of recognition will be attained, provided both consciousnesses involved in the intersubjective relationship not only understand the importance of the other consciousness to their own objective existence, but also, and most importantly, recognize the survival of the other consciousness to their own existence. Hegel named the process that makes it possible, during the process of recognition, to kill the other consciousness while, at the same time, and for the sake of one's own survival, keeping it alive, *sublation*. Sublation is an operation that preserves the lives of all the consciousnesses involved in the struggle for absolute recognition insofar as these consciousnesses need one another for their individual survival. Sublation is a method of cancellation and retention whereby, by canceling his or her otherness, the subject both ascertains his or her own distinctiveness from the other, and releases the other to go free, emancipating, henceforth, this part of himself or herself that is inevitably in the other consciousness. If for the sake of his or her own certainty the subject *must* sublate the other, nevertheless — and since the subject cannot objectively attain affirmation without the other — sublating the other also amounts to canceling himself or herself. Therefore, the subject *should* let the other go free so that he or she can be free, too, through the other's freedom: "For, just as life is the natural 'position' of consciousness ... death is the natural 'negation' of consciousness...."[8] So, according to Hegel, in the master/slave relationship, the consciousness of the master depends on the consciousness of the slave for recognition; and the consciousness of the slave depends on the consciousness of the master for recognition; thus the interdependence of the master's and the slave's consciousnesses. The implication of this reciprocity is that the master's power is also the power of the slave since that power depends for its affirmation on a mutual act of recognition between the master and the slave.[9] This interdependence of consciousnesses explains the importance, for Hegel, of the metaphysical, rather than the physical, nature of the "life-and-death struggle" for recognition.

As one can see, the Hegelian "double meaning" of consciousness — one's consciousness as necessarily contingent upon the other's consciousness — is lacking in the relationship between the doctor and Koumba — and, correlatively, in the larger dialectic of which these two characters are metaphors. The doctor's behavior with his patients, the blacks among whom he has lived for so many years, is wicked and paternalistic. In *The Great White Man of Lambaréné*, Doctor Schweitzer's refusal to confront Koumba's gaze on the bank of the river and his brushing off Koumba's professional aspirations as mere indigenous fantasizing are symptoms of his recurrent failure to engage alterity, to recognize in the other that part of himself of which Hegel speaks in his *Phenomenology*. In his relationship with the blacks, the doctor remains solipsistically shut within himself, his gaze perpetually turned toward white Europe; thus allowing no possibility of any reciprocal engagement with blacks. Each time the local drumbeats fill the nights of Lambaréné, it is as if the doctor were being drawn into a world of dementia, as if the monstrous spirits in the "heart of darkness," to use this regrettable expression by Joseph Conrad, were taking over his reason. So, in order to preserve his sanity, the doctor rushes to his piano and launches into a feverish *solo concerto*, in the hope of exorcising the sounds of Africa with those of Europe.

The idea of Europe is not just one of psychological solace; Europe is also a notion of physical relief. Thus, to his ailing wife (played by Marisa Benrenson), who insists on staying by his side rather than going to Europe for a cure, the doctor offers an imaginary concert, such as those available in big European capitals. "I would like to give you a concert to remember," he says, "London, Madrid, Berlin, and now ... Lambaréné." As the doctor gambols on the beach, leading his wife by the hand and pretending to be a conductor, she happily imagines that they have a whole modern orchestra playing before them. If the doctor has failed to find peace and serenity in Lambaréné, it is less because they are lacking there than because he has never entertained the possibility of adopting what his wife so emphatically calls *les principes indigènes*, that is, indigenous standards, the standards of those who are not "like them."

For Schweitzer—who, in Ba Kobhio's *The Great White Man of Lambaréné*, stands as the ideal metaphor of the imperial imagination—there are two irreconcilable worlds, two species of human beings: whites and blacks. As if at a certain point of human ontological development blacks and whites split and had different evolutions, Schweitzer is convinced that none of the white's invention should carry over to the black's existence, thus displaying a disturbing notion of cultural relativism so prevalent among closet supremacists. Elsewhere, in a much fêted book, *The Psychology of Peoples* (1912), Gustave LeBon, a self-declared advocate of blacks' right to self-determination, made a similar racist argument.[10] Schweitzer seems to share LeBon's argument that whites institutions are ill adapted to blacks, because blacks constitute an inferior race, or at best an exotic one not to temper with, but to preserve as a museum relic. Therefore, in order to keep "[his] primitives" authentic, the doctor will neither use electricity in the hospital and distribute uniforms to the black staff nor observe the basic rules of hygiene. Furthermore, during his unethical scientific experiment, he keeps the blacks' hopes high on placebo and gets rid of the anesthetics donated to the hospital, preferring to perform painful surgery on them, arguing that one day, "[his] research will provide a native African medicine for [his] primitives."

Schweitzer's biological and cognitive relativism, which he readily justifies as prompted by his love for the natives, is, for the character Mikendi (Gilbert Nguema), nothing more than hypocrisy. Mikendi, the only survivor of a group of young Lambaréné soldiers sent to France to help in the Second World War, has experienced first hand white duplicity. Upon returning from a war they fought for Europe, black soldiers were ignored, while white soldiers were acknowledged and decorated. "The whites," Mikendi declares, "take [the blacks] for complete jerks." Consequently, Mikendi does not believe in the possibility of any genuine dialogue between whites and blacks, because from the white's point of view, the black is not worth engaging; he is subhuman. Mikendi's perspective echoes Fanon's beliefs as they have been expressed in two places, in *Black Skin, White Masks* and in *The Wretched of the Earth*. In the colonial context, whites have never regarded blacks as their equal interlocutors. This is where Fanon finds fault with Hegel's theory of recognition, and especially his theory of sublation.

Fanon's Ethics of Recognition

Fanon's commentary on Hegel's tale of recognition deals primarily with its romantic aspect. Although he retains the fundamental precepts of Hegel's dialectic, Fanon contends that as far as the colonizer/colonized relationship goes, only a violent confrontation between the black and the white, the result of which is the physical elimination — not the metaphysical sublation — of the latter, will allow the former to ascertain his/her being.[11] For Fanon, in the context of French colonization in Africa and the Caribbean, "the master differs basically from the master described by Hegel. For Hegel there is reciprocity; here the master laughs at the consciousness of the slave. What he wants from the slave is not recognition but work."[12] The master does not see the slave as his equal. He does not even see the latter as another human being to engage for recognition. The slave is to the master an animal; he is comparable to a workhorse. This is because in the master's racist imaginary the slave and he are not of the same species. The slave has branched out in his development and has turned into a subhuman, a lobotomized human. In Lambaréné Doctor Schweitzer seemed to subscribe to the argument that the colonial encounter is the meeting of two species of men: the civilized white and the primitive black.

The way Fanon goes about debunking Hegel's theory might seem laden with racist implications. Too much emphasis seems to be put on racial identity by Fanon, who, incidentally, has never been shy of expressing his preference for the black race. Nevertheless, the foundation of Fanon's questioning of Hegel's theory stems less from theoretical apartheid than from the need to rectify an ontological *coup de force* lying at the foundation of Hegel's methodological tool; elsewhere, Fanon has strongly dissociated his discourse from any essentialist rhetoric. He has refused to be "the victim of fraud of a black world" and has wholeheartedly recognized the likelihood that blacks and whites will design a common *telos*. Thus in *Black Skin, White Masks* Fanon hints that the struggle for liberation is more nation-specific than race specific. As he writes about the black liberation struggle in the United States of America, Fanon prophesies the gradual erection of a quilting point, a healing monument, rising out of a surrealist and expressionist tableau of torn battlefield, white teeth, black limbs, and howling voices. "On the field of battle, its four corners marked by scores of Negroes hanged by their testicles, a monument is slowly being built that promises to be majestic. And, at the top of this monument, I can already see a white man and a black man *hand in hand*."[13] Nevertheless, as soon as he puts forth his conciliatory vision, Fanon retracts it, announcing that this common understanding will only emerge from violent physical confrontation rather than through mere metaphysical annulment and retention of what is negated, as has argued Hegel.

For Fanon, what is at stake in the failed encounter between the colonizer and the colonized is a system of signs that irremediably loads the dice at the expense of the colonizer. In the black/white relationship, the white is necessarily engaged not with anyone else, but with himself, this by virtue of the language that he has shaped to his advantage and to the detriment of the black. Although a metaphysical engagement between a German and another German or a French and another French — and correlatively a white and another white — is more likely to lead to mutual objective recognition in the Hegelian sense of the term, in the black/white encounter, the black is to the white an *always already absent other*. Fanon shows how, in the black/white relation, Hegel's battleground for recognition, the (un)conscious(ness) is never neutral, but always structured like (the white's) language.[14] From this perspective, Fanon's criticism of Hegel is psychoanalytical, and precisely Lacanian.[15] Fanon seems to argue that if the battleground for recognition must be consciousness, then the black colonized will never reach out to real objective self since the black's consciousness is always already the consciousness of the white, shaped by the white, or by the white man's language. Accepting the Lacanian premise that Language illustrates the structure of the unconscious, Fanon argues that for the black, "...to speak, is to exist absolutely for the other," that is, in the *other's* symbolic order.[16] In the colonies, race is a barrier that prevents reciprocity. The white master sees himself as superior, and the black slave's attempt to engage the white in mutual recognition appears as a quest for lactification or whiteness. That quest is unachievable. On the one hand, blackness is biological and unalterable. On the other hand, in the white's imaginary-ideal — deeply ingrained in the white's personal convictions and private communications — the docile black person, who indulges in the rhetoric of mutual understanding between white and black, assimilation and non-violent transition from slavery and bondage to freedom and independence, will always remain an inferior and childlike character. So from whatever angle one looks at it, reciprocity is impossible in the master/slave relationship. In Martinique, where blacks have been assimilated as French, the prospect of rectifying the prejudice of colonization is bleak. The Martinican black has accepted a "false freedom" disguised as integration. Because he/she was not able to denounce the violence that presupposes this "false" autonomy, the Martinican has undermined the possibility of his/her "absolute" independence. Confrontation is what the black from Martinique — and by extension the black French — needs: "The former slave needs a challenge to his humanity; he wants a conflict, a riot. But it is too late: The French Negro is doomed to bite himself and just bite."[17] For the former slave, Martinique will never be a true home; the supposed freedom that the colonizer offered the colonized on a silver plate will never be an authentic one. Fanon contends that the people colonized by the French, who have accepted freedom, as a gift from the colonizing father, will never again experience this Kierkegaardian dread of liberty that keeps self-determination alive. Fanon himself came face to face with his shattered dream of emulating the white father. He realized his illusory certitude of being French when, once in Paris, he became the object of prying and suspicious white gazes. He became convinced that for blacks to achieve full self-determination, for them to exorcise this depersonalized self full of French dreams, they will have to resort to physical violence, a violence which is purgative, unifying, and restorative:

> The mobilization of the masses, when it arises out of the war of liberation, introduces into each man's consciousness the ideas of a common cause, of a national destiny, and of a collective history ... the native's violence unifies the people. At the level of individuals, violence is a cleansing force. It frees the native from his inferiority complex and from his despair and inaction; it makes him fearless and restores his self-respect.[18]

More than a simple means to win a strategic war, violence is for Fanon a factor of *becoming*. It marks the beginning of a process whereby the ugly ones evolve into the beautiful ones, whereby "the last become the first," the proletariat matures into the ruling class, the slave develops as his own master. Violence, Fanon contends, frees, purifies, revives, and binds the people. Violent confrontation takes the oppressed to new heights, to new appreciation of themselves, and to self-consciousness.[19]

In *The Great White Man of Lambaréné*, Mikendi decides to implement Fanon's program of absolute violence and *tabula rasa*. However, it is clear that violence is not inherently black, as the hot-tempered Mikendi's call to violence hits a snag among the people of Lambaréné, and especially among the women of the community, who have been more tolerant of the whites' eccentricities than the men. Bissa (Magali Berdy), the native girl that the local chief has given to Schweitzer to alleviate the latter's lonely nights in the absence of his wife, epitomizes the patience of the women of Lambaréné toward the whites. Like the African land she metaphorizes, Bissa has been indiscriminately hospitable and receptive to the whites, who, in order to have control over her, have not hesitated to stake their lives in a trial by death against one another. As one would expect from Mikendi, perhaps, Fanon's mouthpiece, Bissa's generosity toward the whites is a betrayal against her entire race. Mikendi and most of the black men in the village consider the Europeans' lack of sensitivity to be an assault on their masculinity and their pride.

In fact, a local chief from a neighboring village, who has been under the doctor's care for a while, is unaware that he does not have much longer to live. Despite the doctor's numerous years spent among the blacks, he has failed to understand the importance, for a chief, of dying an honorable death, of facing his death with dignity in a festive atmosphere, surrounded by his subjects. To remedy the doctor's intercultural ineptitude, his aid, Lambi (Marcel Mvondo), takes it upon himself to break the grave news to the chief, so that the latter can go home and "prepare for the great journey." When the chief learns that the doctor has "betrayed" him, and that Schweitzer was planning to let death surprise him, he collapses. Furious, the doctor strikes Lambi, who falls to the ground, in front of his son, Koumba, and the whole village. When the men of the village witness Doctor Schweitzer pushing his contempt for the black people one step too far by striking a black man, they realize that it is time to strike back. This slap to a black man is one instance too many of the humiliation and injustice done to blacks in general, and, particularly, to the strong heterosexual black males, who, in the Fanonian conception of the liberation struggle, are considered the pillars of the black revolution. Owing to this conviction, Fanon had condemned the black woman/white man intimate relationship as an act of high treason from the black woman; the mere desire of a black woman to whiten her race, which carries the damaging consequence of undermining the struggle for racial freedom. "[T]he race must be whitened; every woman in Martinique knows this, says it, repeats it. Whiten the race, save the race, but not in the sense that one might think: not 'preserve the uniqueness of the part of the world in which they grew up,' but make sure that it will be white."[20]

The *homosocial* nature of Fanon's revolutionary discourse, whose traces persist in Mikendi's own words, has been criticized in many places. Lola Young, for instance, denounced Fanon's position for prefiguring women within an economy of pathology. She decried the fact that black women in particular are, more often than black men, portrayed as the betrayers of the race. In "Missing Persons: Fantasizing Black Women in Black Skin, White Masks," Young argued that, although Fanon's depiction of black women through the Martinican Mayotte Capécia's *Je suis martiniquaise*[21] could be interpreted as a textual hyperbole whose purpose is to shock, "[his] unforgiving analysis of [Capécia]" still gives away his inclination to probe her unconscious, "even without access to her dreams," as the desire of every Martinican woman to whiten the race.[22] Likewise, bell hooks confesses that while Fanon remains, along with Memmi, Cabral, Freire and Malcom X, the "intellectual parents [who] nurtured [her] emergent radical subjectivity," Fanon is, at the same time, a thinker in whose works she perceives a "profound lack of recognition of the presence of the mothering body, of the female body that thinks." It is perhaps this "symbolic matricide"—the fact that Fanon seems to suggest that "all will be well when men are able to reach a level ... of homosocial ... of homophilia: love of men for men, but more profoundly, love of the same"—that precipitated her own conversion into feminist politics as "a journey for the recovery of the mother's body."[23] Like hooks, Kobenan Mercer reads Fanon as not only guilty of suppressing the female body, but also of conferring upon an idealized, essentialized, and fixed-black-heterosexual-male the characteristics of a Master-Signifier.[24]

In Mikendi's revolution, as in Fanon's, women are merely portrayed as marginal characters. When Mikendi decides during a gathering of the men of Lambaréné to make Doctor Schweitzer pay for his insolence and to take back the village, he has everything planned, and the roles distributed among the men, reserving for himself the most crucial aspects of the revolution, that of educating Koumba (the ambassador of the rising generation) and policing the village. Koumba, Mikendi announces, will go to the white man's land as soon as the next day to study in order to become a doctor, a black doctor for the black people, so that no white would ever again raise his hands against a black. In the meantime, all the vestiges of the black's belittlement, derogation, humiliation, and disparagement, which are monumentalized in Doctor Schweitzer's hospital, will be brought down. Koumba should come back not merely as another doctor willing to occupy the white doctor's seat, but rather as a metaphor for a new breed of black leaders, particularly of black male leaders, who will erect upon the ashes of the abusive, self-centered, self-indulgent, narcissistic name-of-the-white-father, the edifice of black pride, betterment, and national development.

In *The Great White Man of Lambaréné*, Ba Kobhio seems to challenge the Fanonian discourse on gender, particularly Fanon's condemnation of the black woman's involvement with white men. Bissa did not initiate her relationship with Schweitzer. The village chief gave her to the doctor. If Bissa serves as a metaphor of the African continent, then there is also the suggestion in Ba Kobhio's film that she is less to blame for the demise of Africa than the indulgent male monarchs who gave her away. While a more daring and controversial analysis of Ba Kobhio's film could start to pose the often avoided question of the role of black people in the abominable slave trade, an immediate, or perhaps preliminary, reading of the film could yield the filmmaker's contention that there has not only been an unfair balance of political power among genders in Africa, but also that the (masculine) gender in power has valued the other gender as mere commodity, failing thereby to take advantage of the great insights that women could have contributed to emancipation and development.

In *Femmes aux yeux ouverts* (1994) (translated in English as *Women with Open Eyes*), a documentary produced by the Togolese filmmaker Anne Laure Folly, a female political activist from Mali makes the same point, arguing that some fundamental differences in the ways men and women tend to conduct politics do exist. Women in politics, she contends, possess a greater understanding of the issues at hand, as they tend to appeal more to their maternal instincts, whereas men tend to be driven by their desire for power and their inclination to use violence as a means of solving crises.[25] In *The Great White Man of Lambaréné*, it is clear that Mikendi is not ready to accept Bissa's suggestion of resolving the natives' crisis with the whites through civil engagement. For Mikendi, only violence will drive away the white invaders, assuage the humiliation suffered by the blacks over the years, and open the door for real independence for the natives.

Is Mikendi not Fanon's alter ego? Did Fanon not maintain that for the wretched of the earth, that is, the historically enslaved, colonized, and subjugated blacks, freedom always implies violence; that true independence presupposes a program of absolute disorder, the replacement of the old order by a new one, a total substitution, without transition, without rational engagement, without friendly understanding? For Mikendi, despite the blacks' so-called political independence, Koumba's successful studies in Europe and his return to Lambaréné as a doctor, and despite the fading authority of the white doctor, as long as Schweitzer or any vestige of his presence remains in Lambaréné, black independence will amount to mere illusion. When Mikendi decides he should be the one to complete the revolution which will make way for absolute autonomy for the blacks by burning down Doctor Schweitzer's hospital, he is fulfilling Fanon's prophecy that the "thing" which has been colonized will become man through the same violent revolution by which it frees itself.[26]

Today, almost five decades after Fanon's death, the Martinican-born writer continues to engender controversies. His ghost still hovers over post-independence and post-plantation debates. For some scholars, he is a theorist and a performativist of liberation; for others, he is a proselytizer of homosociality. Either way, there are some lessons to be learned from Fanon's emancipation discourse. The Cold War is over, and the Eastern bloc has fallen. Since capitalist powers in the Western world no longer fear that the oppressed minorities will capitulate into the camp of Communist forces, they can afford to drag their feet in instituting international justice. In fact, a new Western doctrine with the pompous designation of globalization has replaced the more openly brutal policy of colonization. Nevertheless, the effects of this new doctrine are almost as destructive for Third World countries as those of colonization.[27] The way the black continent will defeat this new tentacular monster is not clear yet. The way it has defeated the monster that preceded it has proven, for the most part, efficacious. In that, Fanon is just as relevant today as he was at the time he wrote his two seminal books. His truth is a disturbing one. If blacks in a country such as South Africa, for instance, had only relied upon the *good will* of whites, would things have changed? If blacks had not, through violent confrontation, made the country less hospitable to international business, and therefore, less profitable for blacks, who never had anything to lose, and for whites, who had everything to lose, would black and white South Africans be sitting at the same table today? There are still many Doctor Schweitzers today who, like ostriches, prefer to hide their heads in the sand of ontological relativism rather than acknowledge their own inadequacies.

On the other hand, what would Fanon's reaction be, were he brought back to life in what he regarded as the quintessential nation; that is, Algeria, the nation to whose freedom he devoted his life, or to the Congo, a nation whose future he saw as inspiring for the whole colonized world? Today, Algeria and the Congo are torn by wars that they wages more against themselves than against imperialist powers, though the origin of the Algerian and Congolese quagmires are very much imputable to insatiable Western powers. If the numerous post–colonial civil wars in Africa are indicative of a syndrome of violence that encourages those holding the machetes, the sticks, the stones, and the gun, in their quest for recognition, to turn violence against their own kind, the hand of the perlocutioner, that is, the hand that makes the hand that holds the gun hold the gun, is as evil as the hand of the executioner.

Ba Kobhio's film is, in this sense, neither a mere regurgitation of Fanon's discourse, for the sake of invoking the cult of Fanon, nor a simplistic overturning of historical "reality" in the name of revisionism, but a complex examination of the dilemma confronting post-independence Africa, where no one, be it the colonizer or the colonized, is left totally innocent or totally guilty. Ba Kobhio leaves his viewers with some very pertinent questions to consider. Koumba (Alex Descas as adult Koumba) has returned from France as a doctor; however, he has chosen the path of politics rather than practicing medicine; while this conversion has rendered him incapable of diagnosing the disease of his dying child, Independence, who was so named because he was born on the day of his country's political emancipation from France, it is nonetheless a necessary compromise. Koumba's conversion can hardly be viewed as a brain drain. It is a compelling call. It is his ethical responsibility towards his country. In the late 1950s and early 1960s, as Africa was swiftly moving from the status of political dependency on Europe to that of supposed partnership with its former colonizers, either as a result of revolutionary violence or as the outcome of peaceful negotiation, it had become imperative that the most educated sons and daughters of the black continent be active participants in preparing their countries for the difficult task at hand: the bold assignment of governing a country in spite of Europe's predictions and expectation that Africans would fail at self-government and eventually appeal for assistance, giving the racist white a chance to say "we told you so."

Such is the dilemma that confronted Fanon himself, who abandoned his position as a clinical psychiatrist in France to join in the Algerian struggle for independence, which, due to his premature death, came too late for him to enjoy. The same sense of duty that inspired many highly educated and competent Africans to commit themselves to politics also led less sophisticated, mediocre strategists and embittered soldiers like Mikendi to take advantage of the shortage of African intellectuals in the aftermath of decolonization, and to proclaim themselves leaders of their people. Mikendi is certainly a war hero — if one believes his rendition of the role he played in the second European war; however, by his unexceptional political skills, Mikendi is an allegory of the many African praetorian leaders, former soldiers in the colonial army who, in the years following decolonization, have moved from the barracks to the presidential palace, making, by virtue of their governing style, a mockery of independence. Mikendi is reminiscent of such African leaders as Mobutu of the Former Zaire, Bokassa of the Central African Republic, Idi Amin of Uganda, Blaise Compaoré of Burkina Faso, and Robert Gueï of the Côte d'Ivoire, to cite only a few. Ba Kobhio's method of making the ruthless and brutal Mikendi the mentor of the sophisticated and poised Koumba is an astute way of making a floating signifier the future of the new African nations whose leaders have the difficult task of reconciling extreme internal tensions (vengeful, anti–European passions vs. conciliatory postures) before or at the same time that they are turning to the outside world. How successfully will African leaders promote an atmosphere of fair discursive emulation whereby these various internal tensions can be resolved? This is a question that continues to preoccupy many who monitor African politics.

2

The Language
You Govern In

*The Rise and Fall of the African
Despot in Balufu Bakupa Kanyinda's*
Le damier: Papa National oyé *and*
Cheick Oumar Sissoko's Guimba the Tyrant

> *This is certainly monstrous and may well be true ... (Of course it is
> true, and it is only a fraction of the truth!) But for God's sake, why
> would someone with even a whit of sense start rubbing the Czar's face
> in the atrocities of his predecessors! Maddest of all madmen!*
> — Jaan Kross, The Czar's Madman

In an article contributed to a volume whose title casts a note of pessimism upon the future of Africa, Blaine Harden had this to say about the African leader:

> If you took a quarter-century's worth of His Excellencies the African Leader and tossed them in a blender, you would come up with a Big Man who looks like this: His face is on the money. He names streets, football stadiums, hospitals and universities after himself. He insists on being called "doctor" or "conqueror" or "the wise old man." He bans all political parties except the one he controls. His off-the-cuff remarks have the power of law. He packs the civil service with his tribesmen. His rule has one goal: To perpetuate his reign as Big Man.... Beneath a facade of democracy, Big Men buy loyalty, using state resources. What they cannot buy, they compel, using state muscle.... A metaphor for the inequality over which Big Men preside is on display outside most African capitals: Alongside a donor-built four-lane highway, there is usually a narrow footpath formed by bare feet. Africa's ruling elite howls down the four-lane road in private automobiles while peasants shuffle along in the dirt.[1]

Harden's remarks are insightful. Any attentive observer of African affairs in general and of West African politics in particular, will agree that the African leader's megalomania has impeded progress and undermined independence.

African Independences: Missed Opportunities

The post-independence exaltation in Francophone Africa was short-lived.[2] By the mid–1990s, most Francophone African countries were ravaged by a wave of widespread political barbarity; which in such places as Benin, Mali, Togo, Zaire (Congo), Upper Volta (Burkina Faso), The Central African Republic, Mauritania, Niger, Chad, Rwanda, Madagascar, and Côte d'Ivoire, served as a pretext for the militaries to seize power, pretending to restore a social order that civilian leaders had failed to maintain.[3] Despite their pretentious claims of good intentions, most of the praetorian leaders proved incapable of implementing democracy in their respective countries. Endowed with practically little, if any, political experience and an inflated will to power, the new leaders ruled their nations as family plantations, reducing the militaries to field workers and the civilian populations to consumers of goods produced in presidential plantations and factories or sold in presidential grocery stores, despite the people's weak purchasing power. The most ambitious dictators, such as Bokassa of the Central African Republic and Mobutu of Zaire, inaugurated themselves President-for-life and referred to and used public funds as their personal assets. These power mongers, most of whom were merely soldiers in the colonial army, became extremely resentful of intellectuals, whom they perceived as threats to their personal authority, and whom they persecuted, executed or forced into exile. Left with no real opposition from within their countries, accountable to no one but themselves, and surrounded by a plethora of praise-singers, these rulers filled strategic political and military positions with their clansmen. They drove their nations into management crises, and they made laxity, nepotism, absenteeism, opportunism, and corruption their governing tools.[4]

In a forty-minute film entitled *Le damier: Papa National Oyé!* (translated into English as *The Draughtsmen Clash*), Balufu Bakupa Kanyinda transports his viewers to a fictitious African nation, exposing the political dealings of a true-to-life dictator. In *Le damier*, an insomniac African leader — and checkers aficionado (played by Dieudonné Kabongo Hashila) — has spent several nights playing with his guards and beating them easily. Now he wants a real a challenge. So, he sends for the best checkers player in the country (played by Yves Mba), who happens to be a destitute poet living in the slums of the capital. What a casual viewer might mistake for a film about a contest between

a bored head of state in
search of exaltation and a
star-struck indigent is, upon
further investigation, a skillful and satirical comment on
the condition of African
states in general and on the
mental disposition of African leaders — although the
target of the filmmaker's sar-
casm may be more fact-spe-
cific than suggested here. In
Le damier, the dictator's distinctive pattern of speech
and intonation, his leopard-
skin toque, his characteristic
scepter, and his dark sun-

Congolese filmmaker Balufu Bakupa Kanyinda
used the chess game metaphor in his *Le Damier:
Papa National Oyé* to illustrate the nature of political discourse in Africa, and particularly in Mobutu's
Zaire (photograph courtesy of congokulture.net).

glasses are all indications that Mobutu, the late Zairian despot, is the subject
of Kanyinda's stinging satire. Furthermore, Mobutu's habit of playing checkers with his subordinates and throwing dangerous temper tantrums — dangerous for his challengers — whenever he lost was a widespread urban tale in Africa.

The Language Within and the Language Without

Kanyinda's genius lies in utilizing the *game metaphor* to illustrate political discourse in Africa in general. From this perspective, political discourse
is a Grand-Narrative patterned according to a structuralist or rigid conception of language as a *game of chess*. It was Ferdinand de Saussure, a Genevian
linguist, who, in a series of lectures he gave between 1907 and 1911 at the University of Geneva, and which were later published as *Cours de linguistique
générale* by two of his students, Charles Bally and Albert Sechehaye, first
formulated the analogy between language and a game of chess. "Of all the
comparisons that might be imagined," Saussure stated, "the most fruitful is
the one that might be drawn between the functioning of language and a game
of chess.... The respective value of the pieces depends on their position on
the chessboard just as each linguistic term derives its value from its opposition to all the other terms."[5] By importing this structuralist understanding
of language, Kanyinda shows how the leading elites in post-independence
Africa perceive political discourse. The analogy between political discourse
and the game of chess implies that to be legitimate, the language of politics
must necessarily function within a closed network of cultural significations,

Swiss linguist Ferdinand de Saussure (1857–1913) was the first to establish the association between language and a game of chess in a series of lectures that would be published in 1916 by two of his students as *Cours de linguistique générale.*

which are often presented as constituting a natural and authentic web that allows no irruption of external events. For instance, as in a game of chess where particular pieces can only be moved in certain ways, in African politics, too, one would dictate that particular words and ideas can only be used in certain prescribed contexts and nowhere else. Conceived this way, political language is as dictatorial as a game of chess is limiting, and the price for violating the rules of the political game could be costly. This is the perceptive parallel that the director of *Le damier* invites the viewers to explore.

Le damier opens with the dictator's televised, sententious denunciation of the West's attempt to interfere in his country's affairs: "All these imperialists who blab about human rights, rights for this or for that," he ramblingly suggests, "why don't they speak about cats' rights, louse's rights and I don't know what?" As he warns his people, there is and will be only one party — *his* — to which one has to belong or leave the country. "[You] should understand once and for all that during my lifetime there will never be a multi-party system in my country." The rules of this party are made very clear, "to serve me and not you."

Generally, when the African autocrat is too "modest" to launch into self-eulogization or to remind the population that he is the supreme master, and his party the only legal political denomination — not that such a stroke of unpretentiousness is likely to occur very often — it is to his ministers that he entrusts this task. In the Houphouët regime of the 1980s in Côte d'Ivoire, for instance, the President's *personal griots* were Laurent Dona Fologo (minister of information), late Balla Keita (minister of education), and Djédjé Madji (minister of health). Their roles consisted in flooding public airwaves with tales of the leader's greatness, monitoring and shaping the contents of knowledge from elementary school to higher education, and organizing a personality cult around the figure of the leader. Many Ivorians still recall Balla Keita's excessive zeal and his coining such phrases as "Nanan Houphouët" (Father Houphouët) or "*un pied dedans, un pied dehors, c'est dehors.*" (One foot inside [the unique party, the PDCI], one foot outside, makes you an outsider). Often, these presidential praise-singers carry titles like "ministers without portfolio" or they act as ministers to the presidency, with huge budgets at their disposal for bribing local chiefs and for organizing marches and demonstrations in support of the President.

In Zaire, Mobutu, the target of Kenyinda's satire, enjoyed a thirty-two-year long crooked and terrorizing reign thanks to *Mobutuism*, a doctrine of personality cult he had instituted. Mobutuism rewarded Mobutu's praise singers and persecuted his foes. It created an atmosphere of self-policing whereby Zairians would report one another's "crimes," either real or invented, in order to live another day. However, what really sustained Mobutu's power was the military and financial backing the dictator received from successive American governments. In fact, Joseph Désiré-Mobutu came to power in Zaire (today's Democratic Republic of Congo) in 1961 as the CIA's handpicked replacement for Patrice Lumumba, the first prime minister of the Congo, who was suspected of anti–Western sentiments and sympathy toward the Soviet Union. Unwilling to see the Congo, this huge and rich territory in Central Africa, fall under Communist influence, the Eisenhower administration coaxed Mobutu, then a young, ambitious, and malleable general, to arrest Lumumba and have him executed in the province of Katanga by his political enemies, Moïse Tshombe and Albert Kalonji (see chapter 9: "There Is No Commerce Going on There"). Initially, the CIA had planned to eliminate Lumumba by means of a biological substance. Later, this plan which appeared too conspicuous was abandoned for one that would not directly implicate the United States. Although ordered by America, Patrice Lumumba's death by the hands of Congolese, which stopped the Soviet's influence in the Congo and put America in the saddle there, avoided placing the Americans in a position where they would have to explain themselves to the rest of the world about their role in the Congo. Thenceforth, Washington's official explanation could be that Lumumba became victim of internal conflicts between Congolese political rivals. Mobutu did the CIA and the U.S. in general a great favor. To reward Mobutu for his obedience, American presidents, from Eisenhower to Bush 41, supported Mobutu's autocracy both militarily and financially and for thirty-two years closed their eyes on Mobutu's reign of terror, corruption, embezzlement, and megalomania. Mobutu was a ruthless ruler. In Zaire, Mobutu had to be the victor in everything; and whoever dared to defy and defeat him was likely to meet with death.

In Kanyinda's film, Mobutu's guards who had been playing draughts with their ruler to alleviate the latter's boredom knew that for their survival, it was important that they lost; and so they never had the courage to win a single game. The dictator was aware of that. He grew annoyed with his appointed praise-singers; so he wanted a challenge. Tired of playing checkers with his immediate entourage, whom he suspected of losing in order to please him, he requested a "real champion." The Leader's insistence to play with "a real champion" is metaphorical of his desire to know what the authentic people of his country — the indigent and poverty-stricken populations — thought of his leadership. As this yearning for "truth" kept him sleepless for nights, the dictator hoped to recover his equilibrium by engaging the greatest checkers player, who came from the slums of the country, and thus represented the best challenge that the ruled had to offer him.

In *Le damier*, the checkerboard, which lies between the dictator and the challenging champion, analogizes the space of political encounter of the two players. The checkerboard is the terrain on which the dictator and the champion will face up. This space, like the Saussurean language or game of chess, is *physically* outside the two players, in the sense that its configuration is not a matter of their will. This space exists before them and irrespective of what they may think of it; and its shape, too, pre-exists them. The checkerboard or the space of the players' discursive engagement is unequivocally well delineated by four sides of equal length. Within the boundaries of this body, the checkers form a system of significations, and the players can only move them according to the laws of that system. The laws of the system that the checkerboard and the checkers form are characterized by *immanence*. In other words, the system being autonomous and self-contained, things can only make sense when they are analyzed from within the boundaries of the system and not from outside these boundaries. Furthermore, the laws of the system are synchronic. Not only should the system be analyzed from within, but it should also be analyzed according to what it is at a given moment rather than according to how it has evolved over time. This principle is important insofar as it gives no license for historical comparison. Instead it assumes that the system is *a priori* valid; and it posits the understanding of the system's internal functioning as what is really at issue. It legitimizes the one-party system. If the *game* of checkers, which pits the Leader against the champion from the slums, analogizes the search for "truth," then the discernible perimeter of the checkerboard might suggest that one can only discover truth within the limited field of the checkerboard. This field is the space of unambiguous significations that the checkers create (here and now on this board) by virtue of the various relations of difference that they share.[6] One important thing in Saussure's theory of language is that the linguistic system is a conventional system inherited by the members that use it. Likewise, in the autocratic regime, the political language that the board represents is a system bequeathed to the community that uses it by the autocratic leader as a Grand-Narrator.

From this perspective, *Le damier* also indicates that such a systemic conception of the game is pervaded by violence. The game as given by the ruler is dictatorial. It is handed down by the ruler as State-form, as State-codification of political discourse along rigid lines. As such, it contains the State's wish for controlling individual idiosyncrasies or flows. However, the State-desire for controlling flows, for restricting speed, for regulating circulation or for relativizing movements cannot arrest the possibility of variability of directions. To emphasize this, Kanyinda causes two forms of political discourses to coexist in close proximity: first, a State-form imposed by the dictator and used in his presence or in the closed quarters of his palace; second, a nomad-form used in the absence of the dictator, which takes advantage of open spaces. The dictator and the State ideology favor the first kind of discourse. The ordinary people, to whom the champion can claim appurtenance, fancy the second kind of discourse. While in the presence of the dictator his guards comply with a rigid State-existence, in his absence, they adopt a suppler nomad-existence.[7] Thus when the guards play checkers out of the master's sight, they deviate from the principle of immanence (which dictates that one can discover "truth" only within the perimeter of the checkerboard), and they introduce into the dynamics of the game para- or supra-segmental events, that is, foreign elements. Henceforth, in the challenge between the Sergeant-Chief and his subordinate, the two protagonists efface hierarchical boundaries, launching into an emulation of taunting and obscenities: "Idiot! You've lost! And my prize is your ugly peasant wife!" Kanyinda's caricature of the dialogue among the soldiers in the absence of their master illustrates the real nature of intersubjective confrontations. Intersubjective relations are playful. They are nomadic. Even in the most structured environments, intersubjective exchanges elude aprioricity; they are predicated on prior and present experiences as well as on a certain sense of unpredictability. Although they may be patterned according to customary paths — such as going from one point to another, as is the case on any checkerboard — intersubjective engagements remain, first and foremost, moments of constant removal and relocation of meanings from their original contexts; that is, they remain moments of constant deterritorialization and reterritorialization.[8] In *Le damier*, the dictator who wishes to know the "truth" by engaging the champion suspects this evanescent and subversive property of the word. The word that is meant to produce "truth" could elude him and evade his control. Consequently, he deliberately restricts the field of production of "truth" by his mere presence. He is a ruler who has never before put up with idiosyncrasies — by the rules which he imposes upon the game, and by his direct threats that "[he] will not tolerate the slightest *écart*."

One Must Be Mad to Be Truthful

Only a fool would dare play checkers with the dictator the way the game ought to be played.[9] The champion, while in his right mind, cannot *play*. The dictator will learn nothing from the champion as long as the latter remains lucid. Upset, the dictator, who understands that the champion is deliberately losing to him, terrorizes his Chief-of-Staff (Jean Lacroix Kamba), who in turn, threatens to have the champion's head if the latter refuses to play like a true champion. "You're playing for your life and mine too," the Chief-of-Staff warns. It is at that point that the champion understands that no matter what the outcome of the game is, the dictator will have his head. So, the champion decides to die with honor. He will play like a champion; but before he does, he will have — like a death row inmate — his last meal. He has not eaten for days, and he confides to the Chief-of-Staff: "I haven't eaten since yesterday ... and the day before. We eat every two days if any." The Chief-of-Staff recognizes that the champion's words reflect the people's opinion on the dictator's failed social policy. However, the Chief-of-Staff is lucid enough to know that reporting them *exactly* to the dictator as they have been told to him could endanger his own life. So, when asked why the champion is hungry, he gives the dictator his own version of the fact.

> "Why didn't he eat?"
> "He fasted for two days ... religion, Boss."
> "Now he wants to eat, smoke and play draughts?"
> "Exactly, Boss!"
> "Ah, that's good!"

The tyrant requests that the champion be fed if that is what it will take for the latter to play — to speak the "truth." Now the champion knows that there is no turning back. He will have to play the game as he has always played it in the popular quarters of the country, like a madman. Playing like a madman within the presidential palace presupposes a mutiny; it implied that the champion should ride difference; that he should think more freely outside the edifice of interiority. For the champion, it implies engaging State philosophy, disrupting the concepts that sustain State authority by taking to task the very architect of that authority, the dictator. This invitation to play, the champion is convinced, will irrevocably meet with tragedy, for the dictator has warned that he will not tolerate the slightest *écart*. In a country where one could be killed for saying the forbidden as well as for remaining silent, the champion decides to die with dignity by telling the truth, his truth, the truth of the people he represents. However, still too clear minded to dare speak the truth, the champion demands to smoke a marijuana joint. Strangely, the dictator, who is now too eager to see this champion play, grants the latter's will; the dictator is so eager to hear what this representative of the people has to say about his governing ability that he opens the field of discourse to the external event by granting the champion his wishes; and now a reality that he can no longer control comes to him in painful shockwaves as the intoxicated champion speaks with no fear. "I'll put you in your place, little draughtsman ... useless, don't you look at me like this ... now play ... idiot ... don't be a sore loser ... are you really the most powerful, the most intelligent man in the country? Poor country ... imbecile, ruffian ... I'll take your gold watch ... and your expensive shoes ... in the slums, you could not even face a beginner." The Champion spews out all the hatred and obscenities that the people in the low quarters of the country reserve for their leader. Though space did not allow the filmmaker to give full account of what the champion could be telling the leader, observers of African politics can easily imagine the drunken champion giving Mobutu a full recollection of his madness; a madness that started the very day Mobutu planted the dagger in the back of Patrice Lumumba, the person that gave him his first important military position, when his name was still Joseph Désiré Mobutu, and not yet a full sentence as Mobutu Sesse Seko Kuku Ngbendu Wa Za Banga (the all-powerful warrior who goes from conquest to conquest, leaving fire in his wake); a madness that kept the Zairian people eating merely one stick of cassava or one plantain as daily meal while Mobutu, his relatives, and his close friends were living in insolent wealth. The champion from the slums must have taken Mobutu back to those days when the dictator would have the Anglo-French supersonic passenger airliner, the Concorde, land on his private airport in Gbodolite, his village, so that his family could go on a Parisian shopping trip. The champion must have recalled Mobutu's reckless policy of *zairianization* the disastrous economic shocks of which further drove the Zairian lower class into scarcity and zombification.

Indeed, as early as twelve to thirteen years after having come to power by coup d'état, Mobutu had personally squandered much of his country's reserves and was hard pressed to find new financial supplies for his development projects. In 1973, Mobutu launched his program of zairianization aimed at giving him more control over foreign enterprises operating in Zaire by adding more medium and small businesses to the list of companies that have been nationalized in the mid– to late 1960s. Zairianization, whose stated objective was to turn farms, ranches, plantations, commerces, and real estate agencies "to the sons of the country," rapidly became a means of enrichment for the dictator, his family, and his close collaborators. Upon confiscating businesses from foreigners, Mobutu turned them to his inept relatives and close associates who were more skilled in draining these businesses off than keeping them running. The new Zairian businessowners failed to maintain the networks of business relations that had hitherto sustained the country's economy. Their irresponsible management style undermined the confidence of private investors, who avoided speculations in Zaire. "Zairianization engendered economic disaster on an unprecedented scale. In a matter of months, commercial networks were utterly disrupted; massive layoffs were reported; and shortages of basic commodities became increasingly widespread along with liquidations of assets."[10] The agricultural sector was the most affected. In a country with generously fertile land where more than 65 percent of the population was involved in subsistence and commercial agriculture, the failure of the urbanized elite to develop agricultural infrastructure and the neglect of existing infrastructures left the agricultural sector extremely archaic, with very small, hardly diversified family plots that were unable to provide for the exponentially growing urban populations. To feed its populations Zaire, needed to import foodstuff from Zambia and Tanzania; which the majority of the people could not afford. Zaire's solution was to borrow heavily from the IMF, the World Bank, and the Club of Paris and to invest poorly or not at all. In the end, Zaire was unable to service its debt and unwilling to abide to budgetary measures imposed by the financial institutions, preferring to bribe foreign governments' officials to delay the application of debt restructuration.[11]

Corruption in Zaire was an art perfected by Mobutu himself. Mobutuism "guaranteed that top functionaries would serve the president, the ultimate source of their livelihood, rather than the nation."[12] Whoever failed to understand this basic principle of Mobutuism could be sure to lose his or her source of revenue; which could be the most lenient of the punishments Mobutu had in store for the renegades. The fact that for the elite no position "offered by Mobutu" was guaranteed to last also encouraged embezzlement. Aware that they could, at any time, depending on the president's whim, find themselves sharing the dreadful standard of living of most Zairians, the elite stole as much money as they could from public funds while they were still in "position of trust;" which further drove the country into financial crisis.

In *Le damier*, the dictator must have heard of these criticisms from the champion. So the dictator's anger soared. His response became reactive and defensive. He could hardly muffle his contempt for the champion, and via him, the people whose truth the champion was speaking. At dawn, the defeated dictator tried to buy the champion's silence by offering him some money. The champion knew too much where Mobutu's co-optation often led to. Too many people have accepted Mobutu's bribes only to turn up emasculated, dismembered or simply hung. For example, "Pierre Mulele [one of Mobutu's opponent, who had once challenged him in Eastern Zaire] was lured out of exile in Brazzaville with a false promise of amnesty and brought back to Leopoldville on Mobutu's luxurious yacht; men of Mobutu's private guard gauged his eyes out of their sockets and tore his genitals off before killing him."[13] The champion, now sober, would like nothing better than to flee the palace as soon as possible; and so, as angry soldiers hauled him away, in a desperate gesture to save his own life, he shouted an affectionate epithet to the dictator:

> "Papa National!"
> "What did you call me?" the Dictator inquires.
> "Papa National! That's the way your people refer to you."

The tyrant liked this flattering sobriquet and decided to offer the champion a position as his personal spokesman in his cabinet. Now the champion understood that even his last effort to avoid the dictator's grip had only produced the opposite effect. The dictator wanted him to play another game whose rules and outcome the latter, once again, had already written. Nobody ever lasted in Mobutu's cabinet. Mobutu's cabinet members were constantly exposed to an exercise of musical chair, whereby "every three months the music stops, and Mobutu forces everyone to change chairs," thus being either tortured, ministers, exiles, ambassadors, traitors, or dead.

> The most remarkable example of this pattern is Nguz a Karl-i-Bond. He served as Zaire foreign minister in the 1970s before leaving that post to serve as the country's only legal political party. However, in 1977, Mobutu accused him of high treason and had him sentenced to death, threatening to shoot Nguz himself. Instead of execution, Nguz was jailed and tortured, including electrical shocks to his testicles. One year later, he was freed from prison, and only a year after that, Mobutu named him prime minister. After two years in that office, he fled to Belgium where he wrote a book attacking state corruption under Mobutu's rule. He then went before a congressional subcommittee in Washington to describe Mobutu's years of theft from public funds. Amazingly, Mobutu invited him back to Zaire, where he was not only well treated, but in 1986 was appointed as Zaire's ambassador to the United States.[14]

Though Mobutu's rule was based on logic of pure chance, nevertheless, the dictator took pleasure in altering the chance game, in loading the dice to his advantage; and Nguz was one of the luckiest players of Mobutu's altered chance game. He tried his luck and lived. The champion would not stake his life in such an improbable game. He would not accept the dictator's offer. Perhaps he could stay alive by just staying away from the palace. Perhaps he could then be forgotten by the dictator and have a chance to live; but the dictator would not have it this way. So, the champion recognized that his fate was sealed: he was a living corpse. Therefore, throwing away the money the dictator offered him for his silence, the champion launched into a defiantly prophetic song as the dictator's men took him away

> Just wait and see
> Change will come
> Just wait and see
> Change will come

In the morning news, the radio announced the champion's "sudden" death. Nonetheless, his prophecy of change was finally fulfilled when, on May 17, 1997, Mobutu's bloody system was toppled by Laurent-Désiré Kabila's rebel forces.

Though irrational, kleptocratic, and brutal, Mobutu's reign lasted more than four decades and survived numerous coup attempts. Mobutu's greatest asset was the Cold War. Western countries' compulsive fear of Soviet permeation in Africa was greater than any revulsion Mobutu's regime could command, and France, Belgium, and the United States supplied Mobutu huge sums of money as well as weapons and military personnel, which helped the dictator to consolidate his hold on power.

Politics of the Africans

Whereas the demises of the African repressive rulers come by way of unforeseen events that dumbfound them as much as they surprise the ruled masses, the tyrants' rises, however, arrive in the form of carefully planned carnivalesque episodes. How better to stage the rise and fall of the autocratic African leaders, if not through a cinema of the burlesque, like Cheick Oumar Sissoko's *Guimba the Tyrant*.[15] In Sissoko's film, an unscrupulous African leader is deposed thanks to the concerted efforts of the people he abused for so long. The movie is an

Malian filmmaker and minister of culture Cheick Oumar Sissoko (photograph by Manfred Schweda, for thisfabtrek.com).

allegory of the reign of the post-independence African power monger, his megalomaniac dreams and his spoliation of independence. However, unlike *Le damier*, whose allusions are clear to the viewer familiar with contemporary African politics, *Guimba the Tyrant* proceeds by circumlocution. The casual moviegoer might mistake *Guimba the Tyrant* for an African adaptation of the traditional American Western full of posses, villains and heroes, horse pursuits in open spaces and through dusty canyons, saloon fights, duels, and, of course, love stories. However, Sissoko's movie is less an imitation of the American Western than a testimony to the rich African culture and human genius that has been tragically laid to waste by the dishonorable twentieth-century African despot whose way of thinking remains mired in his *folie des grandeurs*.

The filmmaker's distinctive alternation of long shots with panning through the architectural wonders and rich social lives of the ancient African city of Djenné that serves as the setting for *Guimba the Tyrant* combines realism with narratological mimesis in order to convincingly tell — or rather show — a story. At one time, Africa enjoyed moments of great civilizations, intellectual and artistic creativity, economic abundance and political stability. What then went wrong and how? Through what circumstances has the black continent come to be known — sometimes wrongly and often rightly — as a barren, poverty-stricken land, where overfed, greedy despots roam insolently unconcerned with their people's basic needs and rights? It is in answering these questions that Sissoko's historical allegory reveals itself as an up-to-date political critique. The contemporaneous nature of Sissoko's criticism is illuminated toward the end of the movie when an anxious Mambi (Balla Moussa Keita) recalls to his daughter Kani (Mouneissa Maiga) that twenty years before, the town was prosperous and everybody lived in harmony until Guimba (Falaba Issa Traoré), "a master of the occult," decided to put his power to evil use. Guimba then killed the village chief and all the eligible men, took over the throne and implemented his dictatorship. Since that day, Guimba's son, Jangine (Lamine Diallo) has not grown an inch, and Guimba himself has been hiding his face from the sun.

Sissoko's tale demands of the viewers an extra effort of deciphering before any clear connection can be established between his main protagonist, Guimba, and the flawed contemporary African leader, such as represented by Kanyinda's dictator in *Le damier*. However, *Guimba the Tyrant* contains numerous clues that facilitate a temporal movement from history to actuality. Guimba's son, Jangine, who "hasn't grown an inch" since his father's occupation of the town, is certainly a metaphor for what has become of African countries since the rise to power of despots who, too preoccupied with filling their own pockets, indulged in mismanagement of national resources or wasted their energies in interminable wars, making their countries poorer than they were at the time of independence. Furthermore, Guimba and his soldiers riddling the architectural marvels of the ancient African city of Djenné with bullets can only bring back memories of the desolation and sorrow which the people of Liberia, Somalia,

From left to right, King Guimba (Falaba Issa Traoré), his dwarf heir Jangine (Lamine Diallo), and the king's griot (Habib Dembélé) at the court of Guimba (*Guimba the Tyrant*, directed by Cheick Oumar Sissoko, Mali, 1995).

Sudan, Zaire, Côte d'Ivoire and many other African countries have experienced in the last three decades; and Guimba hiding his face from the sun is reminiscent of these "Al Capone-like African leaders," who have so much blood on their hands that they can no longer trust anyone and, therefore, must remain prisoners in their own palaces.

The Griot-within and the Griot-without

Guimba's chronicle, which is recounted from the point of view of a griot, a man who is traditionally in the services of the ruling class, is strangely critical of the tyrant's reign. Before the advent of alphabetical literacy in Africa and the Antilles, the particular histories of individuals, families, clans and tribes were mainly preserved and transmitted to successive generations through repetitive telling by the griot, the official repository of the community's narratives. The griot — which is the common French name for the West African Djeli, Djeliba, Mabo, Guewel, Belen Tigui, or the Caribbean Quimboiseur, Paroleur, or Oraliturain — was simultaneously a storyteller, poet historian, and genealogist.[16] Although the griot was not necessarily a notable, his close proximity with chiefs and royalties conferred special regards upon him. In *Guimba the Tyrant*, the fact that the griot is able to speak impartially against the abuses of the very social class in whose members' hands lay his fate is worth noting. This paradox provides proof that in traditional oral societies, the griot was neither an omnipotent Grand-Narrator whose narrative stood as absolute historical truth nor a versatile bard triangulating alongside the axis of popularity and personal safety.

In the traditional oral society, the griot's tool was his voice, speech, which was also available to almost every member of his community. Therefore, with exception to his ascendancy, his legitimacy, which essentially stemmed from his gender and family name (usually Kouyaté in West Africa), could be challenged by just about any person who could speak and was skillful enough to tell stories.[17] It is therefore the confidence the people placed in the griot that legitimized his function; and to sustain that confidence, the griot had to strive for objectivity, operating from both the margin and the periphery. Despite his closeness to the power center, the information that the traditional griot transmitted to future generations could not be warped in favor of the ruling class. Rather, it ought to encompass the community's diverse individual narratives.

In *Guimba the Tyrant*, Sissoko suggests that the griot is a communal story gatherer through the use of three griotic agencies, which illustrate various constitutive layers of the same *reporter of fact* (the griot) — or various modes of production of knowledge — than determining qualities of three different and unrelated individual griots. Thus Sissoko's account of Guimba's reign does not follow a linear rendition by a single narrator. Three griots tell the story: They are, on the one hand, the filmmaker, and the first griot that opens the narrative at the beginning of the film (certainly the filmmaker's alter-ego) and, on the other hand, Guimba's own griot. These various narratives are what are termed in this chapter the discourses of "the griot-within" and "the griot-without."

The use of the term *the griot-within* is meant to name the reporter of fact, insofar as his immediacy to the power center causes his narrative to pass over the multifarious peripheral experiences and to reflect and propagate the philosophy of the center. Such is Guimba's personal griot, whose blind allegiance to his master leads him to excessively eulogize the latter, despite clear evidence of the tyrant's shortcomings. The eccentricities of Guimba the tyrant, a ruler with no regard for the law, are evocative of the follies of some African autocrats, such as Wade, Bokassa, Mobutu, and Bongo — all self-proclaimed fundamental leaders and benefactors of their people. It is from Guimba himself that one learns of his governing method, as he confides in his son Jangine that a great ruler must be ruthless to his people; he must instill fear in them so that his decisions are executed without ever being second-guessed. Guimba himself ruled as if to illustrate these tenets, eliminating his opponents, separating families in order to have his ways with others' wives. However, were Guimba's personal griot, *the griot-within*, left alone to record and transmit history, he would only record and pass on to future generations moments of great deeds by his master.

It is from the *griot-without* that one learns of Guimba's flaws, his taste for the superfluous, his inclination towards the bizarre and the occult, his contempt for morality, justice and legitimacy, and his ineptitude in leading. The filmmaker's juxtaposition of the *griot-within* and the *griot-without* makes the movie into a grotesque art form, a mixture of the farcical with the tragic, the comical with the terrible, whereby the post-independence African subject learns to exorcise the misfortune that struck him/her so hard by laughing it away. Through the griot's expert metamorphoses, through his masterful ability to both straddle the border of the village and reunite with the constituted *crowd* at the center of the *socius*, the segment of the community that venerates Guimba (the courtiers) as well as those who dangerously mock his excesses (the *habitués* of the local bar and of the market place) are simultaneously interpellated into the same experiential field.

The griot's narrative is an assemblage of memories garnered concurrently from different places, synchronously from various individuals, through a technique of digression, repetition and various forms of parallelism. From René Maran to Sembène Ousmane Patrick Chamoiseau and Raphaël Confiant, passing through Senghor and Césaire, black writers and filmmakers of French expression have tried to emulate the griot's rhetorical paradigm. Some intellectuals, such as Senghor, have gone so far as to proclaim and celebrate it as the essence of Africanity. Such is the style that has given this ubiquitous scavenger of remembrances — who has learned to listen carefully when solicited and to eavesdrop when unsought — the reputation of a maker of wonders. In reference to him, Laye Camara, the late Guinean novelist wrote,

> [He] is a man whom no one would have ever dared to interrupt once he had begun to give tongue under the palaver tree, unless he wanted to draw down upon his head trials and tribulations ... his word would make the thatched roof of a hut shift all on its own. Through the magical power of his word, birds ... would stop singing. Those that persisted ... would drop dead.[18]

In his analysis of Camara's autobiographical novel, *L'Enfant noir* (1954) (translated as *The Dark Child*) Jacques Bourgeac deduces from a particular event in the novel, the gold smelting episode, the communal importance of the mystical role of the griot in the Malinké society. According to Bourgeac, the ceremony of fusion and transformation of gold by Camara's father rehearses the birth of the Malinké tribe, and it insures for future generations cosmogony according to the Malinké.[19] In this ritual, as Bourgeac notes, the griot's role is indispensable, for he is an intermediary between the goldsmith and the creation gods. It is his instrument (the Kora) and his powerful incantatory song (the Douga), that actually send the author's father, the goldsmith, into a creative trance.[20] Likewise, in Dani Kouyaté's film *Keita: The Heritage of the Griot* (1995), the griot is a mythical character that communicates with spirits.

This idea of the griot as sorcerer speaks less of an actual supernatural power, than it calls up Derridian rhetorical postures of *double entendre* and Deleuzian and Guattarian movements of *dédoublement*.[21] The griot is an anomalous memory gatherer, a double agent, who has learned to establish alliances both within the center and at the periphery of the political machinery, and who dances perilously on the tightrope of the dividing line. When the griot loses his footing, the part of him that falls into reproduction and representation of genealogy is *the griot-within*, the tyrant's praise-singer, and the part of him that falls into permanent undermining of any relationship of filiation is the *griot-without*. In the first case, he is reactionary, in the second, reactive. Either way, he is a subject of deep *resentment*. As a sorcerer, the griot must learn to swim between tides; he must occupy a position that encompasses features of both *the griot-within* and *the griot-without*. He must cultivate a perfunctory versatility.

This is what Patrick Chamoiseau and Raphaël Confiant, in *Lettres créoles* (1991), point out as the preeminent rhetorical strategy of the *paroleur* of the plantation society. The *paroleur* or *quimboiseur* (the griot in the Antilles) developed a technique of feigned naïveté, of *masquage* and connivance, which allows him to move information from the "*habitation*" to the *plantation*." This strategy is one of false self-erasure, whereby the *conteur créole* or *oraliturain* burlesques himself, mocks his own stories by injecting occasional grotesque exaggerations and vulgarities into them, refusing all responsibility for the sto-

Guimba's guards fight for the king's enjoyment. The loser will be punished at the hands of the master (*Guimba the Tyrant,* directed by Cheick Oumar Sissoko, 1995).

ries he tells and, in a cleverly orchestrated act of derision, even inscribing them under the register of the non-veridical. Through this play, the *paroleur* subverts his master's suspicion and thus protects himself, his function, and the message of resistance that he propagates.[22] This is because the *paroleur* or *conteur créole* is "...*le délégué à la voix d'un peuple enchaîné, vivant dans la peur et les postures de la survie...*"[23] (the spokesman of a people under bondage, living in fear and in the postures of survival).

This is also what, beyond its obvious burlesquing of the dysfunctional African leader, Sissoko's film teaches us about the African griot. The most powerful asset of this great collector of information and disseminator of knowledge is first and foremost his ability to be a great dissimulator. Neither totally committed to the center nor exclusively pledged to the margin, neither an unequivocal insider nor a complete outsider, the griot is but a self-conscious actor, always suspicious of any absolutism, a nomad, a Jew. This condition of *Jewness* whereby the subject's gaze is ineluctably turned both inward and outward, although it is already discernible in the traditional African griot as the very condition of his function, has become a rare occurrence in Francophone African literary and cinematic traditions; these very traditions that have gone to great length to claim their appurtenance to the world of the storyteller.

3

Nostalgic Memories and Nomadic Spirits

Merzak Allouache's Bab-El-Oued *and Karim Dridi's* Bye-Bye

Anonymous stones, buildings rising to the glory of anonymity. O cities where I walk in search of a time before my past, reading in every wound revealed by the thick, cracked walls. Your stones, gagged by cement and concrete, recognize me in spite of you. For, like me, there are not from here and remember only the dense, humid night from which they were extracted.

— Edmond Jabes, *A Foreigner Carrying in the Crook of His Arm a Tiny Book*

There exists in postcolonial literatures a tendency to articulate the self as necessarily anchored in, and rendered discernible through, the collective. Against this backdrop Edmond Jabès teaches us that one is always already a foreign and unhappy solitude despite all efforts toward socialization. The Algerian Merzak Allouache, in *Bab-El-Oued*, and the Tunisian Karim Dridi, in *Bye Bye*, reiterate this Jabesian prophecy by interrogating the postcolonial explicit opposition between supposed rural reciprocal selves and urban exclusive others.[1] By so doing, they disclose the inherent impracticability of any quest for ideological oversimplification and totalization, and they underscore, on the other hand, the nomadic and fragmented condition in which all subjects dwell despite their most passionate claims of purity and wholeness. Allouache's and Dridi's projects bear great contemporaneous pertinence given the *malaise* generated in some nationalist milieus by the increasing rhetoric of technological globalization and economic transnationalism. In many advanced as well as less advanced countries, the fear of being politically and economically engulfed by an imperialist power or culturally contaminated by

40

a weak nation has led proponents of the politics of purity to fortify the edifice of ordered interiority by reinforcing what they perceive as the social glue preserving the spirit of homogeneity. The mid–1990s have witnessed the growing influence of intolerant nationalist movements in countries like France, Germany, Great Britain, and the United States, where partisans of the politics of purity have called for the immediate erection of a dividing fence between the impure *them* and the pure *us*.[2] The movements of Allouache's and Dridi's protagonists unfold as metaphors of the collapse of the spirit that articulates the opposition us/them, pure/impure. The advent of this collapse was previously heralded in several places as the reversal of the hierarchy of identity and difference, inside and outside; but most importantly, it was revealed as a weakness lurking from within the very dialectical apparatus that constitutes the foundation for that hierarchy.[3]

In *Bab-El-Oued*, the target of Allouache's irony is a certain post-colonial Algerian will-to-domination that functions under the guise of Islam. For, when the desire for control is so great as to overflow the immediate domestic space, the conditioning of the subject is performed according to religious, political and ideological imperatives; and the resounding leitmotivs of this grand program of totalization become such sacred signifiers as God, the Nation, the People, the Revolution, the Law, the Truth; words that are sanctimoniously uttered as the points of presumed supreme density of signification against which all gestures, all desires, all utterances must be measured — and above all, toward which they must all strive. By injecting these recurring themes into every aspect of the populations' lives, the advocates of national sameness expect to keep the people in conditions of constant wakefulness and obedience.

Bab-El-Oued starts with a young man's audacious gesture of resistance against Islamic fundamentalism. Boualem (played by Hassan Abdou), a night shift worker in a Bab-El-Oued bakery, for whom it is a matter of practical necessity to sleep during the day, finds it impossible to get any rest under the annoying fifteen rooftop loudspeakers which, day in and day out, loudly broadcast Islamic morals and prescriptions on conduct. In order to avoid being driven insane, Boualem removes the loudspeaker closest to his bedroom and throws it in the ocean. Hardly has he gotten rid of the noisy apparatus, however, than he realizes the gravity of his not-so-secret action. A group of young Muslim vigilantes led by Saïd (played by Mohamed Ourdache), a hot-tempered revolutionary hero who has vouched to rid the city of its filth and sins, have now made it their personal crusade to find and punish the perpetrator, and make it known that no blasphemy against (religious) authority will be tolerated. Although Saïd's special culture police claim that their decisions are dictated by their drive for religious purity, that is, for the Law as

Prophet Mahomet prescribed it, their own daily deeds hardly conform to this degree of perfection. According to the Imam of Bab-El-Oued (played Ahmed Benaissa), Saïd's interpretation and application of the Law is contrary to the teachings of the Koran. Islam, the Imam reminds Saïd, is a religion of tolerance; violence, he warns, can only breed more violence. As Saïd persists on finding and disciplining the perpetrator of what he regards as a great infamy despite the Imam's call for peace, it becomes clear that his determination is fueled more by his own inflated ego than by his religious conviction. Besides, in private, Saïd's culture inspectors have all displayed evidence of their false pretenses. They have proven that Islam is not what actually motivates them.

Saïd's behavior is antithetical to the Muslim credo of tolerance, simplicity and honesty. Saïd is a narcissistic and conceited man with little sense of honor. While he physically brutalizes his young sister and keeps her locked up in the house, lest she should attract men's attention, he himself spends great time in the powder room tending to his facial appearance. Furthermore, Saïd is tied to the mob in Bab-El-Oued and its illegal trafficking. And like any good mobster, he never does his dirty job alone. After Saïd discovers not only that Boualem is the one who stole the loudspeaker but also that Boualem has been dating his sister, Yamina (Nadia Kaci), he orders the gang to hush the young man's relation with his sister and starts sending Boualem death threats. Fed up with Saïd's intimidations and tired of constantly watching over his shoulder, Boualem seeks out Saïd and challenges him to a duel. Instead of fighting Boualem alone as they had agreed, Saïd gets the whole gang to attack Boualem. Like their leader, the gang members are duplicitous characters who rule Bab-El-Oued by threatening, blackmailing, and terrorizing the people as well as mythologizing their roles in a 1988 anti–Communist revolution.

Let's fight the filth that surrounds us!

Boualem (Hassan Abidou) is removing the Islamist rooftop loudspeaker while it is blasting precepts on moral conduct (*Bab-El-Oued City*, directed by Merzak Allouache, Algeria, 1994).

Religion: A (dormant) Machine of Structuration

If religious faith is not at the foundation of Saïd

and his friends' acts, how is one to explain their claim of appurtenance to Islam and their assertion that Islamic faith is the guiding spirit of their decisions? In fact, what really interests Saïd in Islam is also what will draw any despotic mind to an apparatus of control. Saïd has detected a dormant force, an organizing principle in religion, which once put to work, can transform religion into a formidable machine of structuration.

As is well known, the religious institution is one of several organizations in the private domain (others being family, education, communication, legal, cultural, trade-union) which, according to Louis Althusser, functions as an Ideological State Apparatus (ISA). The role of the ISA is to secure the reproduction of the relations of production that insure the survival of the State. The ISA is a third moment that Althusser adds to the Marxist double articulation of ideology as the exercise of 1) State Power (the power possessed by the ruling class) into 2) the (Repressive) State Apparatus (the elements of the society that control the relations of production by repressive or physical means). Althusser suggests that the (Repressive) State Apparatus branches between a body of institutions belonging to the public domain (the Government, the Administration, the Army, the Police, the Courts, the Prisons) that uses *forceful* methods of compliance and a body of Ideological State Apparatuses that uses *persuasive* methods to produce willing methods of compliance. Both the RSA and the ISA work for the preservation of State Power; although the former (RSA) functions "massively and predominantly" by physical repression and only secondarily by ideology, while the latter (ISA) functions "massively and predominantly" by ideology and only secondarily by repression. In this chapter the allusion to Islam as a dormant machine of structuration concerns this predominantly ideological (non-physical but persuasive) characteristic that Althusser identifies in the Ideological State Apparatus. It is in this sense that Islam is *ordinarily* an Ideological State Apparatus.

In *Bab-El-Oued*, the competing interests between the body of institutions (RSA) and the body of Ideological State Apparatuses are so similar that the contours of these two organizations tend to blur. Saïd and his hooligans seek to exploit this tension by coalescing these two bodies by reifying not just Islam but the most fundamentalist branch of Islam as the State's religion, thus legitimizing the use of force in securing its total establishment. The difference of opinion between the Imam and Saïd is significant only insofar as these two men disagree as to whether Islam should be part of the body of institutions and therefore function "massively and predominantly" by repression, or remain an Ideological State Apparatus in the private domain and function "massively and predominantly" by ideology, delicately and very cunningly *interpellating*— as is the method of the Ideological State Apparatus — concrete individuals as concrete ideological subjects.[3] It is through charitable acts, that is, by opting for Islam as an interpellative apparatus, that the Imam wins his followers over and recruits new members. For Saïd, however, Islam must function explicitly by law and by decree as a public institution having control over people's mobility and education. The conflation of the two bodies of the public institutions, on the one hand, and the Ideological State Apparatuses, on the other hand, is not necessarily evident and requires of the ideologist skills that Saïd does not seem to possess.

In order for Saïd to use religion (an Ideological State Apparatus) as if it belonged to the body of public institutions, he must proceed by false pretenses. Only through an act of connivance, which makes his public gestures tangential to Islamic performances, will he be able to move his own agenda forward in the name of religious truth. In co-opting religion, Saïd hopes to rule Bab-El-Oued by imposing himself as the Grand-Narrator or the leader of a great teleological enterprise. Islam, Saïd and his bunch of hooligans anticipate, will silence all voices of pluralism and erect the great Islamic nation of Algeria. Ironically, it is Saïd himself who undermines this unifying project by invoking a religion the principles of which he knows very little about. The conflict between the impatient Saïd and the indulgent Imam also indicates that Saïd's religious competence, which he regards as the ideal competence for all the people of Bab-El-Oued, is only a performance in relation to the competence of the supreme representative of the Islamic faith.

The Fantasy of Purity

Saïd (Mohamed Ourdache) surrounded by his gang of fundamentalists (*Bab-El-Oued City*, directed by Merzak Allouache, Algeria, 1994).

Saïd's failure to perform a *vraisemblabilisation*, a repetition of Islam, is symptomatic of the impossibility of ever attaining purity; for to think *the pure* is to attempt a coup of subtraction of a pure whose contamination is already acknowledged, a subtraction from *an other* whose infiltration is already recognized and whose purity, too, is already undermined. The temporality of the pure origin is as complex as that of the *gift*. "The gift only 'exists' or gives in an exchange in which it already gives no longer. What is commonly called a gift or present is therefore only the trace of a pre-archaic event of donation which can never have taken place as such. The gift is never (a) *present*; it is given in a past that has never been present and will be received in a future that will never be present either."[5] Thus the pure may pre-exist the transcultural, but that moment of purity is never *present* in the past, in the present and in the future, since in that *proto-existential* moment when the pure may be thought as such, it is not yet, and the very moment it is thought as pure, it has already dissolved itself in the transcultural event. That the "pure" does not exist, that it has already *exited* the very moment it was thus conceived, and consequently, that Saïd's project is not safe from any transcultural or transnational contamination, is an idea which subtly traverses Allouache's film in several places, as almost all the characters of *Bab-El-Oued*, in one way or another, yearn for some external event or some *impure* reality. Saïd and "Immigrant" are two sharp metaphors of the fantasy of purity.

One of Saïd's henchmen is Mess (played by Messaoud Hattau), an enigmatic French citizen referred to as "Immigrant," who, trapped in Algeria with no papers and no place to stay, grows a beard and passes for a Muslim as a matter of survival, joining Saïd's gang. To those who hate Saïd's group of bullies, "Immigrant" announces that he does not actually know "these guys," and that his stay in Algiers is only an insignificant transitory stage. To Saïd, on the other hand, Mess represents himself as a fervent believer in Islamic faith. In fact, like many other characters in *Bab-El-Oued*, "Immigrant" is an analogy of the extent to which Saïd's project of simplification and totalization of identity in the name of Islam is actually fraught with tensions. "Immigrant," who claims to be a pure French citizen, has so convincingly played his game of *masquage*, of passing for the "impure" Arab, that he finds himself caught in his own game. No one in Bab-El-Oued takes him seriously when he decides to recover his "true" identity. His efforts to reclaim his *Frenchness* meet with people's conviction that he is an Arab. For the people of Bab-El-Oued, "Immigrant" is perhaps an Arab from a neighboring country, Tunisia or Morocco, maybe; but above all, he is not a French subject. The role of *otherness* that, for the sake of survival, "Immigrant" wanted to assume only temporarily, has stuck and has become his identity. And Mother-France, to whom "Immigrant" enthusiastically pledges allegiance and to whose bosom he wishes to return, is paradoxically the nation that has thrown him out, without papers, without any identity, like an impurity extirpated from the authentic.

The protagonists of *Bab-El-Oued* are all caught in a play that, despite themselves, makes them agents for the destabilization of the notion of unified identity. It is as if both in the presence of mind and the absence of mind of the characters, events themselves were taking turn in satirizing their nostalgia for the pure. Saïd is dreaming of an unadulterated Islamicized society under his control, but he cannot help assimilating authentic holy Arabic with inflections of the infidel's idiom, that is, French; At the bakery of Bab-el-Oued,

Boualem's best friend, Mabrouk's (Mabrouk Ait Amara) "bad habit" of chewing tobacco while mixing his dough causes him to "contaminate" the French croissants and baguettes he makes with the flavor of Algerian tobacco; and yet, as if he were purer than the croissants he bakes, this maker of transcultural tastes is so certain of his pure *Algerianness* that he does not miss the slightest occasion to remind "Immigrant" of his foreignness. Even as they decry the oppressive system "at home" and fantasize about a journey to the land of the *other*, out of the encapsulating Algerian nation, most of the young Algerian men in the film still remain infatuated with their own Algerianness, which they constantly evoke by indexing the other's supposed lack of authenticity.

However, "Japanese," the Bartender of Bab-El-Oued, is about to give these self-sufficient authentic Algerians a taste of their Algerianness. "Japanese" is perhaps not even from Japan, but his physical features are all that is needed for him to be reified as the representative of the whole Japanese nation. None of his clients ever calls him any other name but "Japanese," which stands as a euphemism for the non–Algerian, the inauthentic, the impure, the other. As if to protest against this will to oversimplification that has branded him with the seal of Japanese essentiality and Algerian otherness, as if to say to the so-called "untouched" Algerians, "since you are so pure, have a drink of yourself! Have a taste of your Algerianness!" "Japanese" quenches his clients' thirst with their leftover beer, gathered from their compatriots' half-drunk glasses. What makes "Japanese's" repulsive commercial method a revolution is that it disrupts the underlying teleological assumptions that govern the moment of Algerian unity. It reveals how much the proselytizers of totalization still remain shut within themselves as particular and distinct individuals.

"Japanese's" resistance, one might object, is implicit and veiled. So are most resistances in Bab-El-Oued. In this town run by Saïd and his hooligans, it is *en catimini* that one dares to love, to smoke, to drink, to read, to laugh, to feel, to desire, and to exist. Thus, for example, it is quietly, with her windows shut, that Ouardya (Nadia Samir), the ill-reputed woman whom Saïd accuses of perverting Bab-El-Oued, sacrilegiously receives her male companions or appreciates a glass of the hard-to-find wine that Boualem gets her at great risk to himself. It is unostentatiously, for example, that Yamina, Saïd's sister, can enjoy a French movie in the absence of her bullish brother or meet Boualem, her lover, in the Bab-El-Oued cemetery. It is covertly, then, that the young girls of the town trade love stories, rehearse passages of Western movies, or make timid homosexual passes at one another. It is by unpretentiously nibbling at the central pillars of Saïd's sacrosanct ideological edifice that the people of Bab-El-Oued are causing that edifice to collapse.

Allouache's characters, who, somewhat apprehensively, take timid but effective bites at the center of the Algerian Islamic machinery of subjugation, are reminiscent of Réda Bensmaïa's schizoidal characters in *The Year of Passages*. To paraphrase Tom Conley's insightful words, they all learn to coexist without being crushed by both the internal and the external war machine.[6] Allouache's cinematic gesture, like Bensmaïa's literary posture, proceeds by fragmentation and displacement of political, social and cultural agencies. The subjects of Allouache's movie are always on the move, always (be)coming, but also, constantly dissolved, never arrested, but rather defined only by their involutionary potentials, as if they were moved, not by their own will, but rather by some forces that evade their own authority: They are what Deleuze and Guattari would call desiring-machines; following the lines of flight, they occupy the sites of peripheral desires yet keep dreaming of central desires; they oscillate between unpredictable revolutionary intensities on the one hand and archaic, fascist entrapments on the other, desecrating, in the process, all languages of representation, of pre-established norms, and championing modes of becoming nomad.

Bab-El-Oued ends with a beautiful irony: Mess ("Immigrant") is finally able to obtain a French passport and is returning "home." As he rushes to the harbor to catch his ship, he bumps into Mabrouk (the young baker and another victim of Saïd's gang) and proudly exhibits his French papers. Only then does Mabrouk realize that Mess, despite all appearances, is "really" French and that he has been telling the truth about his nationality all these past months. Mabrouk is happy for Mess and wishes him good luck; in fact, he urges him to hurry to his boat, as if he were afraid that by some strange circumstance, Mess would be stuck, once again, in the Algerian asylum. Mabrouk's hunch almost materializes. In his excitement, Mess nearly leaves his passport with Mabrouk, but the latter hails him and gives him back his papers. Finally, "Immigrant" makes it to the vessel. The ship that is taking Mess "home" is the same one that is taking Boualem into exile. Now the roles are reversed. As Mess thinks that he is putting an end to his nomadism in Algeria, Boualem's wandering in France has just begun.

In Europe, Boualem will be the "Immigrant" that Mess was in Algeria. He will henceforth be the one to live by connivance, to pass for the "pure." He who has failed to be an authentic Algerian will now try to *pass for* pure French. However, is this possible? Can Boualem pass abroad the test he failed at home? "Immigrant" has been on both sides of the fence. Could Boualem only speak to Mess, he would learn of the impossibility of being authentic both at home and abroad. Nonetheless, to learn from Mess would be too easy a counterfeit. It would be a falsification of life for Boualem to appropriate Mess's experience as his. "Immigrant's" experience is only unique and irreproducible — even by "Immigrant" himself. Boualem has to roll his own dice;

he has to write a story of his own. In a remarkably adroit cinematic gesture, Allouache does not make it possible for these two characters to meet on the boat. As they come aboard, not aware of each other's presence on the vessel, the two protagonists choose to go in opposite directions, thus avoiding — perhaps out of the necessity of original experiences — the possibility of an encounter.

All Is Tossed in a Moment of Jewness

If one's voyeuristic desire to develop a sequel to Boualem's experience were so great and irrepressible that one had to invent Boualem's exilic life before the event, it is perhaps to another North African movie, the Tunisian Dridi's *Bye Bye*, that one would turn. Dridi's film could be an interesting follow-up to Allouache's *Bab-El-Oued* since Ismael (played by Sami Bouajila), the main protagonist of *Bye Bye*, opens for the viewers an insightful window on what Boualem's voluntary expatriation in Europe could look like. Having left his Tunisian village, the *bled* as they call it — a word which has now come to signify a desolate little place in the North African desert — Ismael has immigrated in France with his two brothers, Nouredine (played by Ahmed Aderrahim), a quadriplegic, and Mouloud (played by Ouassini Embarek), a quick-witted fourteen year-old boy. One day, as Ismael leaves for work, a fire breaks out in their Parisian apartment, tragically trapping and killing the helpless Nouredine. Haunted by the nightmarish guilt of his brother's death, Ismael decides to take Mouloud back to their native land. On their way to Tunisia, the two brothers choose to stop in Marseilles for two weeks in order to visit their uncle (played by Benhaïssa Ahouari). *Bye Bye* opens with Ismael and Mouloud driving into the cosmopolitan and ethnically tense city of Marseilles, France.

The brothers' arrival in Marseilles is greeted by a number of incongruous developments. Their relatives, who have just spotted them from their apartment window, are waving at them and prompting them to rush upstairs. However, as Ismael and Mouloud are being welcomed, a black family is being evicted from an apartment in the most inconsiderate manner. Their furniture is being repossessed and whatever is of no value to the French landlord is being thrown out the window. As the mother and father are wailing and begging their unforgiving proprietor for mercy, their bewildered children remain strangely calm amidst this great commotion caused by the adults. This situational irony is emblematic in two ways.

First, for those who are familiar with the power of the father in most traditional African societies, it suggests that the displacement of the (African) father from the rural setting to the urban environment has been accompanied by the loss of his authority; the father is alienated from his progeny who, troubled by the lack of a necessary nexus between his boisterous ways and his claim for power, is gradually moving in to occupy his place. The contradiction between the hysteric adults and the poised children rehearses Ismael's inability to properly care for Nouredine, and it augurs trouble to come in his relationship with Mouloud to whom he has become more a failing surrogate father than a brother. In fact, hardly have the two visitors been shown into their uncle's apartment that the veiled indication of Ismael's lurking "impotence" (the powerlessness of Ismael as a father) becomes more explicit through the uncle's struggle to take control of his household. In order to make room for the newcomers, Ismael's cousin Rhida (Sofiane Mammeri) is asked by his father to sleep in the living room for the next two weeks. However, Rhida strongly protests his father's decision, and only his mother's intervention convinces him to give in. This does not please Rhida's father, who directs harsh criticisms toward both the youngster and his mother (Jamila Darwich-Farah). Dridi emphasizes the father's lack of authority within the domestic space by burlesquing the drunken father in the black family, who is chased around and beaten by his wife. Rhida's father is also mocked as not displaying much leadership either. He is an irritable man whose constant rambling causes people to tune him out more often than they listen to him. He has lost touch with his family, and although he suspects that his son, Rhida, is involved in drug dealing, he does not know how to effectively confront him. He throws his arms in the air — when he does not throw himself at his son — and lets his wife deal with what he calls *her* lost child.

As Ismael apprehensively observes his uncle's failed efforts to recapture his manhood, he realizes the task at hand for himself. Worried that his little brother Mouloud could be drawn further into Rhida's dangerous urban lifestyle, Ismael precipitates the question of the "return to the *bled*." For Ismael and his uncle, the *bled* is not just a phys-

From left to right, Rhida (Sofiane Mammeri), his mother (Jamila Darwich-Farah), and his young cousin, Mouloud (Ouassini Embarek) (*Bye Bye*, directed by Karim Dridi, France, 1995).

ical space in Tunisia. It symbolizes, above all, a psychological oasis, a state of congruence between masculinity as a biological and corporeal condition and the gendered expectations that are projected into that condition. However, if for the older generation of men (Ismael and his uncle) the *bled*—to borrow this Glissantian metaphor — is the place of "natural poetics"; that is, the place where sex and gender cohere along an ancient line drawn in the Tunisian sand, for the younger generation, Mouloud, Rhida and Rhida's two sisters, Malika and Myriam (played, respectively, by Farida and Airm Melaab), the *bled* represents the place of "forced poetics." The young protagonists of *Bye Bye* oppose the Metropolis to the *bled* in contradistinction to the Martinican writer Edouard Glissant's opposition of the letter to the word as articulated in *Caribbean Discourse* (1989).[7]

For the younger Tunisian generation more habituated to life in a big metropolitan city than to existence in a little Tunisian village, it is the *bled* that constitutes the place of incongruity, or the locus of what Glissant calls *forced poetics*; and it is the position of the older generation (the uncle, Ismael) that is more in conformity with Glissant's equation. This is why as soon as the *bled* is mentioned to the younger generation, that generation goes into a state of manifest rebellion. This is why Rhida and his sisters refuse to go back to Tunisia, be it only temporarily. And this is why Mouloud runs away from home to live with a drug dealer as soon as his brother suggests that they return to Tunisia. For the young, Tunisia is a lifeless place, a stifling notion, and the idea of physical and psychological numbness. Ironically, the younger generation has inherited this idea of the *bled* from their elders. At one time, the older generation, too, felt this way about their native land, and this is precisely what prompted them, like the Boualem of *Bab-El-Oued*, to pack their bags and leave. The fact that they still remain in exile and speak of their homeland no longer as a permanent "home," but rather as a place for a temporary stay or as a vacation land, is evidence that they now cast upon it a *tourist gaze*. From this perspective, they are reminiscent of the French man in *Bab-El-Oued*, who, after many years away from Algeria, walks his blind aunt back into Bab-El-Oued and tries to convince her that nothing has changed, that the city has kept its beauty and purity, all the while observing the desolation of Algeria, as his aunt can smell the stench of pollution. What then has caused Ismael and his uncle, if not to totally change their perception of homeland, at least to exoticize it as a place of moral purity in opposition to France's "decadent" morality? The answer to this question, I believe, lies in the situational irony that I noted at the inception of *Bye Bye*.

The juxtaposition of shots of flying furniture, crying parents, and Ismael and Mouloud's happily looking up at relatives that motion them to come upstairs constitutes a wise synecdoche — a part standing for the whole — of what Ismael will later come to understand as the incongruity between gesture and feeling in the urban space. In the city, the filmmaker suggests, there is no "real" or "sincere" relationship of equivalence between the gesture and its signification; this relationship is always already one of dislocation, of miscommunication (or missed communication). For Ismael and his uncle, their contrastive experiences of the *bled* on the one hand, and Paris and Marseilles on the other hand, seem to have convinced them that the rural space is the place of "sincere" communicability of consciousnesses. Thus when the rural (the African) meets the urban (the French), their encounter is necessarily thwarted by lack of sincerity, false pretenses, un-met expectations and misapprehensions. When Ismael and Mouloud arrive at their uncle's apartment in Marseilles, the latter insists that they should make themselves at home, and that they should feel free to stay as long as they like. When Rhida refuses to vacate his bedroom for the newcomers, his mother is quick to teach him that random act of hospitality and sharing are traditions of "*chez nous,*" that is, of the *bled.*

In contrast, in the urban space, no gift is ever free. Renard (Foxy) the drug pusher (played by Moussa Maaskri), is an interesting analogy for this disconnection between the signifier and its signified in the urban notion of the gift. Renard never gives anything without expecting something in return. When he offers Rhida and Mouloud some crack cocaine, it is clear that his intent is to hook them and control them. Renard epitomizes the exploitative urban machine (France), which tolerates the rural *other* (the *Beur* as the Arab is called in France) only insofar as that other does its dirty work. Renard, himself a *Beur,* believes that he has understood the rules of the urban game: "When it's violent, it's violent." In other words, one is a man only insofar as one is more violent than the violent urban machine. In fact, that violent urban machine, precisely Paris, has already failed Ismael, Mouloud and Nouredine. In a rap lyric that he wrote the very day he arrived in Marseilles, the young Mouloud indicates that he is not totally naïve about urban France's conniving act. He is aware of his otherness; he is of another color; he is the color of butter; he is the *Beur.* Perhaps the quick-minded Mouloud is not so naïve as Ismael believes. As early as their arrival in Marseilles, Mouloud has understood the irony of the situation, and he knows that their experience in Marseilles will not differ from the one in Paris. Both in Paris and in Marseilles, they will remain *Beur.* He has made up his mind; he will not try to find refuge in the exoticized *bled.* Instead, he is determined to fight back and win recognition in the land of the other. Mouloud has this to say to the narrow-minded, xenophobic French such as represented by Ludo and his associates: "You are not the ones who'll eat us up. We're the ones who'll eat you up."

The character of Ludo (played by Philippe Ambrosini) is the French counterpart of the Saïd encountered in *Bab-El-Oued*. Ludo is the leader of a gang of young French men who are concerned with preserving their racial and national purity. Ludo despises the "foreigner" and believes that the expulsion of the foreigner from France will not come about through mere disorganized, individual random acts of hatred. Instead it should be a systemic and programmatic endeavor. However, Ludo's inability to conceive and implement the program he talks about denotes the lack of sophistication and inadequacy of hate mongers to come to terms with their own societal norms. Ludo's hatred of the foreigner is a subconscious defense mechanism by which he hopes to deal with the frustrations imposed upon him by a France that has taught him to think of himself as superior to the Arab in particular, and the foreigner in general, and yet which still grows increasingly fond of the exotic "East." Yasmina (played by Nozha Khouadra), the girlfriend of Jacky (played by Frédéric Andrau), is the symptom of Ludo's homosocial obsession. Clearly, Ludo is attracted to his younger brother's Arab girlfriend; he makes flattering and bawdy remarks to her each time he encounters her. However, for the sake of his racial purity, Yasmina also embodies the impure other that Ludo must hate in order to love himself, that is, in order to live in total agreement with his myth of racial superiority. So Ludo hates what his society, in the name of racial purity and superiority, forbids him to enjoy, by creating relationships of contiguity and similarity between the term Arab — or foreigner for that matter — and other terms, such as lewdness, loudness, idleness, larceny, depredation and destruction.

Yasmina is not only the symptom of Ludo's malaise; she is also the manifestation of Ismael's delayed *jouissance* or bliss as much as he is hers. To each other, Yasmina and Ismael represent the postponed journey back to the *bled*. Within each other's eyes they see Tunisia, Arab language, customs and mores, which they long for, and whose engulfing embrace they nonetheless try to elude, and whose psychological shelter they nevertheless cannot help yearning for. It is their tormenting desire for home that leads Yasmina and Ismael to betray Jacky's great trust in them and to have a love affair. In fact, Jacky, who befriended Ismael, protected him from his racist brother Ludo, and even went so far as to put his own life at stake to save Ismael from drowning in the frigid waters of Marseilles, was far from imagining that Ismael could "stab him in the back" by sleeping with his girlfriend. However, in the moral solitude of Marseilles, among the many gazes that reminded them of their foreign uniqueness and subjectified them as strangers, the call for home — which caused Yasmina and Ismael to hail one another as subjects belonging to the same ideological sphere — was more injunctive than Jacky's friendship. Yasmina and Ismael's indistinct relationship with Tunisia is exemplified in their own dubious love affair, and their off-again on-again acceptance of the fact that they are seeking one another. Although Yasmina is the one who first made an implicit pass at Ismael, she keeps insisting that he sought her first; and even though Ismael is the first one to have more explicitly pursued Yasmina, he is now torn between his feelings for her and his loyalty to Jacky.

Yasmina and Ismael's fraught relationship is reflective of their equivocal rapport with Tunisia as both a place of spiritual solace and a site of physical entrapment. A total investment in Tunisia as the quintessential home always undermines the characters' relationship with France. This is metaphorized in the breakdown of Jacky's, Yasmina's, and Ismael's friendships through Ismael and Yasmina's betrayal. Disappointed in his two friends, Jacky finds consolation in Ludo and his racist gang. Metaphorically, Jacky returns "home," that is, among his own, as Ismael sets about to find and take back to Tunisia, his brother Mouloud, who, since their disagreement about going back to the *bled*, has disappeared into the Marseilles night.

Ismael finally finds his young brother living with and working for Renard the drug dealer. Renard, who believes that Mouloud has set him up with an undercover agent, threatens to shoot Ismael. However, it is Mouloud who, applying Renard's own concept that one is a man only insofar as one stands on the right side of a gun, saves his brother by pointing a bigger gun at Renard.

This time, the two brothers are determined to leave Marseilles to its violence. They rush to their uncle's apartment to collect their few possessions. As Ismael gathers their belongings and says farewell to their grandmother (Bakhta Tayeb), Mouloud spray paints the words "Bye Bye" on their car. The title of the movie is thus a token of his determination to steer away not just from Marseilles but also from the Algerian community in Marseilles, both sites constituting spaces for coercion and subjectification of concrete individuals. Marseilles and the *bled* are like the city and the desert, or France and Algeria. They are ultimately two Ideological State Apparatuses. Each one has its "clique" (group, gang), Ludo and his gang on one side, the Algerian community on the other side. Each "clique" is self-mystified (formalized), and at the same time, mystifies (formalizes) the other:

Renard (Moussa Maaskri) holding Ismael (Sami Bouajila) at gunpoint (*Bye Bye,* directed by Karim Dridi, France, 1995).

"Hey, you there, you who do our dirty job, you Algerian or Moroccan — what's the importance? You all look alike to me — *Beurs*, hashish dealers, belly dancers, are you looking at me? Do you want a piece of me? This is France; Morocco is on the other side," say Ludo and his "clique." "Hey, you there, heartless ignoramus white racists, I am the color of butter, but I am no butter. You won't eat me up, I will eat you up," say Mouloud and his "clique."[8]

Toward the end of the film, an exhausted Mouloud falls asleep with his head resting peacefully on the shoulder of his brother at the wheel of their two-horsepower Citroen. Mouloud wakes up only to realize that, from a telephone booth on the coast of the Mediterranean Sea, Ismael has been able to convince their parents that they will not be coming back to the *bled*. Furthermore, their car has broken down for good, and whatever their new destination, they will have to get there on foot. Over Ismael's objections, the young Mouloud proposes that they try a new adventure in Spain, of which he has heard a lot of good things.

Mouloud's and Ismael's resolution not to go back to Tunisia, but rather to continue their deliberate exilic quest for selfhood, is suggestive of their coming to terms with the illusory nature of the notion of home and their consequent commitment to displacement. In the Jabesian sense of the term, these two *Arab* travelers, whose dedication to erring, displacement, and relocation is stronger than the interpellative voice of the native land, are *Jews*. Uprooted from a pseudo-objectively and ontologically anchored condition of Arab-ness or *Beur*-ness and cast into the ungraspable, fleeting moment of the formation of the autobiographical "I," they come to function within an economy of difference, which questions the relevance of such binaries as insider/outsider, pure/impure, native/foreigner. What have we learned from Jabès a propos the Jew? Other than the Jew is not a rigidified state of difference, not an identity of difference, but a "foreign I" (un étrange je), a tormented subject, committed to estrangement, to self-erasure, like a poet or writer who writes an interminable book and who will never fully be a writer until the interminable book that he will never be done writing is written. "The Jew ... is the hope and wearing away of a book he can never exhaust. You and me next ... we are ourselves an enigmatic text that we try in vain to decipher, page after page ... having made of the infinite space of this book, the infinite book of our questions."[9]

What the two brothers are hoping to steer away from is the double bind of subjectification whereby they are always already formalized either as *subjects of enunciation* (on the side of the Algerian community that is involved in the act of producing an idealized discourse of the *bled* as the site of congruity and subjective wholeness; a discourse that indubitably interpellates them as concrete ideological subjects) or as *subjects of the statement* (on the side of Ludo's clique and its discourse about the Arab in which the latter metaphorizes strangeness, lewdness, dishonesty and uncleanness). Mouloud and Ismael's task is the daunting project of breaking the double bind of transcendentality and genealogy, of rendering the transcendental quasi-transcendental and the genealogical anti-genealogical. The notions of quasi-transcendental and anti-genealogical, as one knows, are for Derrida and Deleuze/Guattari respectively, various nicknames of the Jew/Jewish quality in all of us; which belongs to the order of deterritorialization and production as opposed to that of representation and reproduction. As Deleuze and Guattari have argued in several places,[10] and as will be shown, in the next chapter analyzing Amadou Seck's *Saaraba* (1988) and Cheick Oumar Sissoko's *Finzan* (1990), this anti-genealogical quality is constantly under the threat of representation, and sometimes, although temporarily, even suppressed.

4

Allegorizing the Quest for Autonomy

Cheick Oumar Sissoko's Finzan
and Amadou Seck's Saaraba

This chapter shall elucidate a question that has only been sporadically touched upon in the previous pages, that of the instability of subjectivity, or better put — and to borrow these Althusserian terms with which we are now so familiar — of the precariousness of both the condition of *concrete individual* and *concrete ideological subject*. The passage from concrete individual to concrete subject of ideology, Althusser warns us, is never definitive. It is always already under constant threat of reversal, only to be, once again, always already reversed in another direction, thus going on *ad infinitum*.[1]

In order to explore the topic of the instability of subjectivity, which has been hitherto identified in *Bab-El-Oued* and *Bye Bye* thanks to the philosophical insights of Althusser, this chapter will borrow a different analytical tool, notably, Lacan's psychoanalysis. This shift from Althusser to Lacan does not constitute so huge an *écart*; for Lacan has illuminated, years before Althusser's 1969 formulation of the Ideological State Apparatus' effects on the concrete individual, the idea that the ideology of the symbolic (the Law-of-the-Father), this vague and insidious dogma acting both in the private and public domains, is mostly, if not entirely, responsible for the formation of the "I."

The Formation of the "I" in Psychonalysis

In a study that spawned his psychoanalytical theory, Jacques Lacan notes that individuals are defined at the discursive (or symbolic) level, itself governed by the Law-of-the-Father.[2] Arguing that subjects are constituted by variegated layers of otherness — of which the father's remains the most influential, Lacan posits that through language, the subject is forever tied to the father, whose discourse is irremediably inserted in the subject's discourse — even when the latter claims to speak on his/her own behalf. Lacan's theory stems from his attempt to return to Freud in order to rescue Freudianism from the psychologism in which the psychoanalyst's obsessive quest for scientificity has plunged it.[3] Unlike Freud — and his modern mutants (behaviorists, phenomenologists, existentialists, psychoanalysts) — who argue that the subject's psychological split is just one stage in the biological development of humans, Lacan maintains that the subjective split is permanent. Thus, by being born into a linguistic system, the subject is — by virtue of the norms which constitute that system, and which are the rules of the father — a permanently split individual, constantly haunted by the desire to be — or to speak — *like* the father.

Lacan argues that the subject's desire to emulate the progenitor is analogical to a yearning to relive the pre–Oedipal moment, that is, the moment of total congruity between the world of the child and that of the mother (the *pre-specular* or *imaginary world*). The imaginary, the world of perfect communication between mother and child, Lacan contends, is irreversibly shattered the moment the child is introduced to language, or to the *symbolic*. The child's acceptance of the gift of language implies a broken promise. By receiving the symbolic, the child also consents to the laws that govern it, which are ultimately under the authority of the father. The symbolic, offered to the child as the instrument of his or her independence from the mother and the means of his or her identification with the father, is in reality that which binds him or her to the father, as slave to master. Thus the subject's desire to be like his or her father is according to Lacan, "desire for a lack" insofar as it is always predicated on the impossibility of finding absolute correspondence between the world of the subject's private yearnings and that of the symbolic; that is, of what is socially acceptable behaviors. Lacan represents this failed connection by the algorithm S/s (the signifier over the signified), whereby the bar separating the signifier (S) from the signified (s) illustrates the gap between the desire for subjective wholeness and the actualization of this wholeness.[4] Lacan contends that this lack of fulfillment is nevertheless the drive for the formation of the "I." It is the desire to (re)capture a lost or impossible sense of unity and fullness that leads subjects to bounce from one form of exposure to the next.

Lacan's notion of the capture of the subjects by the Law and the subjects' vain attempt to free themselves from a Law that is always lying in wait somewhere else to ambush them as soon as they think to have liberated themselves is what is allegorized in the Senegalese Seck's *Saaraba*[5] and the Malian

Sissoko's *Finzan*.[6] While casual viewers of *Saaraba* and *Finzan* are more likely to satisfy themselves with the conclusion that these two films stage the confrontation between tradition and modernity in Africa in the aftermath of decolonization and at the dawn of urbanization, one shall refrain from such a simplistic analysis. *Saaraba* and *Finzan*, produced in 1988 and 1990, respectively, can obviously not afford to ignore the crises that the black continent faces at the crossroads of tradition and modernity. However, reading the central tensions in these two films as necessarily contingent upon the colonizer/colonized encounter does not do justice to their complexity. The dramas that unfold in both films illustrate the general scenario of the subject's constitution; it should only remain accidental that in Seck's and Sissoko's films, the postcolonial context constitutes the primary stage for their development. Thus, the next pages will attempt to elucidate through *Saaraba* and *Finzan*, treatments of the Lacanian motifs of identity, desire and lack in African cinema, more for the purpose of directing attention to how seriously African filmmakers have reflected — through questions of identity construction and social formation — upon the structural complexity of social reality than with the intent of exacerbating African scholars' apparent institutional *malaise* about psychoanalysis and so-called Western theory in general.[7]

African scholars and filmmakers, such as Martin Mhando, Keyan G. Tomaselli or Olufemi Taiwo — to cite only a few — have criticized what they see as most critics' rush to Western modes of interpretation when dealing with

Cheick Oumar Sissoko, an indefatigable fighter for African women's rights (photograph by Banning Eyre, for www.afropop.org.).

African cinema (or literature), and the consequent absence of African philosophy as well as the legitimating of the hegemony of colonialist/Eurocentric philosophy in academia. Mhando, for instance, has argued that Western theories, which tend to privilege content over form, are insufficient and inadequate in explaining the materialist aesthetics of reality in Africa. He contends that a necessary re-questioning of aesthetics and praxis of African cinema narration should restore the importance of form by exploring orality as the defining structure of African cinema.[8]

Insofar as structural psychoanalysis, which developed in France under the aegis of Lacan, falls under the appellation of "Western theory," the very theory that is being second-guessed by the panegyrists of African epistemological autonomy, the use of it in discussing *Saaraba* and *Finzan* could generate some uneasiness. Nevertheless, the aim here is no more to legitimize a so-called Eurocentrist colonialist view than to set the stage for an engagement between European Continental theory and African cinema within cultural studies as a discipline; a meeting which, one should hope, will elucidate some of the ways in which African cinema and (Western) theory support, cancel or illuminate one another in their particular treatments of questions that remain of great concern to human societies in general. Freud and Lacan did not invent the unconscious and its functioning but only found languages which, provided one agrees on a lexicon for the purpose of communication, attempt to render the intricate mechanism of the human being's most passionate quest, that of identity. It is inasmuch as *Saaraba's* protagonists' desires to evade a certain father and to ascertain their autonomy inevitably meet with lack and relapse into the realm of another father, and insofar as, in their pursuits for identity and representation, these protagonists seem to lend credence to Lacan's claim of the subject's necessary attachment to the Name-of-the-Father, that Lacan himself becomes pertinent in the discussion that will take place in the next pages.

The Impossibility of Autonomy

Saaraba begins with the homecoming of the main protagonist, Tamsir (played by Abdoulaye Aziz Diop), who is returning to Senegal after seventeen years in France. Because Tamsir's French education was in great part financed by his wealthy Senegalese uncle (played by Elhadj Abdoulaye Seck), his knowledge is already a gift, a present from two paternal donators, the white colonizing father (France) and the traditional father (his uncle). But these two gestures of donation have duplicity at their core: both presents (the uncle's and France's) have already melted in exchange. By accepting them, Tamsir has alienated the possibility of his freedom; he has become indebted to both fathers, whose laws he is henceforth expected to further. Tamsir's uncle is the owner of a successful construction firm who anticipates that his nephew will use his France-gained Western knowledge to expand his business. A position and an office are made available to Tamsir immediately upon his return to Senegal. Unlike Tamsir's uncle, France does not make its intention overt. However, by virtue of his French education, Tamsir has become France's agent and like so many Africans educated in the French system, he will consequently participate in the dissemination of French ideology. It is by attempting to evade both fathers' authorities and by refusing to pay off his "debts" to his uncle and to France that Tamsir hopes to affirm his autonomous selfhood.

To subvert his uncle's hold, Tamsir sets forth to sabotage the firm's projects either by not coming to work or by destroying documents pertaining to important activities, thus undermining the company's financial viability. In a nation which, to Tamsir's great frustration, is increasingly adopting capitalist postures and duplicating the class divisions, which, he believes, are the fallout of capitalist ideologies, the firm's financial impairment would also mean that it would fail to thrive as another one of France's vestiges. Tamsir's rebellion against his uncle is meant to undercut France's hegemony in Francophone Africa and its negative effects on the African populations.

Since his arrival in Senegal, Tamsir has been relentlessly speaking out against the depersonalizing effects of the West's intrusion into the black continent. From the day he landed in Dakar, he has witnessed first hand the undignified stance of the unemployed Senegalese youth driven to the alluring and deceptive glitters of the city; he has seen the plethora of beggars that the unequal distribution of the country's resources has produced; he has driven through quarters where extreme poverty and insulting wealth co-exist in a "strange" proximity; during the Paris-Dakar car race, he has watched rich white daredevils in fast cars transform the dirt roads of Senegal into muddy ponds. Tamsir is convinced that these conditions cannot be dissociated from the white father's (France's) egocentrism and his compulsive desire for the accumulation of wealth. The more he observes the dreadful conditions in Senegal, the more it becomes clear that France could not have succeeded in reducing so many blacks to poverty without the complicity of the black father. The uncle begins to look strangely white to Tamsir. To Tamsir the uncle is developing a white (capitalist) syndrome. Has not an earlier and mightier black voice prophesied the spoliation of independence if left in the exclusive care of the greedy and opportunistic bourgeois spirit? Has not the author of the *Wretched of the Earth* also devised an anticipatory prescription against the destabilizing force generated by the collusion of post-independence black bourgeoisie and the former colonial power, a remedy in the form of an alert suspicion of the money-hungry elite and a reliance on the peasantry?[9] As if attentive to this Fanonian prediction and to its antidote, Tamsir wants no part of his uncle's collusion with the West. If neither France nor his uncle — the epitome of the urbanized black — is pure, that is, sincere and authentic, then purity lies elsewhere, in the country, within the confines of the authentic father's realm, which Tamsir resolves to find.

Tamsir is now absolutely certain that Senegal, in particular, and Africa, in general, needs a "new man." However, this Messiah is to be found neither in the alienating spirit of capitalism as shamelessly displayed by his uncle, nor in the abdication of his marijuana-smoking cousin and childhood friends. This hero will come not "from the cold" of the West, but rather from the warmth of the country, with country values. So, Tamsir goes to the village in search of a new self, away from the invading other, away from the French and the want-to-be-French body snatchers to whom he refuses to be indebted.

Nevertheless, the hero's effort to reinvent himself hits a snag. As he comes to realize, it is neither easy to evade the white father nor undemanding to live according to the ideals of the "authentic" black father. In his ancestral village, Tamsir is referred to as the relative from France; he is asked to read and translate letters; he has forgotten the way to the river and can no longer keep his balance on the precariously assembled rocks that make up the floor of his family's traditional shower. Tamsir is henceforth standing on shaky ground:

the white father has tracked Tamsir even down to his village, demanding that he pay off his debt to France, who educated him, and to his uncle, who paid for it all. Ignoring his capitalist creditors (France and the uncle), Tamsir still wants to convince himself that the law of the "authentic" tradi-tional father is inalienable. Like the pil-grimage of the prophet whose voice seems to animate him, Tamsir's own trip to the locus of authenticity appears contrived;[10] as he compulsively seeks to champion and to impose upon the peo-ple of the village ancestral laws that they have grown less enthusiastic to uphold, the acts that Tamsir poses become comically less oriented toward predication. Thus, Tamsir insists that his sister, Daba (played by Awa Che-ickh Guey), who refuses to marry the man to whom she is promised, comply with tradition.

Top: Tamsir (Abdoul Aziz Diop), lec-turing his sister, aba (Awa Cheickh Guey) (*Saaraba*, directed by Amadou Seck, Senegal, 1988). *Bottom:* Lissa (Fabienne Joelle Felhio) is promised to an older man, but it is Tamsir that she loves (*Saaraba*, directed by Amadou Seck, Senegal, 1988).

He continues to champion tradition and the "transcendental" law of the ancients until he falls in love with "the forbidden" in the form of Lissa (played by Fabienne Joelle Falhio), a young woman from his village. Lissa, like Tamsir's sister, is already promised to another man, an older man, a powerful Member of Parliament (played by Mamadou Ka) who has been showering her parents with jewels purchased in city shops. Although Lissa loves Tamsir, she cannot marry him. She has to listen to the call of tradition and respect her parents' will. She has to remain a virgin for her future husband.

One might expect that Lissa's great respect for tradition should make a man like Tamsir proud; that he should admire a girl who displays so high a regard for the very custom he has asked his sister to uphold. By Tamsir's own standard, he has fallen in love with a virtuous woman; unlike Daba, his sister, whom he castigated for not listening to the voice of the ancients, Lissa respects the ancestral law. One would expect Tamsir to be proud of her, to praise her devotion to tradition. Instead, he starts resenting his elders' mores and customs. Unexpectedly, the "authentic" father's laws seem to engulf and oppress him. Tamsir's faith in tradition cannot resist the test of love. In rebellion against the Law-of-the-Traditional-Father, Tamsir and Lissa decide to have a child, hoping that this will discourage the MP in his romantic pursuit of Lissa.

Tamsir is the symptom of one of the postcolonial intellectual's greatest *dis-ease:* his tendency to suspect evil intents in any other one of his compatriots but himself; his propensity to suggest that any other solution to the problems plaguing post-independence Africa but his own remedy is deficient. Tamsir illustrates the syndrome of intolerance that has always dwelt in both the precursory struggles for decolonization and the management of the newfound political and cultural autonomy in the former French colonies of Africa and the Antilles. His gestures evoke those of the hypocritical Fanon of *Black Skin, White Masks,* who even when he has made the same decision as his compatriots (that of marrying a white woman), nonetheless manages to detect guilt in others' judgment but never in his own. "...what [the Martinican woman] wants is a kind of lactification. For, in a word, the race must be whitened; every woman in Martinique knows this, says it, repeats it.... Out of the blackest part of my soul, across the zebra striping of *my* mind,[11] surges this desire to be suddenly *white* ... who but a white woman can do this for *me?*"[12] Tamsir's admonitory stance toward his compatriots, who, like him, are trying their best to reconcile the internal tensions created by their encounter with the West, is a pattern, which, beyond Fanon, is also evocative of Senghor's insincere censure against the African critics who do not see eye to eye with Negritude.[13] Tamsir, whose biological father is a "marabout," a teacher of Islamic faith and a respected man in the traditional community, failed to answer the voice of tradition when his own interests were at stake. His flight from the white father (France) has only led him straight into the crushing embrace of the traditional father; and his attempt to flee the traditional father reveals how ephemeral his hatred of France and his love of ancestral customs actually are. To speak like Lacan, Tamsir is only what he is, that is to say, the plaything of his thought, living with the illusion that he is what in reality he can never be; and what he can never be, the object of his perpetual want, is this autonomous subject free from the embrace of the abusing father.

For Demba (played by Diankou Bakhayokho), too, another marginal character in *Saaraba*, paradise exists neither in the world of the white father nor in that of the black father, but rather a place he will arrive at some day, thanks to a bike offered to him by a white priest. Like Tamsir's, Demba's search for *Saaraba* (paradise) outside the realms of the white and black fathers is doomed to failure, as his efforts to assert his difference only end up reifying the white father. Is it merely accidental that Demba hopes to liberate himself from the paternal grip using a donation (a motorbike) from the father (a white priest)? Demba's ambivalence is what has been pointed out elsewhere, and which has just been identified above in Tamsir/Fanon/Senghor, as the postcolonial subject's inextricable oedipal entanglement with the West.[14] Is it coincidental that Demba spends most of his time searching for the bike's missing piece (a chain) and devotes a great part of his energy and effort to repairing the father's broken present? Demba's constant tinkering with his broken present conjures up images of the French speaking African people, who, in the aftermath of decolonization and independence, are left struggling to upgrade the very scarce and at best archaic infrastructures that could not be transported back to the *métropole* and which France, so grudgingly, bequeathed them as it was reticently withdrawing from its lost empire. The fact that the broken gift, which chains Demba to France, was a present from a missionary supports Fanon's indictment of the entire colonial system as a monstrous exploitative machinery whose parts comprised the military, the education and the religion.[15] The chain that Tamsir ultimately offers Demba, and which is symptomatic of a binding contract chaining the latter to the white father, suggests that Demba has entered a binding law the terms of which evade his authority; and this act of donation by Tamsir is indicative that Tamsir, in spite of himself, desires the white father whose gesture he extends, via Demba, to rural African populations. Ironically, when Demba and Tamsir leave their village in order to reconstitute their wholeness away from all the fathers who desire them, it is by means of the bike — the father's gift — that they travel. When they have finally reached the place which Demba mistakes for paradise, it is the city of Dakar, glittering under neon and headlights, which Demba has fallen in love with. Tamsir and Demba's fate seem to be unavoid-

ably tied to the Name-of-The-Father. Their desire for recognition is inex-
orably tied to their desire for the *Other*, the father, who acts as the "guarantor of truth."

In the psychoanalytical register, both Tamsir and Demba would be
regarded as failed subjects, disappointing characters that have missed an opportunity to make productive use of the gifts they received from their father(s).
Here, one would argue that both subjects, having abdicated the roles and
spaces designed for them in the societies that raised them to be productive
members, lost their sanity. It is henceforth incumbent upon the community
at large to protect them in spite of themselves by capturing, curing and then
restoring them to the moral entity. Such a view is often anchored in the logic
that one can only be either *all self* or *all other*, either all A or all B, either normal or monstrous.

This operation of registration into degree zero of monstrosity, that is to
say, into state philosophy or normality, is less subtle in Sissoko's *Finzan* than
it is in Seck's *Saaraba*. Both in *Finzan* and *Saaraba*, it is clear that marginal
characters — those who do not abide by societal rules — are treated like patho-
logical subjects, and the community's attitude toward them is the conde-
scending posture of the healer. However, while in *Saaraba* the process of
restoration of the marginal subject or the socially insane to sanity takes place
at the discursive level — the dialogic relationships between Tamsir, Lissa and
the elders is analogous to that of the reluctant analysand and the almighty
analyst — in *Finzan*, the therapeutic method combines discursive violence
with physical brutality. In *Finzan*, a whole community, scandalized by the
drifting of two women (Nanyuma and Fili), makes it its duty to forcefully
restore them from a life of profligacy and immorality to the life of reason.

Sanity Is Male as Insanity Is Female

If Sissoko's *Finzan* stages the confrontation between reason and unrea-
son, the film makes it plain that sanity is male and insanity is female. By refusing to comply with the rules of her community, and by allowing both her
voice and her body to question the ancestral symbolic order of the Bambara
people, Nanyuma (Diarrah Sanogo), the main protagonist in *Finzan*, makes
herself a monster and offers herself to the community's wrath. For this very
old Bambara society whose daily life Sissoko projects on screen, the threat of
the enemy from without (the oppressive Western capitalistic ideology and its
brutal black political and military agents) seems to cause less concern than
the malaise stirred by the monster from within (in the form of the rebellious
Bambara women). The madwomen undermine the Bambara *socius*, the ances-

tral gift in accordance with which the Bambara people has lived for centuries, and which has sustained its life. Within the confines of this *socius*, that is, the set of attributive judgments that for each individual defines a space and a role, the law is inviolable. Consequently, every voice and gesture should function to reflect, mirror and recognize the *socius*, rather than contradict it.

Nanyuma, the third wife of an old Bambara man, has just become a widow. According to Bambara customs, she must show her affliction and pain by lamenting and crying. However, Nanyuma's protest starts in the first scene of *Finzan*, as both in her voice and gesture she adopts a non-traditional stance during her husband's agonizing moments and in the aftermath of his death. Unlike her two co-spouses, who seem to launch into a wailing contest, Nanyuma shows little emotion and utters no cry, because, as she remarks, she has shed all her tears during eight years of a marriage whose burden she bore like the trauma of slavery. The Bambara custom also requires that the youngest wife of a deceased husband be remarried to his surviving brother, who should then take care of her children; Bala (played Namory Oumar Keita), the unscrupulous younger brother of Nanyuma's late husband, is not shy in making his intention known to the village chief (Balla Moussa Keita). He has always desired Nanyuma. Now that she is a widow, he intends to fulfill his "duty" by taking her in his home as his third wife. The chief agrees that the traditions should be respected, and Bala, the village drunk, is given permission to marry Nanyuma. However, Nanyuma, who has hoped that her husband's death would be the defining moment for her own freedom, has vowed not to submit herself once again to a marriage arranged without her consent. She tries unsuccessfully to find refuge and support, first at her father's compound in a neighboring village, and then at her brother's house, in the city. Each time, she finds no strong ally in her protest, and the concerted efforts of men succeed in returning her forcibly to Bala.

The community's exceptionally unified desire to exorcise the threat of Nanyuma's protest stands as a metaphor for the analyst's presumptuous clinical gesture of rehabilitation into a supposed ideal social space or the Grand-Narrator's un-avowed desire to lead a herd of individuals con-

Nanyuma (Diarrah Sanogo) in mourning. She had hoped that her husband's death would free her from an undesired marriage (*Finzan*, directed by Cheick Oumar Sissoko, Mali, 1989).

tained by moral institutions.[16] In Nanyuma's world, the Grand-Narrator happens to be the transcendental *griot*, the African praise-singer and genealogist. It is *he* who defines the grid of attractors, the abstract categories that constitute the Bambara individual. The griot is an Ideological State Apparatus (ISA). His function is to turn concrete individuals into subjects of ideology. So the griot's praises, his rituals, the education he gives, and the information he disseminates are not necessarily innocent. They are intended to hail subjects, to manipulate them, and by complementing the family education individuals of the community receive, transform these individuals into perfect ideological subjects. The griot's praises run something like this: *scratch yourself here! Give a smile there! Shake a hand now! Look! A woman! Can you recognize her? Say woman! Good boy! Say it again! Very good!* When one is done listening to *him*, one is also done being formed and amazed at oneself: *is that me? Is that really me? Yes, that's me! I am so proud of me! If you are the other, you are not as good as me! I feel so sorry for you for not being me! But you know, not everybody can be me, the me that is the correct one!* This is why the griot is not — cannot be — a neutral signifier. He is a male character working for the reification of the masculine corporeal. This is why the term "griotte" can only be an oxymoron. The griot's interest is in his permanent erection, and consequently, anything that suggests, even slightly, the collapse of the masculine erection, becomes the target of his wrath. The griot, this Ideological State Apparatus working to turn individuals into ideological subjects acquiescent of male supremacy, does not operate alone. He has an army of believers working for him. He recruits his most passionate supporters among women; for who else can better convince women of men's superiority than women themselves?

In *Finzan*, the character Fili (uncredited), Nanyuma's niece, can testify to this if she survives her ordeal to talk about it. Fili's tragedy illustrates the insidiousness and pervasiveness of patriarchy's authority, which has so successfully invaded all the layers of the Bambara *socius* that the Bambara man can be assured that even in his *absence*, he can still rely on the Bambara women to keep a vigilant eye on one another and enforce *his* law. In fact, Fili's family has a medical history of hemophilia. So, Fili's father, who would not risk losing his daughter under the blade of the village excision woman, raised Fili in the city. Fili grew up without undergoing the ritual of excision to which all Bambara women are to submit. However, to punish his daughter for supporting Nanyuma's rebellion, Fili's father sends the young girl to the village, so that she can be chosen a suitable and respectable Bambara husband there, far from the denaturalizing city. In the village, as Fili is showering with another girl, her friend discovers that she has never been excised, and she relays the information to the older women who are scandalized and sickened by what they regard as "unclean." After reporting Fili's "monstrous" condition to the men of the village, the latter give the women permission to take the necessary measures to *rectify* Fili's "abnormality." Despite her loud protests and her struggle, Fili is captured and mutilated. The movie ends on a tragic irony, as Fili's father, having learned that his daughter is about to be excised comes running to the village, but arrives too

Fili (uncredited) has just learned that her lover will not marry her, because she is not excised (*Finzan*, directed by Cheikh Oumar Sissoko, Mali, 1989).

late, only to witness her hemorrhaging profusely. By restricting his daughter's space, by strictly confining her within the social boundaries determined by the griot's narrative, Fili's father has not just killed his daughter's plastic power; he has also undermined the possibility of his own freedom. The Bambara *socius*, which the Bambara man so proudly accepted as a gift from his father, turns out to be that which chains him to his own subjugation. By holding on to this gift, by making himself the watchman of woman, man has also restricted his own movement.

Tamsir, Lissa, Demba, Nanyuma, and Fili are all living proof that, as Deleuze once suggested, if human beings have lost their freedom, it is less because their fundamental values have been violated than because their movements have been restricted. If the *socius* is the myth that binds man/woman to the crowd, to the vertiginous *folie circulaire* and causes him/her to walk *kurmagati* in the company of men and women who think and act uniformly, then there is reason to believe that Nanyuma and Tamsir have offered the measure of what it takes to act otherwise, that is to say, *gangasrotagati*.[17] Breaking the antiquarian chains of submission and coercion and traveling uncharted paths in the "*écart*" of traditional *trace*—causing tradition to stand on its head — they take upon themselves to defy the almighty father by overturning his law, and by overstepping the boundaries that he so officiously prescribed.

With Tamsir, the insubordination reaches a certain paroxysm. Approaching the father from behind, this time, he would not try to stab him in the back — such is the revolution of predictable men and women. Tamsir's insurgency will be more subtle, less foreseeable: he would give the father a child that is too monstrous to be recognized by the father himself, a supple individual born out of his *qualitative* and vortex-like collision with Lissa — herself already a vortex — a thousand plateaus of judicial, economic, political, social and bureaucratic intensities. Tamsir's union with Lissa, although it produces a child, is less concerned with sexuality as a process of filiation, of reproduction of the original familialism, than it is an alliance for the breaking of procreation of the concrete ideological subject and the opening up of the possibility for a line of beginning, for the birth of the Jew-child. This child — far from reiterating a movement — will only seek to duplicate a process, the continuous and creative development of disjunction and exclusion, of becoming *affirmatively* schizophrenic.

For this anti-genealogical child, for this child that is born to scuttle the father's reason-plated fortress, there already is a disgraceful name made available in the recesses of this coldest, most extreme, most passionate, and most self-centered entity that is the *Cogito:*[18] that name is *the anomalous.* The anomalous, which, within the stronghold of reason, in the familial or societal citadel, stands as the proper name of insanity — Tamsir's flight from the Law of the father leads him to drug addiction and to irrationality — or of asexuality — within Bambara tradition, Fili's preservation of her clitoris makes her both a non-woman and a failed man — we are told elsewhere, is the nickname of the individual resisting ideological interpellation, exorcising normalization.[19] The terms to designate such *involutionnary* individuals as Tamsir, Fili and Nanyuma could easily be borrowed from both the deconstructionist critique of the signifier and the schizoanalytical criticism of reason, respectively as arche-trace or point of flight. As arche-traces, these various protagonists are the names of what — within the very systems of representation that seek to erase them, that seek to write them only insofar as they are insane or absent agencies — mark the place of their presences by the very uneasiness they stir within their respective communities, and therefore, allow a possible relationship of those communities with their alterities — be it even a mere relation of misprehension or *méconnaissance.* Tamsir's, Nanyuma's, and Fili's passages in their societies bear profound implications. They are the absences by which society defines its own presence; they are the very conditions of society's presence, the absences that need to be (present) for society to ascertain its presence; a presence which, until they were indexed as absent forms, was itself absent.

> The trace, where the relationship with the other is marked, articulates its possibility in the entire field of the entity [*étant*], which metaphysics has defined as the being-present starting from the occulted movement of the trace. The trace must be thought before the entity. But the movement of the trace is necessarily occulted, it produces itself as self-occultation. When the other announces itself as such, it presents itself in the dissimulation of itself.[20]

The revelation of this incongruity within society has become one of the primary preoccupations of marginalized groups, and especially of African women writers in their denunciation of patriarchy. One can see it at work in Mariama Bâ's *So Long a Letter* (1980),[21] Fatou Keïta's *Rebelle* (1998) and Régina Yaou's *Le Prix de la révolte* (1997).[22] This incongruity, this *dédoublement* of the pure into the impure, and vice versa, we are told, is always already lying in wait in any system of representation. To think the pure as wholly constituted amounts to wishful thinking.

> To think the unique *within* the system, to inscribe it there, such is the gesture of the arche-writing: arche-violence, loss of the proper, of absolute proximity, of self-presence, in truth, the loss of what has never taken place, of a self-presence which has never been given but only dreamed of and always already split, repeated, incapable of appearing to itself except in its own disappearance.[23]

On the question of the eccentricy of subjectivity, of its multiplicity, of its multi-layered constitution, of its split between concrete ideological subjectivity and concrete individuality, psychoanalysts (Lacan), neo–Marxists (Althusser), deconstructionists (Derrida) and schizoanalysts (Deleuze and Guattari) are in relative agreement: Society's obsessive quest for unicity only ends up revealing its weaknesses. This is a reflection for the guardians of the social edifice to ponder on: to so carelessly create the conditions for its own destabilization, the Grand-Narrator, reason, that is, *Cogito*, must have gone insane.

5

Writing the *Soxual* Order

Ousmane Sembène's Faat Kiné *and Ngangura Mweze's* La vie est belle

In his film *Faat Kiné* (2000)[1] late Sembène, arguably the leading Sub-Saharan African filmmaker, attempted a critical analysis of social status founded on gender, thus re-examining, from his traditionally privileged masculine position, the cultural aprioricities that have established an association between the dichotomies masculine/feminine and lord/vassal. However, Sembène's project in *Faat Kiné* is an arduous and torturing endeavor that reveals, if anything, the filmmaker's internal dilemma: on the one hand, the pressure exercised upon him to catch up with a new filmic tradition, such as the one practiced by younger African filmmakers like Cheick Oumar Sissoko or Amadou Seck — a cinematic tradition that seeks to uncover gender inequity in Africa and social injustice against African women in general — and, on the other hand, his difficulty to totally severe ties with the old school of cinema characterized by phallogriocentric conventions. As if to suggest, as did Ngangura in *La vie est belle* (1987),[2] that all is well when sexual responsibility is diligently exercised, Sembène sets about to resurrect social order by first restoring sexual harmony. Thus, sexual orthodoxy, the cultural yardstick, is for Sembène, as it is for Ngangura, the rigid designator in a series of equivalences of social imperfections comprising such collective flaws as corruption, illegitimacy, theft, non-respect of human rights, among others. Like Mweze in *La vie est belle*, Sembene, in *Faat Kiné*, would have us believe that restoration of sexual "normalcy" is the sine qua non condition for the unraveling of all other societal insufficiencies. Thus, although both films decry the degeneration of cultural mores, what they actually deplore is the loss of traditional sexual formality. In other words, if society has gone bad, it is less because people are fundamentally imperfect than because men and women have indulged in new sexual positions.

70

In *La vie est belle* Kourou (played by Papa Wemba), a successful traditional musician with a faithful rural audience, dreams of making a splash on national radio and becoming a star in the big city. So, he leaves his loyal audience and his traditional instrument behind him and travels to the big city. After a few nights erring in the city, Kourou lands a job as a domestic

From left to right, Mongali (Kalimazi Lombume Riva) and Kourou (Papa Wemba) (*La vie est belle/ Life is Rosy*, directed by Ngangura Mweze and Benoît Lamy, Congo, 1987).

in the home of a successful music producer, Nvuandu (played by Kanko Kasongo). Though financially successful, Nvuandu is sexually deficient. So he consults with the local healer Nganga (Bwanando Ngimbi), who advises him, as a solution to his impotence, to marry a second wife, a virgin, with whom he should have no intercourse during the first thirty days following the marriage. Nvuandu's marital choice has fallen on young Kabibi (played by Bibi Krubwa), a graduate of a secretarial school whom Kourou, passing for a successful man, has also seduced. In order to punish her husband for taking a second wife, Nvuandu's first wife, Mamu (played by Landu Nzunzimbu Matshia), not only encourages Kourou's affair with Kabibi and facilitates their encounters, but also takes as lover Kourou's cousin Mongali (played by Kalimazi Lombume Riva). The plot of the movie is thus articulated around Nvuandu's laughable attempts to manage his life as a polygamous man and to take control of his wives who are making a fool of him. In Sembène's movie, Kiné (Venus Seye), a middle-age successful Senegalese single mother of a a young girl, Aby (Mariama Balde), and a young man, Djib (Ndiagne Dia), recollects her life as the children she raised alone have successfully completed high school and are on their way to college. As a young girl, she was impregnated by her teacher who refused to make her his wife and left her to face alone the wrath of her dishonored father trying to burn her. Instead, it is Kiné's mother (Mamé Ndoumbé) that is burned and severely scarred, as she shields her daughter. Later, Kiné is once again impregnated by a swindling fiancé who runs away with her savings and winds up in prison. Nevertheless, Kiné works hard at an entry job as a gas station attendant and, over the years, becomes the successful manager of the business and a proud homeowner. Henceforth in position of power, Kiné refuses the propositions of married men seeking to add her to their harem, as is very common in Senegal. She decides that she really does not need a permanent man in her life, because she can now pay for their favors. Kiné's lifestyle does not necessarily meet the endorsement of her relatives, and especially her children, who try to find her a suitable husband.

While on the surface *La vie est belle* and *Faat Kiné* appear critical of polygamy and its debasing effects on women, neither Sembène nor Ngangura condemn the institution of polygamy as such. The critique of polygamy appears as nothing more than a pretext for a historical nostalgia — the good old sexual order — and an excuse for the condemnation of sexual dysfunction as it is practiced in the modern African society. That is why the place to find Ngangura's and Sembène's sexually deviant characters is the city. The city is the locus of sexual/social chaos and the site whence to restore traditional sexual/social order. What should that *soxual* organization look like? Despite the fact that *La vie est belle* and *Faat Kiné* indicate that this new structure should be gendered, and although Sembène and Ngangura hint at the structuration of "conventional" feminine sexuality, both filmmakers remain ambiguous as to the form of "normal" masculine sexuality.

The evasive male sexuality on the one hand and the ordered female sexuality on the other hand, as they are treated by Ngangura and Sembène, are not accidental if one agrees, as has been said elsewhere, that "one pays a price for being the child of one's parents."[3] While accounting for male and female sexualities, Sembène and Ngangura have only fallen into reproduction of a phallocratic discursive agenda; thus viewing women as sexual animals whose sexuality should conform to the strict, unsophisticated orthodoxy of reproduction and men as more sophisticated beings whose sexuality ought to be an exuberant quest for psychological fulfillment, that is, for eroticism.[4] It is only to the extent that man has usually thought of woman as being an animal that her sexuality is analogized to the inert, unquestioned and unquestioning and supposedly natural animal sexuality; and it is only to the extent that man has always thought of himself as an extraordinary being not submitted to the Law *he* writes that he places his sexuality in the register of the erotic.

Thus, orthodox feminine sexuality, of which Kabibi is the epitome in *La vie est belle*, is expected to remain quiet, subdued and kept under lid until the moment of tolerated transgression, that is, until marriage; for feminine sexuality is first and foremost a sexuality dedicated to reproduction within the institution of wedlock, and to a certain extent, put at the service of man's desire. Ngangura shows this clearly when he opposes Kabibi, the virtuous graduate of a secretarial school to Nzazi (played Lokinda Menji Feza), the unemployed, opportunistic single mother who preys on unsuspecting men in search of fleeting erotic moments. While Kabibi has "chosen" to remain virgin until marriage, Nzazi, as for her, has elected to satisfy her urban needs by leading an unprincipled lifestyle of sexual promiscuity, theft, lies, abuses and drunkenness. Like Mama Dingari, Kabibi's mother (played Mazaza Mukoko) and the "liberated women" of the Musiki Club to which Mamu belongs, Nzazi is part of this class of

From left to right, Mamou (Landu Nzunzimbu Matshia) and her husband, Nvuandu (Kanko Kasongo) (*La vie est belle/Life is Rosy*, directed by Ngangura Mweze and Benoît Lamy, Congo, 1987).

women that one so easily refers to in some Francophone milieus as "mal baisées" (desperately seeking what men supposedly find in each sexual intercourse, orgasm). The suggestion is that their social lives are chaotic because their sex lives are in shambles; so their devastating sexual experiences or lack of orgasmic satisfaction, create a negative hormonal reaction that causes them to take their frustrations on the rest of the world. Thus, Mama Dingari's exploitative and ruthless commercial methods and Nzazi's abusive tendencies, for instance, have a common root cause. As single mothers with no men of their own — Mama Dingari for example has to pay for the sexual favors of a midget, a metaphor of masculine abnormality, phallic imperfection and orgasmic insufficiency — they are sexually unfulfilled, and their *jouissance en reste* maintains them in constant mood swings and makes them incapable of relating positively to people around them. In *La vie est belle*, for instance, Mama Dingari is a crooked landlord who raises the rent on a whim with no rational justification.

As deceiving as the notion of the hysteric single woman can be, the suggestion that marriage constitutes necessarily the site of feminine orgasmic consummation is even more misleading. Orgasm is, even so slightly, tied to the erotic, to a sense of sinfulness; the erotic implies first and foremost transgression of the interdicted; and marriage is essentially the watchdog of the forbidden, that which insures the continuity of societal taboos, most of which are sexual. Because marriage is the site of permitted transgressions, the kind of eroticism that the legal conjugal space allows can only be a non-erotic one, a clean and sanitized sexual engagement, which is fulfilling only insofar as it satisfies a collective need to belonging to a moral culture. Nothing behind the close doors of a conjugal bedroom is secret or appalling anymore. Everything is expected and tolerated to the point where the fear of not performing to expectations, of not living to the anticipation of being a "gifted husband or wife" could be so stressful as to inhibit pleasure. Marriage is the institution of ordered interiority, the incarceration of the erotic, the suppression of *jouissance*, the latter of which needs, in order to flower, explorations in the realm of the repulsive, violation of the censured, infringement of ordered life. The erotic, pleasure, is outside marriage. So, too, can be feminine monstrosity.

In Sembène's *Faat Kiné*, it is out of their desire to prevent their mother from falling into monstrosity, it is with the intent of rescuing her from the uncontrollable state of *mal baisée* that Kiné's children set about to find her a suitable husband. She, too, like Mamu and Mama Dingari of *La vie est belle*, has been paying a man, a failed man in the form of a compulsive gambler, for sexual favors after two unsatisfactory relationships, both of which resulted in a child for her alone to raise. Kiné's encounters with men always bear a burlesque aspect. When she is not shouting at them, she is ordering them around in the most conspicuous manner. Sembène seems to burlesque the methods by which Kiné expresses her found independence. Like the bellow she uses to summon her subordinates, every gesture in Kiné is grotesque and ubuesque. As if Sembène wished to suggest that Kiné has trouble managing her new status as an emancipated Senegalese woman, at the end of the day, she would leave her office barefooted were it not for the reminder of her male subordinate.

Naturally, it is not Aby, but Djib (aka Prési), her male child, foreseen by his high school friends as the future president of Senegal, who proposes to link Kiné with an established man. It is no accident that Prési should become the filmmaker's mouthpiece. He is a man in the making. He represents the new generation of African leaders, just as his older sister, Aby, epitomizes the new breed of African women. Through Kiné's two children Sembène offers us his vision for a new Africa. Sembène's perspective should not strike us as very optimistic, as it suggests that composed and cool-headed men like Djib will rule a continent whose stability could at any time be thwarted by the disgraceful behavior of truculent, sexually promiscuous women fascinated by the West and its failed conception of femininity. Fortunately, however, male wisdom will triumph and peace will ultimately prevail. It is thus from Djib's mouth, and neither from Kiné's nor Aby's, that the filmmaker's dream of a new Senegalese *soxual* order unfurls, precisely because Djib represents less the birth of a new social force than the restoration of an old and dignified Afrocentrist might. Djib possesses a lion's heart. He commands the authority of his grandfather, his grandmother reminds the viewers.

Djib is Sembène's rescuer of an old and authentic era threatened of erasure by the seductive gaudiness of the West. He carries the voice of griotism. This is why he can afford to castigate these flawed men of the modern age who, by soiling the importance of manhood, have caused women to think that they could emancipate them-

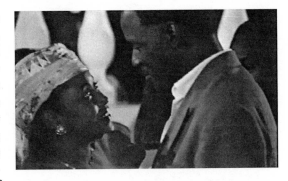

Faat Kiné (Venus Seye) finally finds sincere love in a man of her son's choice (*Faat Kiné*, directed by Ousmane Sembène, Senegal, 2001).

selves from man's authority. Consequently, when Djib reprimands his half sister's father and his own father, the former for having impregnated and abandoned Kiné while she was just his mere student and the latter for having robbed Kiné and left her with a pregnancy to support, his criticism is meant more for the preservation of manhood than the protection of women's rights. Sembène's criticisms are directed less against the polygamy that has steered man away from his familial responsibilities than they are meant to consolidate the institution that has so effectively served man as a cover for his erring.

Ngangura's and Sembène's films produce less new ideas than they reproduce an Afrocentrist masculinist discourse of the kind heralded in most traditional African homes. What these films say is that man is the quintessential master and his acts are always already justified by virtue of the Law that he alone writes, and which submits everyone else but him. Why would Sembène, at the dawn of the new millennium, shoot a film that says nothing new, that introduces nothing new? To his credit, let us assume that he really wanted something novel to come out of his art. Unfortunately, however, Sembène has grown too old in the trenches of antiquarian idealism. He has waded for too long in the waters of fossilized beliefs. As says this African proverb, no matter how long a tree trunk has remained submerged, it will never become a crocodile. It is therefore to a crocodile, rather than a submerged tree trunk, that one must turn in order to have a crocodile's perspective. It is to a woman that one must turn in order to have a woman's perspective.

6

Cogito Must Have
Gone Crazy

*Construction and/as Deconstruction of
Masculinity in Nouri Bouzid's* Bent Familia
and Mufida Tlatli's The Silences of the Palace

Two Tunisian films, Nouri Bouzid's *Bent Familia*[1] and Moufida Tlatli's
The Silences of the Palace,[2] allegorize perceptively well how both in pre-independence and post-independence Tunisian society language has come to function to the advantage of the Tunisian male, by overcoding the unorganized
field of desires along the axis of gender. These films forebode a conviction
enunciated elsewhere, and which posits that "there is no ideal speaker-listener,
any more than there is a homogenous linguistic community.... There is no
mother tongue, only a power takeover by a dominant language within a political multiplicity."[3]

Deleuze and Guattari have insisted that strata, the acts that capture and
organize the flows or free singularities of the body without organs into a system of redundancy or a system of reproduction of habitual gestures, are not
necessarily language based. They can be, and are often, movement based.
However, it is also a fact that in their critique of structural semiotics laid down
in *A Thousand Plateaus* Deleuze and Guattari have pointed out that, when it
is besieged by linguists and psychoanalysts, language becomes the quintessential apparatus of organization of desires; when language is overtaken by
linguists and psychoanalysts, it becomes a partial *abstract machine* used by
ideologists eager to advance particular regimes of signs as natural and imma-
nent and to devalue others as illegitimate and occasional.[4] Like Deleuze and
Guattari's *A Thousand Plateaus*, Bouzid's and Tlatli's films denounce language
as means of subjugation; but they do it precisely in the context of Tunisian
society's gendered discourse. They expose the linguistic artifice by which all

76

aspects of Tunisian life, up to the very notion of existence, are subject to codification and control under a governing male authority. What is thoughtfully shown in both movies is the subtle nature of patriarchy's grip on women, which makes of their rebellion a simulacrum, insofar as women's most insurrectionary postures are always already thwarted by their inevitable invocation of patriarchy.

In *Bent Familia* viewers are introduced to women with various degrees of attachment to men, and who share the same tragic reality: Their lives are put on hold by men's tacit or manifest desire for self-assertion. Aida (Amel Hedhili) is the single mother of two children, a young boy and a little girl. She has been divorced for seven years. Since her ex-husband refuses to pay her any alimony, lest she should be independent enough to start dating other men, Aida is trying to raise her children the best she can by earning a living outside the home. Aida's unorthodox lifestyle — the fact that she is both divorcee and a "working woman" — makes her the subject of mischievous gossip by women and constant harassment by men. However, despite the neighbors' *on dit* that she is a woman of little virtue, Aida has been waiting for only one man, her Palestinian lover, Mahmed, held hostage in Gaza by a protracted peace negotiation between Palestinians and Israeli. For that man, Aida has gently rejected the advances of Slah (Kamel Touati), a good-natured divorced man who has been courting her for some time. Mahmed constantly deferred arrival delays Aida's enjoyment of life as well.

Unlike her sister, Aida, Meriem (Hassiba Roshdi) is still married. She has given two little girls to her husband, and although she claims that one should "accept everything the Lord gives," and that her daughters have brought good luck to her husband, it is clear that Meriem, like her sister, is still waiting to experience her own happiness. She has a sense of incompleteness because she has not been able to give her man the son he so desires. So, to subvert the game of God, to curve the misfortune which somehow seems to make her a failed woman by causing her to give birth to girls only, to load the dice of fate so that she shall become a "true woman," one that can play God by giving her husband the child of his wish, that is, a thing in his likeness, she asks her sister, Aida, to take her to a fortuneteller and maker of wonders. It is on their visit to the oracle that Aida comes across an old friend, Amina (Leila Nassim).

Amina, too, has come to see the fortuneteller to keep her husband at home. She is afraid he is deserting her for other women: He eats outside, comes home late, laden with the scents of other women. Amina is convinced that her husband is having an affair. However, the old oracle's advice to Amina is only a reiteration of the traditional Law of the father: Amina should neither listen to the voices of jealous persons who tell lies and gossips nor spy on her husband. Instead, she should make herself attractive, remain submissive and be grateful that her husband returns to her every night.

Thus, despite their seemingly individual concerns, Aida, Meriem and Amina all long for the same thing: the figure of a male character (Aida longs for Mahmed; Meriem desires a boy child, and Amina wants to retain her husband on her own terms). Until they can find it, their own existences will be held hostage. On the other hand, that they be able to find it remains highly problematic, insofar as it could be argued that the masculine figures these women are looking for are only metaphorical of life, that is, of being itself. Man is only a pretext. What they want through man is confirmation of their own existences; even better, what they want is to exist. However, because in this Tunisian patriarchal society one *apparently*—let us say apparently for reasons that will be discussed later—exists only insofar as one is a man, for these women to exist presupposes that they be men; hence the unattainable nature of their wish. Were we good enough disciples of Lacan—that is, as pessimistic enough as Lacan—to call upon him as a witness, we would concede with him that these women's desire is desire for a lack, as they will come to realize how difficult, how impracticable, it is for women to just pretend to exist through mere mutiny, by simply seizing life in the *absence* of men.

In *Bent Familia,* tired of waiting for men to consecrate them as beings, Aida, Amina and a young Algerian refugee, Fatiha (Nadia Kaci), decide to drive to the Ocean. However, this act of "going out," because it is performed by three women alone, in the absence of man, bears at its center a characteristic of falsity. It is a parasitic act, an inauthentic performative, an act of theatricality, in the Austinian sense of the term.[5]

In fact, what John L. Austin defines in *How To Do Things with Words* as a performative or a speech act is a statement that executes an action the very moment the sentence is uttered. One example of performative is "I do!" (I do take this woman as my lawful wife), "I do!" being said during the marriage ceremony. As an utterance, the performative differs from such utterances as constatives in that it is not meant to describe, to report or to establish a fact; instead, it is uttered to perform an act. However, the simple fact of uttering a performative does not suffice to perform an action. Some necessary conditions need to be fulfilled such as the appropriateness of the circumstances in which the sentence is said, the authority of the speaker to say them, the appropriate gestures to accompany the performatives, and so forth. Austin insists that the *true* performative must be uttered with sincerity and in the *presence* of the necessary circumstances. Sincere performances, Austin warns, excludes the theatrical performances, or the poems, which are fictitious actualizations. If the utterance "I exist" is a performative, in the traditional Tunisian unconscious, insofar as it is uttered by a lone female subject—in the absence of a male subject — it becomes automatically a failed performative, that is, a parasitic act. It is so because the most important missing element from the situational context is the presence of a masculine *signata*.

In *Bent Familia*, the women's pure act of "going out as women" is already thwarted as their whole conversation to and from the Ocean is invaded by the mourning of man in the absence of men (as they recall their first lovers) or the conjuring up of man in the self-presence of men (as they maneuver to elude two harassing male motorists). It is this inescapable presence of the masculine referend that undermines a pure feminine existence, and which sabotages the possibility of a female bond. In *Bent Familia*, the constant masculine intrusion into the *female trip to the Ocean* almost leads to the breakdown of the women's unity. After they escape from the harassing motorists, the three women become hypersensitive; they take their frustration out on each other. For a few seconds they stand on the beach a distance away from one another, facing different directions. However, as if to suggest that just as brotherhood is global and united in the subjugation of women, sisterhood, too, should be united in the fight against patriarchy, the three women iron out their differences right away, and the beach on which they stand holding each other becomes, once again, the space of reciprocity, of shared narratives, of mutual understanding. However, how long will these joint feminine efforts last before the lurking destabilizing force of masculinity comes blowing in, like a hurricane in a fine china shop? *Bent Familia* seems to suggest that in their fight against patriarchy the feminine subjects need to remain in a constant state of sleeplessness, in a permanent condition of self-consciousness, as patriarchy will not miss an opportunity to turn them against one another. The precariousness of the "feminine nature" tells a story: It is indicative of the extent to which, even in the absence of man, everything has been historically arranged so that, through the *gift of culture*, man's permanent preeminence is assured.

Nonetheless, as hinted earlier, this preponderance of masculinity is only *apparent*. By overcodifying language for the subjugation of femininity, patriarchy, too, finds itself trapped in its own *language game*. By its inability to control the free flow of language the patronymic reveals the ephemeral condition of its authority. In *Bent Familia*, for instance, Slah, the divorced man, confesses to Aida that the notion of a "divorced person" is as degrading for men as it is for women. For men, it connotes a state of *ex-ness*, that is, ex-powerful, ex-potent, and ex-respectable, ex-man, and thus ex-being. It is the fear of falling into this state of nothingness that leads Majid (Raouf Ben Amor) to take some drastic measures against his wife, Amina, when she unexpectedly announces to him that she wants a divorce.

By seizing Amina's car as well her identification papers, Majid hopes to reduce his wife to nothingness, to make her existence even more contingent upon his presence, before she has the opportunity to "ex-ify" him and reduce him to thing. Majid seems to hint that there is something about movement that language does not possess; a certain liberating agency, which, despite Majid's orders that his wife remain silent, nonetheless, allows her to steer clear from his zone of influence, to remove herself from his authority. By repossessing Amina's car, he hopes to have also taken away her ability for motion. As Amina takes refuge at Aida's, she finds an ally in Slah, the ex-man, the non-man, who understands her revolution, and who infuses some strength in her so that she can continue to fight for the right to exist. It is because Slah has been to the other side; he has been both a man and a non-man; it is because, as a desiring-machine, he has crossed the gendered boundaries, bypassed the dominant Tunisian semiotics of the body, put himself in a position of homosexuality, that he is able to understand Amina's struggle and to inspire her. For he, too, has been branded by language, by the system of representation, as a non-being, and he now seems to realize that the notions of manhood and womanhood are mere linguistic or cultural constructs, illegitimate *coups de force* on the irreducible and indomitable multiplicity that language is. Amina does not need to hear from Slah any sententious declarations about her absolute right to freedom, about the necessity to take arms in rebellion against patriarchy. Slah's mere *passage* as a man becoming-feminine, as a heterosexual becoming-homosexual, as a phallocentric-*jouissance* becoming-bodily-*jouissance*, as the product-of-a-psychoanalytical-system-of-inscription-and-representation-and-production becoming-production-of-productions, is enough to unleash Amina's own flow of desires, to reconnect her with her fluidity outside the realm of structuration, that is, outside the organization of sexuality, that is, before the Law and the erection of the walls of gendered spaces and roles, before the *one is woman insofar as ... and one is man inasmuch as...*, before *movement*, that is, *freedom entails motion from point A to point B*, before the conception of *point A* and *point B*. For before "motion from A to B," freedom, in the form of affirmative production of desires, exists, even better, pre-exists the authoritarian regimes of signs that abstract particles from the multiplicity in order to allege a universal Law of representation of desire. Through becoming-feminine, Slah liberates himself by liberating his flow of desires from the encapsulating regime of the Law-of-the-Father and inspires Amina to not fear, to the point of criminalizing, her own desires anymore.

It should be emphasized that the Slah who, by understanding her struggle, inspires Amina to free herself is no longer a man; it is not a man that frees a woman, but a becoming-feminine; no longer a heterosexual, but a becoming-homosexual; a body traversed by a thousand intensities and semiotic flows rather than a body organized according to a semiotics of desire. When Guattari (and Deleuze) say that becoming-other, becoming-feminine, becoming-homosexual, is the prime gesture toward liberation of the subject from the oedipalized moment, this should not be equated to saying that the other in the form of the feminine and the homosexual — as they supposedly exist within the taken-for-granted system of representation, the system that psychoanalysis names the symbolic — already occupies a position of freedom coveted by the heterosexual male other.[6] It is, I believe, such misunderstanding of the Deleuzian and Guattarian concept of *devenir féminin* that has triggered the philosophical xenophobia on the part of some feminists who, by interpreting *becoming-woman* as a male desire to appropriate women's position, seem to be saying "*the other gender is moving in and occupying our space. What is going to become of us?*"[7] It seems rather clear, from my reading of Deleuze and Guattari, that the woman who complains of losing her position to man is far from being the *devenir féminin* promoted in schizoanalysis. This woman is an Oedipalized *product* (Aïda, Amina, Meriem, for instance) constituted according to the blue print of the semiotics of the body, that imposes upon her "...the ideal of a certain restrictive or exclusive use on [her] ... here is where mommy begins, there daddy, and there you are — stay in your place."[8]

Despite the "slip of Oedipus" into her body nibbling efficaciously on the continuum of flows of desire, integrating her into the exclusive notion of Tunisian womanhood, Aïda pretends that she is different; that she can brush aside her neighbors' indicting gazes and foul remarks. However there is no doubt that she has already sunk deep into representation and reproduction: "I don't want the neighbors to gossip about your frequent visits," she says to Slah. This woman is living her life according to the oedipal shibboleth of womanhood. *Devenir-féminin*, on the other hand, pre-exists the body. It is a process of transfiguration whereby what matter is more the *devenir* than the *féminin*. It is the disjunctive synthesis that antedates the psychoanalytical organization of the body's functionality and the identification of desire with pleasure, and lack. Becoming-woman, homosexual, and plant, is not becoming homosexual-product, woman-product, plant-product. It is a process whereby the subject "is not simply bisexual, or between the two, or intersexual. He is transsexual. He is trans-alivedead, transparent-child. He does not reduce two contraries to identity of the same; he affirms their distance as that which relates the two as different."[9] Perhaps Deleuze and Guattari's most illustrative example for this state of passage, of becoming-plural, is sado-masochism.[10]

Thus, it is not a man (Slah) that frees a woman (Amina) from the crushing embrace of another man (Majhid) and vice versa. In the Deleuzian and Guattarian conception of experience, the factor of freedom is movement,

movement of becoming. But this movement, as I mentioned above is not necessarily motion from point A to point B, but rather the indescribable incandescence that makes us pass through variegated states. In *Bent Familia*, because the proper language of cinema is motion, because cinema came to life the moment it became possible to put pictures in motion, this movement is indicated as the possibility of actual motion; thus the importance of going out; thus the significance of Amina's recovering her car keys from Majhid; thus the synecdochical weight of the car keys (freedom) that Amina passes on (extends to) her friend Fathia. In order to (re)make themselves bodies without organs, the protagonists of *Bent Familia*—men and women alike—have to destroy the phallocentric man that dwells in each one of them as well as in the other. For they all have participated in reinforcing the system of representation by making themselves available pillars of the Tunisian socius. The men by being men on the side of men and the women by being women on the side of women, they have worked together as pieces of the well-oiled Tunisian repressive machine. Within that socius, they have desired their own repression; for, as Deleuze and Guattari point out, there is a strange fascination for the socius from both victims and victimizers.[11]

The repressive machine constituted to perpetuate the socio-political preponderance of masculinity is secured by means of *patriarchy's takeover* of language. This power takeover perverts language, dilutes its inherent political and social multiplicity, and causes it to "stabilize ... around a parish, a bishopric, a capital."[12] In *The Silences of the Palace*, the Tunisian filmmaker Moufida Tlatli's illustrates this symbolic *coup de force* in the form of language stabilizing inside the iron gates of a Tunisian Palace, where, besieged by controlling monarchs, who break it down into internal structural elements with overcoded and distributed boundaries, it functions as a State signifying apparatus, a device for rigidification and subjugation of will.[13] From within the perspective that makes of language a State-model, any word can be made to signify whatever the besieger wants it to represent. However, this assignation of a fixed meaning to a signifier is only a tyrannical endeavor, a power takeover on the asignifying multiplicity that constitutes language.

Tlatli's film is the tale of a young servant coming of age in Tunisia in the 1950s. Born under bondage, in the Palace of the Beys, the last monarchs of this French protectorate, of a slave mother, Khedija (Amel Hedhili), and an unknown father, Young Alia (Hend Sabri) grows up amidst the songs, cries, laughters and gossips of the many servants of the palace, who try in vain to exorcise their sorrows. Like them, Alia is expected to serve her masters' needs and desires for the rest of her life. Like them, too, she longs for freedom and for a true family life outside the stifling gates of the Palace, away from the authority of the Beys.

In the Palace, each servant has her own house or her personal unit. Nevertheless, there remains a network of interactions between these units, which ultimately falls into the same point of accumulation: the masters' watchful gaze. The servants' "territories" are all codified and assigned by the masters according to geometry of subjugation.

Young Alia (Hend Sabri) dreams of a life outside the gates of the Beys' palace (*The Silences of the Palace,* directed by Mufida Tlatli, Tunisia, 1994).

The territories mimic the general outline of a camp or fortification. Following a pyramidal model of hierarchization, the Beys' rooms are upstairs, and the slaves' downstairs, by the kitchens. Each time a female servant is summoned upstairs, she knows that she is being sent for to sexually gratify the masters. The language of the Palace has codified upstairs as the space of coercion and submitted all the servants to that linguistic codification. Thus, the masters have only to mention to the slaves that they want their "herbal tea" upstairs for the slaves to be prepared to satisfy the masters sexually. The slaves have become so habituated to the voice which chains them to their own servitude that they can only expect freedom to be uttered by that very voice. So, they live in the anticipation that the masters will offer them their freedom some day, even though it is clear that the masters have no intention of freeing their slaves.

However, unlike her mother and the other servants, who have been waiting for the miracle of emancipation to happen through the magic of the masters' voice, Alia is determined to allow herself small freedoms. For her, freedom seems to imply autonomy of movement more than it does freedom of speech. For Alia, freedom is infinitude of desires. How much more schizophrenic could she be? Does she not give credence to this Kierkegaardian motto espoused by Deleuze and Guattari?

> [T]hat there is no movement that is not infinite; that the movement of the infinite can occur only by means of affect, passion, love, in a becoming that is [a] girl, but without reference to any kind of "mediation"; and that this movement as such eludes any mediating perception because it is already effectuated at every moment, and the dancer or lover finds him-or herself already "awake and walking" the second he or she falls down, and even the instant he or she leaps. Movement, like [a] girl as a fugitive being, cannot be perceived.[14]

"Movement," "girl," "fugitive," "eludes mediation," "lover," "dancer," "falls," "leaps," so many states applicable to Alia, who, as a servant that is not allowed to go anywhere she wishes within the Palace, nonetheless forbids herself no space, no corner of the Palace. Thus, walking in the footsteps of her play-mate, Sarra (Khedija Ben Othman), the little princess, Alia allows herself as much freedom as Sarra is afforded. To her mother who reminds her of *her place* in the kitchens of the palace, remarking that she cannot "take Sarra as an example," Alia replies that she hates pots and pans; in essence, that she hates her condition of slave. So, moving about in the palace, Alia ascertains her freedom not through words — as she talks little — but through movements, that is, by annexing spaces.

Alia seems to have understood that if people are oppressed, it is less because language has failed them than because their movements have been restricted. She seems to have comprehended that in order to subvert patri-archy's will-to-domination, which is, as one has learned from Lacan, staged through language or the symbolic, one has to be inhabited by a multiplicity of movements — movements of deterritorialization (uprooting) and reterrito-rialization (re-rooting). To escape the *coup de force* of patriarchy, Alia seems to suggest, one has to be governed by a principle of connection and hetero-geneity, whereby from any point, one can — and must — be connected to any-thing other. Deleuze and Guattari have termed this self-vibrating, asignifying, and unorganized gesture rhizomatics, schizoanalysis, nomadology or desir-ing-machine. Alia is a desiring-machine. She is a machinic synthesis in the factory sense of the term; that is, assemblage of variegated parts, each func-tioning differently. As desiring-machine, Alia's investment in the social field is from the order of production of production rather than from that of mere representation or reproduction. She does not seem to imitate anything pre-existing (her mother, the servants, or even Sarra the little princess). She seeks to create new intensities; and this quest for the new, she is convinced, is not vain pursuit of an unattainable, "un-namable ... beyond."[15]

Alia is a rhizome. She can claim no known genealogy. It is as such that she is able to steer away from — but also connect to — the code of language, which, according to *Palace-Philosophy*, is one of bi-univocity, whereby "herbal tea," signifies "sexual gratification" when it is voiced by the master, and "upstairs," is overcoded as "the chamber of domination." The rhizome, we are told, is antigenealogy.[16] So, too, is Alia; a girl claimed by no identifiable father, by all indications a bastard child of an abusive rapport between a slave mother and an all-powerful master, Alia is necessarily "meant" to escape Freudian holy unified trinity (the father, the mother, and the castrated child). This bastard child speaks no father's language; she speaks not at all. Instead, Alia walks, trots and runs, leaps, dances, dreams of love, where no girl is expected to run, where Sarra, the legitimate child, the good princess, Daddy's precious little girl, is not supposed to run; where movement, excessive movement for that matter, is not girl-like, is not, in other words, in the *order of things*.

From this perspective, then, Alia's *imitation* of Sarra is not representative or reproductive. It is not mere tracing. Rather, it is a connivance that ends up generating productive movements. On the one hand, Sarra goes by the *book* of the palace's masters; she remembers to do everything according to Daddy's Law of castration —"A girl should not run ... my parents found me a husband ... my cousin ... it does not matter that we love one another...." She starts from the beginning of the book of the father's law, and, methodically, thoroughly, works her way toward its end. Alia, on the other hand, seems to unfold everything from the middle —"I like to run ... do you love him? ... I am dreaming of love ... outside the gates of the Palace"— Alia has no beginning or end. Always in the middle, she constantly seems to overthrow the *good* order of things, like the day she almost *ruined* a *perfect* family photograph by surreptitiously inserting herself among the members of the royal family. Constantly between things, she overflows the father's shibboleth of good manners; like the day she ruined Sarra's wedding by singing a revolutionary song that denounced the royal family's collusion with France and their betrayal of the Tunisian people and subjugation of Tunisian women.

It is not inherently contradictory that Alia will undermine the ethics of the very family she desperately tries to belong to. There is nothing incongruous in the fact that she wishes to inscribe herself in the royal family's genealogy while, as a bastard child, she can remain free to elude oedipalization and castration. Alia is not the strict opposite of Sarra — even if, for the convenience of expression, while speaking of them, one is *compelled* to use such dichotomous terms as "like" or "unlike" or "on the one hand" and "on the other

Alia is not allowed to be part of the Beys' family portrait. From left to right, Sidi Bechir (Hichem Rostom), Sarra (Khedija Ben Othman), Sarra's fiancé, and Alia (Hend Sabri) (*The Silences of the Palace*, directed by Mufida Tlatli, Tunisia, 1994).

hand," which tend to suggest a substantive opposition. Both Sarra and Alia are the products of the father's desire for decoding, comprehending, penetrating femininity; and both epitomize, respectively, how the father succeeds and fails to control the free flow of information that his desire unleashes. Sarra represents what the father has been able to structure and organize through language. Alia on the other hand, is a machinic movement or a rhizome; she contains, like Sarra, lines of segmentarity, which urge her to enter the organized structure. Nevertheless, she also possesses stronger lines of deterritorialization, which compel her to scramble the father's symbolic codes, to flee the organized structure. Alia and Sarra are like the two strata or layers of the same plane of consistency; each serving as a substratum for the other. They both contain the same qualitative characteristics, however in varying degrees. Qualitatively, Alia is as susceptible to modes of encoding as Sarra is prone to modes of decoding, and vice versa. However, *quantitative-qualitatively*, Alia is more *supple*, more molecular, whereas Sarra is more *rigid*, more molar and organized, that is, more receptive to unification, integration, hierarchization. They are a double articulation in that they each contain the terms of the other. However, the identity of the terms that constitute them does not necessarily mean an identity of their compound substances. This only means that their differences are differences in organization rather than augmentation or reduction. For instance, as a substratum, whatever Sarra can bring — such as the experience of the Father's voice — to Alia (her substratum) is not substantially foreign to Alia's composition. It is only more organized and more organizing (the prince wants his daughter to behave like a little princess). Likewise, as a substratum whatever Alia brings — such as the silence and movements of a slave mother — to Sarra (her substratum) is not substantially extrinsic to Sarra's constitution. It is just less organized and less organizing in Sarra.[17] Alia must have had a father to be born, and Sarra must have a mother that effaces herself in the presence of her father; hence the double articulation of Sarra and Alia. It is such polymorphous composition that leads Alia to seek in one of the Beys, Sid Ali (Kamel Fazaa), the father figure. At the same time, it is this multiplicity in her that keeps Alia's gaze fixed beyond the gates of the Palace and allows her to ultimately steer away from the Beys' authority the very day her mother dies aborting another bastard child.

In the end, however, the difficulty of Alia's life outside the gates of the Palace makes her realize that women's prison is not merely a physical reality; it is a conceptual one. Insofar as women enter into a binding contract with men, the terms of which are written by men to maintain women in a condition of dependency, they will remain slaves and will be entitled to nothing — not even their bodies. Alia, now an adult (Ghalia Lacroix), arrives at this conclusion after a visit to the Palace, many years later, on the occasion of Sid

Ali's death. It is the flashbacks prompted by this not-so-happy "homecoming" that allow the viewers a glimpse of Alia's life within the Palace. This visit also makes Alia understand that both inside and outside the Palace her life has always been dictated to her by Patriarchy, by the Beys inside the Palace and by her live-in boyfriend outside the Palace. Alia's stopover at the Palace is a cathartic event that helps her regain control of her mind and her body, as she becomes aware that all her life, her body has been violated by men and abused by too many abortions. This time, she has made up her mind. She will object to her boyfriend's demand that she abort her child. She will keep her pregnancy as a token of independence. However, does not Alia's ultimate gesture of emancipation, too, have at its core a degree falsity, some may wonder. Is Alia not reproducing an antiquarian familial order?

7
Keita: The Heritage of the Griot
Economic, Social, and Cultural Organization of Ancient Africa

Je suis moi-même griot de naissance. Je suis de ce fait garant de l'histoire de mon peuple vis-à-vis des générations futures. Le thème de ce film s'impose donc à moi comme un devoir. Mais j'ai de la chance, j'appartiens au "siècle du cinéma," c'est un instrument fabuleux pour un griot!

[I, myself, am a griot by birth. I am thus the guardian of my people's history for the generations to come. I take the theme of this film as a duty. But I am lucky; I belong to the age of cinema, a fabulous instrument for the griot.]

— Dani Kouyaté

The Burkinabé filmmaker Dani Kouyaté, a descendant of traditional West-African genealogists, storytellers, and historians known as griots, does not make any mystery about his first film. *Keita: The Heritage of the Griot¹* is a film meant to educate today and future generations of Africans, schooled in Western cultures, about Africa's past. The pretext for this archeology of African memories is simple. Like many African children, Mabo Keita (Hamed Dicko), a young and intelligent Burkinabé boy, who lives in the city of Ouagadougou with his parents and goes to a French school, has never been taught the famous origin of his name. So, a ghostly ancestral figure sends Djéliba (Sotigui Kouyaté), the family griot from the village of Wagadu, on the mission of instructing Mabo about his glorious ancestor, Sundiata Keita, King of the 13th century Mali Empire. In the city, where he is resolute to carry out his responsibility, Djéliba is confronted with the disapproval of Mabo's mother, Sitan (Claire Sanon), and teacher, Mr. Fofana (Abdoulaye Komboudri). The griot's captivating teaching style and the fascinating stories that he tells mesmerize the child so much that the schoolboy starts daydreaming in class when he is not missing school at all. Mabo's mother and teacher find the griot's presence disruptive and complain to his father, who sees no reason to be alarmed. However, as Mabo repeats his ancestor's epic to some of his classmates, his excitement rubs on them, and they, too, become distracted from school, as they spend hours in a baobab tree listening to their friend. Mabo's father, Boicar (Mamadou Sarr), becomes the target of some parents' anger. To avoid any further disruption of Boicar's relationships with his wife and neighbors, Djéliba, who is now convinced that he has implanted a strong enough seed in Mabo for the child to want to investigate other aspects of his history, returns to Wagadu, insisting that no one can ever stop the course of the story.

Djeliba's way of telling Sundiata's epic is very typical of what has been discussed elsewhere as characteristic of Francophone African rhetorical pattern.[2] That pattern is one of digression and repetition, the continuance of which has persisted in Francophone writing thanks to the efforts of the precursors of the Negritude movement, passionate advocates of Black African ontological and teleological specificity. The griot's gesture of rememorying is a pertinent reminder that the global, to which one is sometimes too incontestably attached these days, should not discard the local; but that global history, rather than being the dilution of individual local accounts and the reification of a hegemonic narration, should be inspired by the multiple local narrations and integrate them as its necessary complements. *Keita: The heritage of the Griot* cannot pretend to be historically accurate. It is told in the playful manner of a children's story, with a lot of humor and wonders. Nonetheless, the film can be historically instructive and could help establish a precise connection with Africa's past, provided one is willing to trace the numerous clues that the filmmaker, as a griot, has sparsely planted in the décor

The griot, Djéliba Kouyaté (Sotigui Kouyaté), is instructing young Mabo Keita (Hamed Dicko) about his family history (*Keita: The Heritage of the Griot*, directed by Dani Kouyaté, Burkina Faso, 1994).

and the narration of the film. This work of connection to the past via exploration of signs will be the concern of this chapter. Kouyaté's movie makes
wide-ranging conjectures, not just on the Mali Empire, but also, on thirteenth century West Africa, its socio-political organizations, its population
movements and settlements, its market system, its industrial, pharmaceuti-
cal, and artistic knowledge, its physiography, and its system of resource production and management, so many elements which deserve to be understood.

The Old Mali Empire: 800–1550 C.E.

The Mali Empire of which it is question here is not modern-day Mali
with its capital in Bamako. It was an ancient empire that existed between 800
and 1550 C.E. Its original founders were Mandé-speaking people (Bamana,
Sénoufo, Dogon), who can be found in almost every country in West Africa
today. At its peak (1200–1300 C.E.), the Mali Empire covered most of today's
Mali as well as western Mauritania and Senegal. However, it did not have
categorically defined boundaries by Western standards. The Mali Empire con-
formed instead to the precolonial African notion of a state as a political organization of people whose cohesion was based less on the boundaries within
which they lived than on the languages they spoke, the cultural rituals and
the economic activities they practiced, and the sovereign to whom they pledged
allegiance, paid excises, and from whom they consequently expected protection. The Mali Empire rose to prominence as a consequence of the fall of
another great African state, Wagadu (or Ghana as it is often referred to by
historians).

One hundred years before the birth of Mali, in 700 C.E., the Wagadu or
Ghana Empire, located more than 1000 miles north of today's Ghana, was
the most important state in Sub-Saharan Africa. Arab travelers who wrote
about the empire referred to it as the land of gold. Yet, the precious metal
was not mined in the land of Ghana, but in a territory southwest of the
empire. The people of Ghana were farmers, fishermen, herdsmen, and warriors; but they were mainly dealers who traded salt brought from up North
against gold from the South. The well-traveled Moroccan legal scholar, Ibn
Battuta, noticed during his 1352 trip to West Africa that salt was as expensive in the South as gold was costly in the North. He reported that "[A] camel
load of [salt] was sold in Iwalatan [Walata] for from eight to ten *mithquals*,[3]
and in the town of Malli from twenty to thirty mithquals, perhaps the price
reaches up to forty [mithquals]."[4] People who were fortunate to have salt
would even cut it in pieces and use the pieces as currency. On the other hand,
gold was so abundant in the South that traders would often give equal weight

in gold for the salt they obtained. Other products traded against gold were copper, dried fruits, cowry shells, and cloth.[5] Clues for the fall of Ghana could be found in Ibn Battuta's account of black Africans' social and religious practices. As he entered Walata, the city he called "the first district of the Blacks," Ibn Battuta was shocked by the "strange and outlandish manners" of its inhabitants, who, though Muslims, had little consideration for the guidelines of their Holy Book. He recalled that, like unbelievers, men did not get their genealogy from their fathers, but rather from their maternal uncles; sons did not inherit from their fathers, but from their mothers' brothers; women lacked modesty, did not veil their faces, and were not required to follow their husbands in their trips; women could have male companions without their husbands showing any jealousy, and men could, likewise, have female companions without stirring any suspicion in their wives. Ibn Battuta offered an impressive anecdote of what he perceived as the blacks' immoral lifestyle.

> One day I entered upon Abu Muhammad Yandakan.... I found him sitting on a mat and in the middle of his house was a bed with a canopy. On it was a woman and with her a man was sitting, and the two were conversing. I said to him, "Who is this woman?" He said, "She is my wife." I said, "What is [the relationship of] the man with her to her?" He said, "He is her companion." I said, "Do you accept this when you have lived in our country [with the Arabs] and have known the matters of the shar [divine law]?" He said to me, "Women's companionship with men in our country is honourable and takes place in good way: There is no suspicion about it. They are not like the women in your country." I was astonished at his thoughtless answer and I went away from him and did not go to him after this. Though he invited me many times, I did not respond.[6]

It is certainly such bigoted impressions about matriarchal black Muslim societies by fundamentalist Almoravids from North Africa that precipitated the demise of the Ghana Empire. The religious and cultural "careless" that Ibn Battuta denounced among the Blacks in 1352 must have been more pronounced and even more upsetting to dogmatic Muslims two and one half centuries earlier. After several raids on Ghana, whose people they saw as too liberal on the precepts of the Koran, the Almoravids succeeded in submitting Ghana in 1076. Though short, the Almoravids' reign in Ghana heavily taxed the empire, weakened it cohesion, and disbanded its army. Frail, Ghana fell under the influence of King Sumanguru Kanté from the neighboring Susu Empire, who had been coveting the riches of Ghana for many years. Later, around 1250 C.E., Sumanguru was himself defeated and executed by Sundiata, the King of Mali, hero of Kouyaté's film.[7]

With the collapse of Ghana, the Mali Empire progressively asserted itself as the major power in the Niger Delta region. By incorporating the territories of former Ghana and Susu into the provinces under its administration,

Mali also grew in size and population, and it diversified its exchange commodities. Around the 14th century, the population of Mali was said to be
between 40 and 50 million people living on 439,400 square miles of land.
Not only did traders in Mali pick up the commercial exchanges of salt and
gold as they were practiced in the former Ghana Empire, but also, the highly
itinerant trading actors, by traveling southward, mixed with populations of
the coastal rain forests. They expanded the trade of kola nuts, shea butter,
textile, while converting a few communities to the Muslim religion brought
to them by the Almoravid invasion; and they disseminated products of the
forest to the northern parts of the empire, and even beyond. Ibn Battuta,
despite his usual small-mindedness, gave nonetheless a picture of the empire
as a land of bounty. He recalled that upon his arrival in Mali, the *quadi* and
the interpreter offered him, respectively, a cow and a bull to welcome him.
The *faquih* sent him two sacks of rice and a calabash of *gharti*. From the sultan, he received food, which he did not think was valuable, and one hundred
mithquals of gold; all acts which speak to the hospitality of the people of Mali,
and of Ancient Africa in general, people that some colonial literatures have
not hesitated to characterize as backward and bloodthirsty savages.[8] Ibn Battuta described the sultan's cupola as one made of elaborate woodwork and
covered with silver and gold plates. Three hundred men slaves carrying valuable bows, spears, and shields always escorted the sultan.[9]

Technological Inventiveness in Ancient Africa

The various accounts one gets from oral literatures about the Mali Empire
and the empires that preceded and followed it point to the existence of great
African civilizations endowed with technological, cultural, and artistic inventiveness and innovation. One of the recurring observations these narratives
make is that of the mastery of metal work, and especially of the techniques
of metallurgy in precolonial Africa. The movie *Keita: The Heritage of the Griot*
makes several allusions to, not just the question of the existence of metallurgy
in precolonial Africa, but also, and more importantly perhaps, the issues of
the quality and organization of metallurgic activities in ancient Africa.

In *Keita: The Heritage of the Griot*, a hunter-soothsayer arrived one day
at the court of Mandé King, Maghan Kon Fatta, and prophesied the coming
of a young and repulsive woman that would give the king a child who will
inherit the Mandé throne. The news left King Maghan Kon Fatta puzzled
and Queen Sassouma Bérété both skeptical and despondent, as she had always
hoped that her son, Dankaran Touman, would be the future Mandé King.
The fortune-teller's prediction turned out to be true. A hideous woman,

offered as reward to two hunting brothers for their prowess in the neighboring land of Do, was brought to the King of Mandé, who immediately recognized her as the woman of the prediction and married her. That woman, Sogolon Kédjou, gave King Maghan Kon Fatta a prince, Sundiata, who, against all expectations, would not walk. Years passed and Sundiata grew into a handsome young man; but he was still crippled and could not help his mother as much as he wished. Upon the death of his father, who had wished that Sundiata be his successor to the throne, the king's first wife, Sassouma Bérété, maneuvered to convince the council of elders to bypass the handicapped prince and to appoint her own son Dankaran Touman as new King of the Mandé. Relocated from the palace main buildings to an insignificant corner of the court, Sogolon and her crippled son were subjected to many abuses by their neighbors, and especially by the Queen Mother. One day, as she was cooking, Sogolon realized that she had no more baobab leaves left. So, she went to ask the Queen Mother for some. In a gesture of contempt, Sassouma Bérété threw a basketful of leaves at Sogolon's face and told her that her seven-year-old son, who could walk, had picked those leaves, and that Sundiata, too, should stand on his feet and run errands for his mother, instead of crawling like a reptile. Extremely hurt by the Queen Mother's remarks, Sundiata's mother run home crying. When the handicapped prince witnessed his mother's sorrow, he decided that he should stand up and walk and be her protector.

So, Sundiata sent his griot, Balla Fasséké, to the palace's master smith, Farakourou, to order an iron rod. The griot found the smith working with his apprentices around the forge. As soon as the master smith saw the griot, he knew what the latter had come for, and he told him that before dying, his own father, whom he succeeded, had forged the rod for Sundiata. The griot then ordered that the rod be taken to Sundiata. The shunned prince crawled to the iron bar and grabbed it, and with the encouragements of the drummers and his griot's praises, Sundiata supported himself and painstakingly started to stand up. The iron rod bent and broke under the force of the prince's pressure. A ghostly figure appeared and ordered that a branch from the sunsun tree be fetched for the prince in replacement of the broken iron rod. Supporting himself on that branch, the prince stood up and walked to the amazement of the bystanders, and to the great sorrow of Sassouma Bérété, the Queen Mother who had wished never to see Sundiata walk.[10] Then Sundiata went outside the palace walls and deracinated the baobab tree whose leaves the women of the palace would pick, and he planted it right in front of his mother's hut so that she would no longer have to go far to fetch some leaves.

This short passage of the movie raises some interesting questions as regards the nature of iron technology in Ancient Africa. Adopting a skeptical posture and leaving aside all metaphorical tropes, one could rightly ask what kind of iron was produced in Ancient Africa that could so easily bend and break under the pressure of a human being. This question has found diverse answers among Africanists. Among scholars of African cultures and civilizations, the existence of iron technology in precolonial Africa has never really been at issue. Empirical and archeological evidence in Sub-Saharan Africa tells of intense metallurgical activities on the continent before the arrival of the Europeans.

> When the Germans arrived [in the Bassar region of Northern Togo] in 1885, they were struck by the size and extent of smelting operations in Banjeli: to one writer, the noise of the blacksmiths' hammers and the fires from hundreds of furnaces burning through the night recalled his native Ruhr. Just before the turn of the twentieth century, a German official (Von Doering 1895) estimated the number of working furnaces in the area to be in the hundreds.[11]

Terry Childs and William Dewey's research on the production, uses, and meanings of ancient iron axes in Zaire (today's Democratic Republic of Congo) and Zimbabwe are in great part based on objects recovered at previous archeological excavations of ancient burial sites dated as far back as 600–700 C.E.[12] Excavations carried out earlier in Sub-Saharan Africa by the Hiernaux team, then by Jacques Nenquin, and later by Pierre de Maret exposed a variety of ornamental artifacts, among which pottery, ceramic, copper, and iron items.[13] Childs and Dewey's research, if anything, demonstrated the existence of a highly structured iron smithing activity in precolonial Africa. Candice Goucher and Eugenia Herbert's endeavor to understand the place of women and men in the highly ritualized iron production activities among the Bassari people of Northern Togo reproduced a characteristic ancient smelting furnace; which is evidence of metallurgical occupation in precolonial West Africa.[14] Peter Schmidt and Donald Avery surveyed ancient iron furnaces in Western Tanzania[15] and even David Kellick, the not-so-easily trusting of African ingenuity, had to admit that "the evidence shows beyond any doubt that many African bloomery furnaces produced steel blooms."[16] In light of so much substantiation, no serious scholar today can deny the existence of iron technology in precolonial Sub-Saharan Africa.

Africanists' disagreements have more to do with the origin and the quality of that technology. Archeological research in Sub-Saharan Africa yields a variety of dates, all of which seem to place iron activities in Sub-Saharan Africa as far back as the first 3 to 5 centuries C.E.[17] The pattern of excavations, which have mostly been undertaken in East Africa, continues to push back these dates, thus suggesting that iron activities in Sub-Saharan Africa are much older than it was previously thought; but precisely how old is the Iron Age in Africa? This question still remains unanswered. In the face of such incertitude, some researchers have simply decided to ignore the fact that excavations in Africa are in their early stages, and they have proclaimed the birthplace of iron technology to be anyplace but Africa itself.

This *diffusionist* tendency, the inclination to see the origins of iron technology anywhere else but in Africa, though uncorroborated, has gained many adepts. Overwhelmed by the great number of smelting techniques found in Africa toward the end of the 19th century, and unable to isolate a single point of departure for African iron technology, mainstream archeologists have chosen the easiest path by ruling that metallurgy arrived in Africa via Madagascar, from East Asia or up the Nile to East and West Africa.[18] One such groundless diffusionist assumption — which does not withstand the tests of history or science, but which has gained wide acceptance in Western scholarship to the point of preventing archeologists from studying metallurgy in Africa as proper to the continent rather than a technology derived from the Eurasian tradition — is the declaration by the French Raymond Mauny, in 1952, that iron technology was introduced in Africa by Phoenician settlers in North Africa.[19] Often the subject of origin and the question of quality have gone hand in hand.

Those who have argued for an exogenous source to African iron technology have also insisted that precolonial African metallurgy was nothing more than an outdated type of the kind of metallurgical technique practiced thousands of years earlier in Europe, especially the prehistoric European bloomery method. In fact, in order for high-grade steel to be produced, iron ore, the unrefined raw material of iron, must be melted into a furnace at very high temperature, beyond 1600° C, which is the melting point of iron, until it is reduced into a flow of liquid slag. For that to happen, preheated air must be forced into the furnace through various devices to quickly elevate the furnace temperature and accelerate the smelting process. In the absence of preheated air, furnace temperatures have rarely been measured to go beyond 1400° C, which is the upper limit of ancient European bloomeries. When a furnace fails to reach the adequate smelting point of 1600° C, the substance that comes out of the furnace is a porous substance that includes iron, charcoal, unreduced ore, clay, ashes, and other contaminants. This aggregate iron substance is known as bloom or bloomery iron, wrought iron, or low-grade steel. It is characteristic of the kind of iron produced in the early age of iron technology in Europe. A number of archeologists have claimed that, not only is the origin of African iron technology to be found in Europe, but also that, African iron technology is only a continuation of ancient European bloomery process.

Schmidt and Avery's ethnographic, technological and archeological experiment conducted among the Haya people of Western Tanzania has refuted the notion that Sub-Saharan African iron technology lacked sophistication, and that it was a prolongation of prehistoric European bloomery technique. Their elaborate reconstruction and testing of Haya furnaces have shown that these furnaces were able to sustain temperatures in excess of 1800° C, which is well over the 1350–1400° C registered in non-preheated European furnaces. The instruments used by Schmidt and Avery to measure the temperature at the nose of the furnace (a platinum/radium thermocouple) melted during measurement. Given the 1820° C melting point of the thermocouple, it is undeniable that the furnaces' temperatures were well above 1820° C. The Haya furnaces, Schmidt and Avery contended, were able to reach that high a temperature because of their singular structure, which too hasty surveys of African furnaces tend to miss. There exists a rampant homogenizing tendency among archeologists that makes them overlook variations in African furnaces and causes them to assume that African furnaces, supposedly vestiges of ancient European bloomeries, cannot sustain heat at temperatures above 1200° C. Haya furnaces, like some furnaces in Southwestern Nigeria, were equipped with tuyeres (blowpipes) inserted up to 50 cm into the furnaces. These tuyeres transferred heated air directly into the furnaces and helped quickly raise the temperature of the furnaces and accelerate the smelting process, thus making it possible for the furnaces to yield high-grade, high-carbon steel. Schmidt and Avery estimated the preheated air in the tuyeres to be in the range of 600° C or more. Their conclusions are telling. "We find in traditional Africa an Iron Age technology process that was exceedingly complex, and in historical and relative terms, also advanced."[20] For Schmidt and Avery to make a case for preheating technology in precolonial Africa was to dismantle one of European proudest inventions, as preheating air technology was not disseminated in Europe until J.B. Nielson's patent, in the 1820s. This constituted too bitter a pill for some proselytizers of European technological superiority to swallow.

Among the fiercest critics of Schmidt and Avery, are J. E. Rehder and David Kellick. Rehder challenged Schmidt and Avery's conclusions that the high temperature registered in the Haya furnaces was caused by preheated air blasted through the furnaces' internal tuyeres. He maintained against all predictions that temperatures as elevated as 1950° C could be obtained in furnaces with charcoal bed without any preheating. Furthermore, Rehder found unproven Schmidt and Avery's statement that the flow of preheated air in the tuyeres reached 600° C. His own calculation yielded the much conservative temperature of 22° C in the tuyeres. He thus concluded that preheating had never taken place in the Haya furnaces, proof that African iron technology was primitive, as the title of his intervention so resolutely foreboded.[21] The problem with Rehder's analysis was that his calculations were flawed. Rehder assumed that the flow of air in the tuyeres was continuous, while in fact it could not be. The bellows that Haya smelters used to blow air in the tuyeres during Schmidt and Avery's experiment had no retaining valves; which caused air to reverse in the tuyeres in an intermittent turbulent motion each time the diaphragm opened to let air into the tuyeres. Nevertheless, Schmidt revised his calculations under conditions of continuous turbulence of the air flow in the tuyeres — because of the lack of adequate mathematical model for calculating intermittent reverse turbulence — and came up with a very cautious preheating temperature of 300° C in the tuyeres, still a much higher temperature than Rehder's faulty method arrived at.[22]

As for Kellick, he was so convinced of African technological inferiority, and consequently of their inferiority complex, that he naively quoted the Martinican poet, Aimé Césaire, as witness of the African's supposed lack of self-esteem, thus failing to understand the obvious ironic tone in Césaire's poem.

> One of the major puzzles in the economic history of Sub-Saharan Africa is the apparently low rate of technological innovation in the subcontinent over the last 1500 years, relative to that of Asia, the Near East, Europe, or the Americas ... public awareness of this disparity shapes the contemporary attitudes of ... Africans toward themselves. Africans are, as the Negritude poet Aimé Césaire noted in 1956,
>
> > *ceux qui n'ont inventé ni la poudre ni la boussole*
> > *ceux qui n'ont jamais su dompter la vapeur ni l'électricité*
> > *ceux qui n'ont exploré ni les mers ni le ciel*
> > *mais ceux sans qui la terre ne serait pas la terre*[23]
>
> [those who invented neither powder nor compass
> those who never domesticated steam or electricity
> those who explored neither seas nor skies
> but those without whom the earth would never be the earth]

He conceded that some bloomery furnaces had used preheated air registered between 288–800° C, but quickly added that, no, they were not African furnaces; they were American furnaces located in New Jersey and Upper New York between 1830–1900.[24] Even when faced with the undeniable archeological evidence that African furnaces in such diverse places as Tanzania, Ghana, Ethiopia, Nigeria, Côte d'Ivoire, Burkina Faso, Malawi, and Zambia have produced steel blooms and even high-carbon steel, Kellick still wants these achievements to be, not the results of purposeful processes, but the consequences of accidents. "Some of the blooms cited above are very high-carbon steel, containing more than 1 percent carbon. African iron workers have also produced cast iron (greater than 2 percent carbon) *on occasion*."[25] When, unable to sustain his usual incredulity about the Africans' inventiveness, Kel-

lick is forced to recognized some spirit of innovation to the African, O does
he do it with such a lackadaisical attitude!

> Some ironworkers among the Northern Mafa of north Cameroon smelted
> Magnetite sand to produce a mélange of cast iron, steel, and wrought iron.
> In a successful reconstruction of this process, arranged by Nicholas David in
> 1986, about 40 percent of the product was cast iron, with the remainder high-
> carbon steel, low-carbon steel, and carbon-free wrought iron.... The produc-
> tion of cast iron was clearly not a mistake, as the smelter went on to decarburize
> the cast iron to steel in a strongly oxidizing forge fire. *This technology, the only
> one of its kind yet confirmed from Africa, is therefore a curious hybrid of the direct
> and indirect methods of making steel.*[26]

The archeological and scientific evidence is overwhelming. Precolonial
Africans, from East to West and South to North, had a technologically
advanced mind. They were inventive and innovative people who did not wait
for the arrival of Europeans to discover iron industry and use and trade iron
tools. Evidently, Kouyaté's small budget movie cannot afford the luxury of
giving the full measure of this lively and sophisticated iron industry that has
been unearthed by archeologists. *In Keita: The Heritage of the Griot*, the King
of the Mandé's forge — a small workshop staffed with just a handful of workers — is hardly representative of what travelers have reported upon arriving in
Mali or what researchers have found in Africa. Kouyaté's deficit of information on this matter — dictated, perhaps, by budgetary constraints or thematic
focus — is balanced by D. T. Niane's 1960 written version of the epic, *Sound-
jata, ou l'Épopée Mandingue*, translated by G. D. Pickett as *Sundiata: An Epic
of Old Mali* (1965). "The royal forges," Niane writes, "were situated outside
the walls and over a hundred smiths worked there. The bows, spears, arrows
and shields of Niani's warriors came from there."[27] Old Mali was a site of
dynamic metallurgical industry.

In *Keita: The Heritage of the Griot*, the collapse of the iron rod should
not be viewed as indication of low-grade iron metallurgy in precolonial Africa.
It is a metaphor that bears profound mythological value. In Mandé mythol-
ogy, Sundiata, like most kings, was not just human; he was prodigious. As
such his rise to power could not happen like any ordinary event. Sundiata's
advent had to register in Mandé history as enigmatic. So, the mystery starts
with Sundiata's pitiable beginning. His mother Sogolon Kédjou, or Sogolon
the hunchback, as she was commonly known, was the most repulsive woman
of the land of Do; she was offered as a royal reward to two hunters that had
rid King Mansa-Gnemo Diarra of a terrorizing mystic buffalo woman. The
hunters' attempts to possess Songolo having failed, they offered her to the King
of Mali, who had been warned of her arrival by a hunter soothsayer. The
soothsayer had advised the King of Mali to marry Sogolon and give her a child
that would become the greatest ruler the Mali Empire would ever know. How-

ever, Sundiata's mother was unapproachable, and it is only by frightening her to unconsciousness that King Naré Maghan or Maghan Kon Fatta [Manghan the handsome] of Mali was able to make her conceive a child. However, that child, Sundiata, when he came, was not the perfect

Sogolon Kédjou (Blandine Yaméogo) languishes over the physical disability of her son, Prince Sundiata Keita (Seydou Boro) (*Keita: The Heritage of the Griot*, directed by Dani Kouyaté, Burkina Faso, 1994).

prince of popular storybooks. He was crippled and had no chance of becoming the great conqueror that the Mandé had been expecting. So, Sundiata, like any messiah, had to overcome his humble beginnings and verify the tale that great things often come in small packages; that the strongest man or the world's most formidable conqueror would not necessarily come under the best circumstances. He could be a crippled, but a crippled that was to make even the fiercest of monarchs bend and break under his authority, as easily as did the strong iron rod that came from the skilled forges of Mali.

Iron: The Great Instigator of Occupational Specialization and Urbanization in Ancient Africa

The mastery of iron technology contributed to developing other areas. Metallurgy insured military might to those who mastered it. Certainly the wealth and longevity of great African states had much to do with the mastery of metallurgy. The army of the impressive Ghanaian empire, for instance, was reported to be about two-hundred-thousand-men strong, equipped with bows, arrows, swords, lances, and daggers. Thanks to this military advantage, Ghana operated numerous successful raids on its neighbors. Also, for half a century, the military superiority of Ghana helped the empire defend itself against the many raids that its envious neighbors launched against it. The Ghanaian army was so formidable that, when the Almoravids fundamentalists started their attack against the Kingdom of Ghana in 1062, it took them five years to reach its gates and another ten years of fighting to finally submit the empire, in 1077. The impressive Ghanaian armory suggested that there was a high level of occupational specialization in this ancient empire. Only some people, not everyone, were specialized in smelting iron and smithing weapons and tools, whereas others were skilled in fighting, farming, trading, building, and more.

In fact, iron smelters and smithers, in their desire to have monopoly on their occupation, have initiated, if not the first occupational specializations, at least, the first occupational castes.[28] Occupational and economic special-izations in Sub-Saharan Africa are reported to be the direct outcome of a long-distance trading activity with its sources in Sub-Saharan Africa rather than the Mediterranean or Middle East, around the second millennium B.C.E. This endogenous development of commerce is attributable to the rapid adop-tion of metals (copper, but especially iron). The need to produce metals, transport them, and exchange them against other goods has also generated other necessities. It became indispensable that some people should be avail-able to grow, transform, and sell the food that would feed the traders; there needed to be people to build the houses that would lodge both the sedentary populations and the traveling merchants and people to entertain the travel-ers; there needed to be people to maintain order and administer justice to ensure the smooth functioning of the empire. So, some communities started to make themselves more and more available for specific tasks. The first stage of productive specialization took place around the first millennium B.C.E. and was more ethnically driven.[29] Around 1000 B.C.E., in the wetlands of the Niger Delta, the Bozo people (ethnically related to the Mandé, an ethnic branch from the Soninké founders of the Mali Empire) specialized in catching and drying fish, an activity passed on to them by their ancestors; while in the wet soil of the Niger, the Marka concentrated on the production of African rice.[30] Today, the Bozo people are still practicing their ancient trade in West Africa

During the age of iron prosperity and the great African empires, when trade increased between Northern Africa and the Middle East, on the one hand, and Sub-Saharan Africa, on the other hand, occupational specializa-tion increased, too. Between the 9th and the 11th centuries, the Mandé of Ancient Ghana traded salt from the North against gold from Wangara min-ers north of the empire. In the 14th century, the Djula of the Mali Empire traded gold against forest products with the Akan from the South. The Djula have remained the preeminent ethnic group in West African commercial life today. While iron weapons helped protect the great African empires against jealous neighbors, secured their commerce by making the circulation of peo-ple and merchandise safe and efficient, enforced tax rules, and gave the empires political stability, iron tools expanded agriculture, stimulated the augmenta-tion of food production, which in turn made it possible for populations to settle in one place rather than moving around in search of new resources; the mastery of iron technology led to the burgeoning of large urban centers in Sub-Saharan Africa. Archeologists have been able to link the survival of permanent settlements with the spread of iron technology and its consequent increase of food production.[31]

Iron was undeniably a vital commodity in ancient Africa; the mastery of its production conferred one high prerogatives. To protect the privileges associated with their profession, ironworkers surrounded the iron smelting and smithing process with secret rituals; which kept the knowledge of iron processing in particular castes and families and out of the public sphere. Goucher and Herbert have documented the ritualistic aspects of iron production among the Bassari people of Northwestern Togo during their rebuilding of ancient furnaces and reconstruction of early smelting process. The process is one of elaborate ceremonies of purifications and incantations. As they report, women are not allowed at the furnace-building site. As women, the researchers were admitted on the location only because they were observers, thus provisional males. Participating males were forbidden from having sexual relations until completion of the furnace. Once the furnace location has been determined, the chief smelter would offer the ancestors a libation of beer to drive away evil spirits and bless the process. Then, he would go naked at night in the surrounding mountains to gather some plants, which he would mix with some ground porcupine skin and hippopotamus hide. This mixture, which was meant to strengthen the furnace, would be progressively added to its superstructure as it is being built. Once the furnace completed, the chief smelter would then cover the interior wall of the furnace with the remaining concoction. Because menstruation was considered detrimental to the smelting process, a widow, who has passed childbearing age, assisted by two girls previously purified who have spent the night under her supervision, would cook a ritual meal and bring it to the site. The chief smelter would present the food to the furnace and urge the furnace to be fertile and give birth to quality iron. The chief would then grab a young boy and beat him until he cried, thus simulating the first cry of a newborn. The furnace was a woman; the smelters were her husbands, and the whole process was meant to imitate life creation.[32]

> As the furnace took shape, it was regarded more and more as human being. The bosh or midportion was referred to as *apo* (belly); the stack is *debend* (chest), and the top is *dyerekan* (se) *kem* (head), with a mouth through which the charge was fed. The interior with its charge was known as *m'poyo* (the lung), and when the smelting had begun, *mfomfotem* (respiration) was said to be taking place ... the furnace was breathing. The master smelter was regarded as the "father" of the furnace; he and his assistants would also become its husbands as the furnace became more explicitly a female being who could deliver the iron bloom from her womb.[33]

The life-creating aspect of metal smelting has survived the test of time. In his autobiography, the late Guinean author, Camara Laye, whose father was a blacksmith, recalled the ritual associated with gold smelting in a language whose allusions to lovemaking, child conception, and creation are only metaphorical. In Laye's autobiography, *The Dark Child*, a woman in need of a trinket comes to see his father. All the ingredients for child creation are figuratively present in Laye's description of the moment. The woman comes to the blacksmith with raw and muddy grains of gold she has collected after months of toil. In order to yield life, these grains, which are a veiled representation of eggs, will need to be fertilized by man. So, accompanied by a go-between — for she will have a lot of convincing to do in order to be squeezed in the blacksmith's busy schedule — the woman seeks the help of Laye's father. She finds him in his busy workshop, with his mystical little black snake coiled by him, under a sheepskin. Before starting his work, the goldsmith "never fail[s] to stroke the little snake stealthily as it lay coiled up under the sheepskin ... this [is] his way of gathering strength ... for the most trying part of his task;" a task that is spiritual in its nature — as is all life-creating endeavor.

> The craftsman who works in gold must first of all purify himself ... and abstain from all sexual commerce during the whole time ... it would have been impossible for my father to ignore these rules ... it was obvious that forewarned in a dream by his black guiding spirit of the task which awaited him in the morning, my father must have prepared for it as soon as he arose, entering his workshop in a state of purity, his body smeared with the secret potions hidden in his numerous pots of magical substances.[34]

As it added a new being to the social fabric, this task was also communal. It concerned the whole society, and so the community participated in it with an interest that could seem voyeuristic if things were to be taken literally rather than emblematically. The griot, along with bystanders, witnessed the process of gold smelting and trinket forging. The griot, as historian and recorder of genealogies, had an important symbolic role in the creation process. His task was to document for future generations the birth of the new metal — which was the birth of the new Mandé child — to detail the circumstances of that child's coming to life, so as to name that child accordingly; for to name was more than to attribute a person an arbitrary signifier of identification. In Mandé tradition, the patronymic is always full with meaning. To name is to celebrate a person's life through his/her deeds and to commemorate the events that occasioned that life through multiple nicknames. To name is to nickname. Was not Sundiata Keita also So'lon Jara (Sogolon's lion), So'olon Ma'an, Ma'an Sunjata, Mari Jata, Danama Yirindi, or Simbon? To name is to praise. The griot, the quintessential praise-singer had to witness the birth of the child in order to better praise it, hence his presence at the gold smelting ceremony.

However, the community, too, has to witness the birth of the new child to become one of them. From this outlook, the griot's story, as collective history, is meaningful only insofar as it incorporates the experiential narratives of all the members of the community to which the new child is to belong, hence the community's presence at the site of creation. Aroused by the *douga*, the mythical chant of the griot, which is sung to and danced by celebrated men only who have ceremoniously prepared for it, the entranced smith creates life to the joy and amazement of his observing community. "No sooner had he finished, than workmen and apprentices, friends and customers in their turn, not forgetting the woman for whom the trinket had been created, would flock around [the smith], congratulating him, showering praises on him and complimenting the praise-singer at the same time."[35] The mythologizing of metal smelting and smithing has successfully kept the profession enigmatic and has guaranteed the social preeminence of the few people who practiced it. To safeguard the secrecy of their profession, male smiths trained their sons in the technical and mystical aspects of the process; and to guarantee the continuance of their social status, they married women of their own groups, avoiding exogamous unions as much as possible, since women from other groups were likely to spy on them and reveal the smelting secrets to their relatives. Soon, the smelting occupation became a family business, and there developed strong castes of ironworkers. In *Keita: The Heritage of the Griot*, the smith's claim that he knew the purpose of Balla Fasséké's visit participates in the enterprise of mystification and preservation of a line of work within a family or a caste. Just as his father Noumoufaïri had preserved the occupation of smithing into the family by way of mystification and passed it on to him, he, too, must preserve it within his family and pass it on to his sons by surrounding it with rituals and taboos.

Mystery as means of securing one's occupation for one's progeny or family members was intrinsic to most trades. Like the ironworkers of Ancient Africa, the masons of the Ancient Malian city of Djenné, known for their fabled mud structural designs, have inherited their skills from their elders thanks to esoteric rites that they, too, still practice today as essential parts of their work. A typical Djenné mud house is built to bring abundance and fecundity to the people who dwell in it. As such, it reflects those expectations by having on its top, above the main entrance and conveniently noticeable, some emblems displayed in a row. The outer two emblems, shaped like two phalluses or two men wearing hats, represent the power of men. Five smaller structures representing women stand between the two phalluses; below the women are even smaller structures standing for the prospective children or the navels of the prospective children of the house. In order to give force to these life-creating symbols as well as to warn off any curse that could befall the house by the hands of Satan or the "many bad spirits that frequent build-ing sites," the mason performs an ancient magical ritual that was captured on camera. For this ritual, the mason uses a ceremonial polished wooden wand with a leather band at its end, which he passes around his wrist. Holding the wand firmly, he draws some shapes on the floor, first standing up and then kneeling down. Then the mason places the wand in front of his knees, gir-dles his waist with a magical belt, and his prayer beads in his hand, he whis-pers a secret incantation. Afterwards, he pulls some dust to himself from the four cardinal points invoking the name of Allah. Gathering this dust, he then uses it for his ablution, as he would water. Then, he kneels down again to pray, casting quick glances at the four cardinal points. After another secret ritual that he "will not reveal to any non-mason," the mason takes the gath-ered dust to the worksite, which he adds to his construction mud.[36] Many occupational castes still live in specialized villages today and trace their ori-gins to ancient Africa. Some examples are the Katiola potters and the Toumodi weavers, respectively, in northern and north-central Côte d'Ivoire. These occupational castes owe their exclusivity and their survival to the esoteric rites that have surrounded them since ancient times as well as to the safe environ-ment in which they were allowed to prosper.

The Administration of Justice in Ancient Africa

At its height, like any big urban center, the Mali Empire must have attracted all sorts of people, many who were in search facile gains. Yet by wit-nesses' accounts, the routes leading to the empire were safe, and so was the empire itself. Ibn Battuta notes,

> When I decided on the journey to Malli ... I hired a guide from the Massufa, since there is no need to travel with companions because of the safety of the road.... It is their customs to prevent people entering the city except with per-mission. I had written beforehand to the white community.... When I Arrived at the [Sansara River],[37] I crossed in a ferry and nobody prevented me.... [T]here are no thieves in their country.[38]

Clearly, Mali owed its safety to the impressive presence of its fierce army patrolling the empire and its periphery. That safety could also be credited to the implacable administration of a system of justice that took advantage of fear of imperial authority, a Muslim ethic of honor, threat of banishment, and menace of divine intercession. The inhabitants of Mali proved to be almost as reverential of their sovereign as they were afraid of the justice of Allah and the loss of their reputation in the community. The Malians were very fearful of their sovereign's verdict, and when guilty of a grave fault, it was only by taking refuge in a holy place that they could hope to avail themselves of their emperor's compassion. Battuta recalls that "[I]t was their custom to take refuge in the mosque and if that were not possible, in the house of the preacher."[39]

Justice in Agadez, a documentary by Christian Lelong, chronicles the kind of justice system that was probably available in the 13th century Mali Empire.[40] In this post-independence era, the society of Agadez, in Niger, which has been influenced by traditional animist, then Arab, and later French cultures, still holds on to a long-established Koranic system of justice that functions alongside the jurisprudence inherited from French colonization. The cadi (also *qadi* or *quadi*), a man appointed for life by the sultan, administers justice in a little vestibule adjacent to his house, assisted by two or three helpers. All day long, he renders justice to people who come to him with a variety of complaints. The cases he has to settle range from those of battered women to cases of exploited workers, passing through allegations of witchcraft. In each case, the Koran has served as foundation for resolution. When a man accusing his employer of not paying him his due is asked by the cadi to warn his relatives that he is going to swear on the Koran, he suddenly changes his mind. Rather than informing the whole community that he is a deceiver upon whom the wrath of Allah might fall, he prefers to acknowledge privately, in the cadi's court, that he has lied about the amount of money his employer owes him. When an elderly violent husband summons his young wife to the cadi's court because she refuses to go to bed with him, she reveals, in her own defense, that the petitioner has often used blasphemous language against Allah and has not been praying for almost seven years. This revelation turns the tide against the plaintiff, and he is urged by the cadi to rectify his lifestyle by going back to praying or else his wife will be granted a divorce. When the police of Agadez are unable to solve a case of women accused of witchcraft, they bring the accused women to the court of the cadi to have them swear of their innocence on the Koran. The cadi's judgment is irrevocable. The police who refer some cases to the cadi, just as he refers cases to them, too, recognize his authority. That Koranic authority conferred to the cadi comes down from the early days of Africa's islamicization by the Almoravids. In Ancient Mali, this Koranic system of justice administered by appointed cadis has regulated life in the big urban centers that have sprouted thanks to the development of iron technology.

The Ecological Cost of Urbanization and Industrialization in Ancient Africa

In ancient Africa, the big urban centers that mushroomed under the impulse of ironworkers must have had some great environmental implications. *Keita: The Heritage of the Griot*, as oral and visual literature, hints at the ecosystem of the area covered by the Mali Empire between the eleventh and the thirteenth centuries. That ecosystem sharply contrasts with the kind of ecosystem that is present today in the same area. In the movie, two hunting brothers are tracking an evil creature, a buffalo woman that has been terrorizing the people of the land of Do. They finally corner her at the foot of a big tree. Accepting her fate that she should finally die by the hands of these two hunters, Do-Kamisa, the creature, gives them some advice and devices to use in their escape. She will surrender her life to them and reveal the secrets to escape unharmed if, as a reward for their prowess, they demand that her nephew, the ruler of Do, offer them her adopted daughter, Sogolon Kédjou, the ugliest woman of the land, who will bear a child that will rule over the savannah. The hunters agree, and Do-Kamisa asks them to gather a stick, a stone, and an egg, which they should successively throw behind them, as they run away from the fatally hurt buffalo-woman. In their escape, as the hunters throw the stick, the stone, and the egg, these elements become, respectively, a thick forest of palm trees, a rocky hill, and a muddy swamp; which protect them from the monster. The important information emanating from this episode has to do with the ecological makeup of Old Mali. The environmental picture of Ancient Mali that one gets from this section of the film is a very diverse terrain constituted by lush woodlands, swamps, grassy and desert plains, and high plateaus, all coexisting in a proximity that is not recognizable today. How could the discrepancy between the ecosystem described in *Keita: The Heritage of the Griot* and the environment observable today be accounted for?

Two plausible explanations offer themselves. The first one is of the order of the mnemonic trope. The griot that tells the history of his people from memory only proceeds by adding together singular family and individual stories. Thus the clan's history as recalled by the griot is a quilt in which are weaved together singular family or individual experiences, each experience functioning like a sub-text that serves as roadblock or insertion point. These insertion points signal to the griot when to add a particular narrative to the collective quilt. It is an effective way for the oral historian to maintain a level of regularity each time he tells the same story.[41] The story of the egg, the stone, and the stick in *Keita: The Heritage of the Griot* could be inscribed in that register. It reminds the griot to record, though in a condensed form, the vast precincts of the state, and thus the greatness of the empire and the authority of its ruler.

In fact, under Sundiata, the Mali Empire had reached great ecological range. During Sundiata's reign, between 1230 and 1255, the empire extended 1250 miles from the Atlantic (West) to the borders of northern Nigeria (East), and 600 miles from the southern Sahara commercial towns of Awdaghust, Walata, and Tadmakka to the borders of Guinea forests in the southwest.[42] This is a huge territory with a multiple environmental makeup that is consistent with the griot's description. The griot's condensation of these various ecosystems is dictated by the trope of mnemonics. Nevertheless condensation is not of insignificant importance, for it registers the essential at same time as it compresses it; and perhaps, it registers better the essential, precisely because it compresses it and makes it a roadblock. By making the essential a roadblock the griot also renders it requisite, inerasable, and therefore necessarily mentionable. To Mabo, Djéliba thus says "look at the extent of your ancestor's patrimony. It was vast, diverse, rich, and to the measure of his power; for only a powerful ruler, like your ancestor Sundiata, could reign over such an immense estate."

The other possible explanation to the ecological discrepancy could be the effect of human actions on landscape over the past several hundred years. Some recent palynological researches have offered better understanding of landscape transformations over the past 2500 years. Palynology, which measures the layers of pollen that is deposited each year at the bottom of lakes, gives information on the type of vegetations that might have existed in a given environment. This deep longitudinal information can then be dated thanks to radiocarbon measurements. The researches done in the Great Lakes area have demonstrated that forest landscapes, for instance, which were until recently thought to be pristine, had in fact been affected by human interventions. Around between 300 B.C.E. and 300 C.E., the environment has witnessed some decline in tree type pollen and an increase in pollen of agricultural and grass species, which point to the effect of clearance of land for agricultural practices.[43]

This research, though not directly related to the area in Kouyaté's movie, could help make some inferences on the physiography of Old Mali. One could, cautiously, surmise that the conception of iron implements has been determining for land domestication and for agricultural progress. As the tale of the chicken and the egg, the increase of metallurgical knowledge and practice played a great role in the clearing of land for agriculture. Iron implements facilitated land domestication and agricultural innovation, which were essential for sustaining the immense urban centers that ironwork has led the way in creating in the Mali Empire. Ironworkers were the instigators of specialized villages by creating family monopolies. Other artisans later emulated them and created more specialized centers. In Sub-Saharan Africa, prosperous specialized villages of artisans and scholars mushroomed as far back as 1000 B.C.E.[44] Several centuries later, these thriving urban centers were still observable. Ibn Battuta, among other uncomplimentary remarks, reported on them as he traveled to "the land of the Blacks" between 1352 and 1353 C.E.[45] Djenné (in the Delta of Niger) was one of these ancient specialized urban centers. The city was a commercial crossroads for the exchange of salt and gold and a scholarly town during the prosperous days of the Mali Empire. People traveled from everywhere to study with learned religious men of Djenné. Another important urban center was Timbuktu. Founded by Tuareg herdsmen around the eleventh century, the first rulers of the city were the Malians. Timbuktu became a holy town and a sanctuary town for people fleeing religious persecution. A commercial crossroads for caravans and boats, the town quickly developed into a cosmopolitan city, and its architecture shifted from mere huts of straw to mud huts and grand architectural buildings.[46] These big urban centers in Ancient Mali with their thriving populations must have dramatically affected the environment, as vast lands had to be cleared for agriculture and for settlement. Again, it is metallurgical technology that helped solve this predicament by providing the settlers with iron implements. Thanks to iron tools, hard soils could be broken and tilled for agriculture; wood could be cut for domestic fuel and for construction; clay could be quarried and collected for more elaborate buildings (as evidenced by the edifying constructions in Djenné, Walata, and Timbuktu); grass and reeds could be cut for roofs. Iron was the solution; but iron was also, beside natural causes, part of the problem. If anything, the mastery of iron technology and the specialization in metallurgy alone were enough to exert great stress on the environment of ancient Africa.

> The African iron industry paid a high price for the levels of production it achieved: each furnace consumed as many as three trees or 180 kg of charcoal per smelt. A single furnace could therefore consume between one hundred and three hundred trees annually. If the Germans correctly estimated that the overall production of the region exceeded four hundred tons of iron per year, the smelters would have required some one hundred tons of charcoal or a minimum of 18,000 trees.[47]

Ancient iron smelting furnaces were — to borrow these words from Schmidt — "a forest stew." Furnaces consumed a variety of trees of all sizes. More than sixteen different genera of trees were used in iron furnaces. Scientific analysis of charcoal types excavated at ancient furnace sites indicated that around the first century B.C.E., ironworkers exploited for fuel first-growth wet-forest trees, such as African mahogany, uapaca, and African celtis (with wide distribution range in countries like Kenya, Tanzania, Uganda, in East Tropical Africa, Cameroon, Congo, Congo/Zaire, in West Central Tropical Africa, South Africa, Southern Africa, Comoros and Madagascar, in Western Indian Ocean). According to scientific indications, however, three to four centuries later, that physiography changed. The scarcity of trees became evident. Study of excavated charcoal types at practically the same site showed that only two moist-forest species were used as fuel for furnaces. "...over the several centuries after the first practice of iron smelting along the coastal hills, the environmental plenty of moist forests diminished to the point that iron smelters were obliged to use only a few remnant moist-forest species and some secondary regrowth and were ranging farther afield to exploit the swamps for supplementary fuels."[48] That pattern of forest depletion could easily be projected elsewhere, notably in the area covered by the Old Mali Empire; and one could reasonably infer that a palynological analysis of swamps contiguous to hillsides and forests would give a comprehensive picture of the landscape of Old Mali and some of the disturbances that the area has undergone since ancient times. In all evidence, abundant cutting of forest and swamp growths for industrial and domestic fuel as well as for construction, hillsides quarrying for iron ores, and extraction of clay for architecture and furnace building in ancient Africa have affected the physiognomy of Africa's landscape. Thus, a combination of these human interventions with natural ecological disturbances could explain the difference in the ecological compositions of Old Mali's landscape as the griot recounts it in *Keita: The Heritage of the Griot* and as it is observable today.

Ancient African Pharmacological Knowledge

Another ancient African practice that could have affected the environment of Old Mali — though at a lesser coefficient — is the utilization of African plants for pharmacological reason. The exponentially growing populations of the big urban centers of ancient Africa had to be protected from the variety of diseases that affected them. The range of the Old Mali Empire — which spread from tropical forests to bushy savannahs, passing through swamps and hilly lands — exposed the area to tropical diseases as well as to infections from semi-desert and desert regions. *Keita: The Heritage of the Griot* hints at several instances of plant use for pharmacological purpose in Ancient Africa. In the film, the mother and sisters of the crippled prince rub his paralyzed legs with a concoction of leaves. The exact nature of the plants used is not explicit to the viewers; which begs the viewers to ask what medicinal resources Sogolon Kédjou, or any 13th century Malian mother for that matter, could have in her medicine basket.

One plant that is at the source of Sundiata's resolve to walk is the baobab tree. It was the humiliation inflicted to Sundiata's mother when she went to Sassouma Bérété for some baobab leaves that triggered off the crippled prince's willpower to stand up. Moreover, it was by supporting himself on a sunsun branch that Sundiata was finally able to stand up. These two plants are among thousands of other plants with alimentary and medicinal virtues that Africans have been using since times immemorial. Adama Doumbia, a descendant of the noble Mandé people founders of the Old Mali Empire, conveys better than anyone his ancestors' reliance on roots, plants, and herbs for their survival.

> We rely upon thousands of plants to serve our needs. We drink concoctions of herbs, inhale their steam, shower with them, and apply them externally. We burn herbs and inhale their smoke for medicine and protection. We boil mixtures and bathe with the tea. We extract the juices, saps, or resins, and apply them to our bodies. We place them in bundles and mix them with other ingredients for amulets and talismans. We make use of every part of a plant; seeds, leaves, flowers, and roots.[49]

Doumbia goes on to explain the virtues of some very popular plants in West Africa: The Jala (*Khaya senegalensis*) is a plant consumed for energy and intestinal cleansing. Tea made from its bark fights fever and alleviates constipation and general fatigue. A twig of this plant tied around the waist of a newborn is believed to fend off evil spirits. A tea of Kinkéliba (*Combretum micrathum*) fights fever, cold, flu virus, aches, and pains. It lowers blood pressure, prevents malaria and treats infections. The neem (*Azadirachta indica*) is one of the most versatile plants. It works as antibacterial, antiviral, and antiseptic. Its leaves treat wounds, burns, sprains, bruises, rheumatism, fungal infection, yeast infection, gum and tooth diseases. The neem also alleviates earaches, fever, fatigue; it treats allergies, sore throats, cold, flu, viruses, digestive problems and food poisoning. The oil from its fruit cures cramps and ulcers. Another plant with multiple virtues is the shea butter plant. Its fruits are edible; its nuts provide the shea butter, which serves as cooking oil, ointment or skin moisturizer. It heals aging skin or serve as muscle relaxer, aftershave, and hair-

A young Ivorian healer displays his collection of curative barks, roots, leaves, herbs, and fibers. In Ancient Africa the traditional shamans would have hundreds of plant gatherers scouring the forests to supply the local pharmacies. This has also contributed to transforming the physiography of Africa (photograph by Julia Dresen-Coulibaly).

balm. The sunsun, also known as Mandesunsun (*Diospyros mespilformis/ Annona senegalensis*), the plant whose branch Sundiata uses as a support to stand up and walk in Niane's version of the epic, is also known among the Mandé as the tree of abundance. It is believed to contain a concentrate of Nyama or supernatural power. Crushed, its leaves protect against wasp stings. Boiled, it heals arthritic joints. Pulverized and mixed with shea butter, the bark of the sunsun is a powerful healing ointment. Its root is consumed by women during pregnancy to avoid complications. Mixed with other ingredients, the sunsun cures impotence and mental illness. The kalakari tree (*Heeria insignis*) also known as the tree of luck, is believed to have some magical virtues. Its powdered bark is used by women looking for a suitable mate. Of all the trees used by the Africans of the Old Mali Empire, the baobab tree (*Andansonia digitata*), which was at the foundation of Sundiata's resolve to stand up and walk, was certainly the most resourceful. The baobab served for food, water, clothing, shelter, medicine, tools, and cosmetics. Even today the Mandé people continue to make use of the versatile virtues of the baobab. As notes Doumbia, the fiber from the baobab's bark is source of rope, mats, baskets, strings for musical instruments, and paper. Soaked in water, the baobab fruit releases some sweet nectar that makes a tasty drink. Eaten, its fruits help fight diarrhea and fever. Spread around the house, the baoba shells repel geckos. Boiled, its leaves make a succulent sauce. A tea of baobab leaves is efficacious in treating asthma, kidney and bladder diseases, worm infestation and pains. It also cleanses the blood and sanitizes it. Roasted and crushed, the baobab's seeds provide a good paste against teeth and gum infection and aches. Oil extracted from the seeds of the baobab can be used as pain reliever or ointment against rheumatism or skin conditions. Ash from the bark of the baobab serves as salt or soap. The pulverized root of the baobab tree is used as makeup or skin moisturizer. The baobab root also cures malaria. Its trunk is a rainwater collector; sometimes, too, it serves as burial sites for traditional shamans.[50] Of the baobab tree, Battuta wrote,

> [The road to Mali] has many trees which are tall and of great girth. A caravan can find shade in the shadow of one tree; some of them have no branches and no leaves, but the shadow of its trunk is such that a man can find shade in it. Some of those trees have rotted inside and rainwater collects in them. Such a tree is like a well and people drink of the water which is in it. Bees and honey are in some and people extract the honey from the trees. I have passed by one of these trees and found inside a weaver with his loom set in it — he was weaving.[51]

The baobab tree, widely spread in West Africa, still plays this sociological function. Around it are organized the social lives of many villages today. Depending on its spread, its shade can serve as a market place, a Koranic school, a mosque, a wedding or baptism site, or a tribunal. The baobab, also known in Africa as the tree of life, is a majestic tree that lives hundreds of years in the most extreme tropical conditions. Many baobabs have survived Ancient Africa's hunger for wood. This cannot necessarily be said about the other trees. Thousands of vegetals, such as the acacia, the kola tree, the ntomi (*Ficus carpensis*), the roselle (*Hibiscus sabdariffa*), and more, were used by specialized healers to tend to the health of the growing populations that the expanding urban centers, following the boom of metallurgy, occasioned in Ancient Africa. In order not to be in short supply of dried leaves, roots, herbs, fruits, nuts, and barks, the hundreds of shamans and healers of the immense urban centers must have had crowds of plant hunters armed with machetes, axes, and hoes, scouring the countryside to collect the vegetals that would constitute the pharmacies of Ancient Africa. The effect, though not comparable to what the hunt for furnace charcoal was, had certainly contributed to transforming the landscape and changing the ecosystem of Ancient Africa.

Like the baobab tree, Dani Kouyaté's *Keita: The Heritage of the Griot* is a resourceful movie for understanding ancient Africa, its history, its peoples, its cultures, and its political and social organizations. In the style of the griots of his culture he emulates, the filmmaker tells his story by propagating roadblocks. At each roadblock, depending on the interest of the viewer, one can choose to travel literary, linguistic, historical, anthropological, archeological or sociological, routes. No matter what itinerary one chooses, the aven-

The African Acacia. In Ancient Africa this tree with multiple curative faculties was always part of the traditional pharmacological supply (photograph by Julia Dresen-Coulibaly).

ture promises to be instructive and exhilarating at the same time. This chapter has only partially uncovered the rich heritage of the griot. Much more remains to be revealed, provided one patiently follows the many clues that the African historian has skillfully scattered in his tale.

Burkinabé filmmaker Dani Kouyaté is a descendant of the griot caste. For him, directing is telling a story in the tradition of the griot (photograph by Robert Millié).

8

Crisis in French Africa as Hexagonal Possibility
Globalization à la française

...Since the collapse of the USSR, the dynamics of empire has changed. The World is now more multipolar and mercantile, with China and Europe emerging to compete against the U.S. Empire is more driven by multinational corporations, whose interests transcend those of any particular nation-state.
— Steven Hiatt, "Global Empire: The Web of Control," A Game as Old as Empire

General Charles de Gaulle, this most beloved French president and iconic figure of French resistance and morality, once formulated an aphorism whose hideous veracity is only equaled by the unscrupulous zeal with which France put it into practice throughout history. "France," he said, "has no friends, but only some interests." This Gaullist maxim, which foreboded an unchanged paradigm of philosophical disinformation, economic strangulation, military persecution, and political destabilization, if it has proven factual over time and has helped France accumulate a colossal fortune to the detriment of its former colonies, is today being challenged by most French-speaking African countries (Algeria, Chad, Rwanda, Cameroon, Haiti, and Côte d'Ivoire). Perhaps, the most powerful counter-hegemonic social movement of the twenty first century witnessed in French Africa is the resistance movement taking place in Côte d'Ivoire since 2002, and which Sidiki Bakaba, the Ivorian filmmaker, has documented in his *Bare Hands Victory*.[1] Bakaba's documentary chronicles the mobilization and struggle against French disguised neocolonial agenda of several Ivorian youth movements gathered under the banner of *La Galexie Patriotique* (The Patriotic Galaxy) and led by the charismatic former student association leader Charles Blé Goudé.

Ivorian filmmaker Sidiki Bakaba during the making of *La Victoire aux mains nues/ Bare Hands Victory* (Abidjan: Kepri Production, 2005) (Photograph by Ayala Bakaba).

To refer to Blé Goudé's movement exclusively as a youth movement would not really do it justice. The *Galexie Patriotique* is actually a spontaneous multigenerational, multi-gendered, multi-party, and multi-professional bloc that has formed to unveil and defeat France's imperial economic and political scheme wherever it will manifest itself in Côte d'Ivoire and under whichever form it will hide. On closer analysis, the movement is a resistance against a tripartite collusion represented by the United Nations, the northern countries, and local informants/collaborators, all united for the continued pillaging of developing countries. Côte d'Ivoire, the *patriotes* often chant, will be the graveyard of France's deceitful policy in its former colonies. What they really mean is that, at least in Côte d'Ivoire, they are determined to put an end to the French arsonist policy by which France has historically schemed to set multiple fires in Africa in order to hire itself as emergency management agency via the United Nations and the world financial institutions.

No matter under which form they come into view, the various French interventions in Africa have never had a philanthropic thrust. French intrusions in Africa have always been driven by logic of maximum wealth through minimum or no effort. Historically, the French Republic has seldom won a war. In fact, the French have systematically lost most wars, even the ones that they confidently declared on their neighbors; and each time France was defeated, it turned to Africa or to the Caribbean with the most destructive designs to assuage its bruised ego and to rebuild its broken finances. An understanding of the French policy in Africa — and the Caribbean — whereby in moments of political and financial distress at home crises are implemented abroad as possibility for Hexagonal improvement could inform a discussion of the contemporary stance against France's brand of globalization in Africa in general, and in Côte d'Ivoire in particular.

In 1871, in the aftermath of the Franco-Prussian War, a war that France declared and seemed so confident to win on its Prussian neighbor, France emerged a broken and demoralized nation with a diminished territory, a poor economy, and an injured reputation. The German Alliance had just defeated the army of Emperor Napoleon III, annexed French territories of Alsace and Lorraine, and handed the French government a reparation invoice the equivalent of one billion dollars to be paid within three years. Despite its drained reserves, France managed to acquit itself of the enormous bill long before the scheduled deadline. France's alacrity to make good on the German humiliating tab would have seemed a casual occurrence if, almost fifty years before that event, a less powerful country, Algeria, asking that France reimbursed a loan it had owed for too long, had not paid a heavy cost for its impertinence.

The Wolf and the Lamb

The immediate economic outcome of the 1789 French Revolution was catastrophic. Agricultural methods in France had remained archaic. Unlike British farmers, for instance, French farmers had not been able to develop large agricultural exploitations to sustain the local markets and garner much-needed revenues. The small French farms could hardly feed the French populations; furthermore, the price of grain and firewood had skyrocketed; bread, the quintessential French food, was being rationed. France was on the verge of famine, and an even more dangerous prospect was lingering: Napoleon's hungry armies in Italy and Spain were getting irritable; a mutiny could break any time. Subsequently, France turned to two Algerian commercial houses, Bacri and Busnach, for a loan in money and grains in order to remedy the country's hardship. However, Bacri and Busnach, too, owed some money to the Algerian sovereign, Dey Kodja Hussein, and they were waiting for France to honor its tab, so that they could settle their debt with the Dey. In 1815, by the end of the Napoleonic failed war, France's debt to Algeria was about 18 million francs. Perhaps the merchants had asked Dey Hussein to use his authority and recover the money from the French authorities on their behalf. Whatever the case, Dey Hussein grew impatient with France's tergiversations.

In 1827, during a heated argument he had with Pierre Deval, the French consul in Algeria, regarding France's long-due balance, Dey Hussein hit Deval with his flywhisk. King Charles X, who had by then been on the French throne since 1824, was not very eager to pay off his country's delinquent debt to Algeria. So, Charles X seized this occasion to protest what he perceived in the Dey's gesture as lack of respect for the French Crown. Despite Dey Hussein's explanation that his gesture was in response to Pierre Deval's personal insult to him rather than condescension toward the King of France, 600 French ships landed 37,000 troops in Algeria on June 14, 1830. The French soldiers engaged in the most despicable acts of religious vandalism and human right abuses. They raided mosques and transformed them in cathedrals. They destroyed private properties; they raped women, and executed hundreds of Algerians. Less than a month later, on July 5, the French deposed Dey Hussein. By February 1831, Algeria became effectively a French settlement colony, and French authorities invited 4500 French colonists to farm the fertile coastal lands of Algeria.[2] The French occupation of Algeria did not remain without any response, nonetheless. The Algerians offered the French a prolonged resistance. Finally, in 1962, the Algerians handed the French one of their most crushing defeats in history and seized independence. Germany of 1870 was not 1830's Algeria. France understood that it was not in its interest to delay its obligation toward the Germans. So, France paid its debt promptly and spent the ensuing years thinking of ways to assuage its defeat and to brighten its tarnished image in Europe. Many social engineers suggested that France should concentrate its efforts overseas and build itself an empire that would both replenish its depleted coffers and extend to "inferior races" its ideals of civilization.

Globalizing Otherwise: From Slave Trade to Colonization

France, it should be noted, had been present in Africa as early as 1642. France had actively participated in the slave trade that sold more than 28 millions Africans in Europe and in the Americas between 1650 and 1900. At that time, the purpose was clearly economic, and no one spoke of extending French "superior" civilization to the "inferior races" of Africa. In the later years of the 1800s, however, the world's opinion on the Trans-Atlantic Slave Trade was changing. Many voices, among which the Quaker settlers in America, John and Charles Wesley (founders of the Methodist Church), the poet Samuel Coleridge, the Evangelical writer Hannah More, had openly questioned the humanity of the slave trade; and an abolitionist wave initiated by Denmark in 1804 started to sweep Europe and America. In 1848, France reluctantly abolished the official practice of slave trade. Among the people who had expressed disapproval of the slave trade, was Olaudah Equiano, a former slave. Equiano was also a former slave owner who had understood that slavery could only be stopped if there could be an incentive for not practicing it. So, he tried to convince slave owners that slave trade was depleting Africa of potential consumers of European goods, and he urged Europeans to turn instead to disseminating European civilization to Africa, as they exploited the many African raw materials from which slave trade had distracted them.[3] The functioning semantic pair was thus launched, commerce and civilization, which would henceforth be seized on as determining the scope of French — and European — new interventions in Africa. Taking Equiano's suggestions to globalize otherwise at heart, European countries raced for the riches of Africa. Ivory, gold, timber, cocoa, coffee, rubber, palm oil, nuts, and tropical fruits, and not slaves — even though some "lawbreakers" were still trading in slaves, for seventy years went by between the Danes' abolition of slavery in 1792 and the effective stop of slave importation to Europe[4] — became the new commodities that brought huge profits to European markets. By the late 1800s, Africa became so crowded with European fortune seekers that conflicts were inevitable.

In the absence of roads, rivers were the principal communication means, and Portugal, which had first claimed the Niger River and the Congo River, would not share navigation rights with other European countries. British trading companies were also scheming to have exclusive control of the whole Niger River. Among the British shrewdest traders was George Goldie, founder of the National African Company. Goldie was so profit-driven that he coerced local chiefs along the Niger to sign treatises that would "for ever" cede their territories to his company and to the descendants of his shareholders. Goldie's deceitful commercial methods were not that much out of the ordinary. They were common occurrences among traders and constituted the sources of many international frictions. To better regulate trade in Africa and to avoid conflicts among the international actors in the region, the European powers held a conference in Berlin between November 15, 1884, and February 26, 1885, under the chairmanship of German Chancellor, Otto Von Bismarck. Although the European powers publicized the conference as a meeting for discussing issues of humanity, peace, and the "civilizing" and "welfare" of the native populations of Africa, what actually dominated the talks was definition of the rules that would govern the Europeans' claims of territories in Africa. The Conference resolved the question of territorial conflicts among European countries by deciding that any European nation that formally gave other nations notice of its occupation of a territory would be recognized as the rightful owner of that territory; and so, the rules of the game settled, European powers rushed to slash as larger morsels as they could of the African pie.

However, still haunted by the specters of defeat, the French had yet to be convinced. Their 1870 humiliating loss to the Germans had dampened all their previous enthusiasm for overseas conquests. Furthermore, their Algerian colonies had not turned out to be what India had been to Great Britain. Algerians continued to oppose long-drawn-out resistances to the French occupation, and the North African colony had cost more headaches to France than it had brought in profits. French financiers were hesitant to spend money in more African adventures; they preferred less uncertain governments bonds, and French politicians preferred for their constituencies a good *pot-au-feu* to the bad bread that they ate during the 1870 German siege of Paris. On the other hand, the wounds of dishonor inflicted by the Germans were slow to heal, and many government officials believed that France could shine again if only it could secure for itself a large African empire. Five months after the Berlin Conference, a debate between proponents and opponents of colonial expansion was raging in the hall of the French *Assemblée Nationale*. The two most memorable protagonists of this debate were Jules Ferry and Georges Clémenceau. On July 28, 1885, five months after being driven out of office for overseeing the failed 1885 Chinese-French war in China, Jules Ferry was making a case for colonialism in the chamber of the National Assembly.

Ferry invoked three arguments in favor of France's colonial expansion. Economically, within the logic of its industrial aspirations, France needed to find new markets outside Europe and the United States for its export commodities, as Germany and America had become increasingly protectionist at the same time as they had been flooding France with new agricultural and industrials products. Economists like Leroy-Beaulieu, who tried to establish a nexus between Britain's wealth and its possession of an overseas empire, and who argued that the acquisition of a colonial empire would indubitably bring economic wealth to France, supported this argument.[5] The lack of knowledge on the interior of Africa often led to sizeable exaggeration about what the continent could offer Europe. During the French colonial campaign of the 1880s, for instance, some government officials elatedly estimated that Sudan had a consumer market strong of 88,000,000 people at the disposal of the French economy. In fact, they were only 10,000,000 people.[6] From a humanitarian perspective, Ferry argued that, as a member of the "higher race," France had a divine right and a duty to civilize the "inferior races," perfect them, and improve their backward morals as was successfully the case in Algeria under the French, and in India under the British. From a political and patriotic perspective, Ferry insisted that France needed to ensure its place in the world by performing acts of grandeur. For Ferry, amidst the European rush for territorial expansion, any politics of abstention on the part of France would amount to abdication. To ascertain its position on the international exchequer, France would have to start exporting its language, its customs, its flag, and its genius.[7]

In a reply to Ferry, Clémenceau charged that Ferry's dichotomy of superior race/inferior race was suspect and reminiscent of the German social engineers' discourse in the days preceding the Franco-Prussian war. The Germans, like Ferry was doing then, had argued for racial superiority. German scientists had asserted that because the French were an inferior race, France was doomed to lose the war. So, Clémenceau urged his fellowmen not to repeat this German axiom against African nations by trying to disguise violence under the cunning designation of civilization. For him, the excuse of right or duty to civilize was nothing but a right to brutality that scientifically advanced societies tend to claim presumptuously in order to take possession of less advanced nations and torture their citizens and exploit them for the benefit of so-called superior races. Clémenceau concluded that to make civilization a justification for colonization was to adjoin hypocrisy to violence.[8] In any case, the early 1890s witnessed the rise of a multitude of strong pro-colonialist pressure groups, such as, the *Comité de l'Afrique française*, the *Comité de l'Égypte*, the *Comité de l'Asie française*, or the *Comité de Madagascar*, all unified under the banner of the *Parti colonial*, which made the case for a revival of France's place in the world. Their argument was less to sell an African business venture to French investors than to sell an African empire to the state. By the end of 1890, a colonial consensus was already in place in France. It advocated, as H. L. Wesseling notes, less emphasis on treaties with local chiefs, and a more forceful military approach that would lead to the subjugation of West African empires, such as Dahomey and the empires ruled over by Ahmadu and Samory.[9] Against all apprehensions, the French colonization of Sub-Saharan Africa turned out to be more lucrative than even the pro-colonists had previously thought, especially in West Africa where, prior to the Berlin Conference, and in combination with the Trans-Atlantic Slave Trade, Europeans had been dealing in great resources of foodstuffs and profitable market products, such as, gold, ivory, timber, gum, and vegetable oils.[10]

When the dust of the European imperial dash to Africa settled, the continent was parceled into fifty territories, and most European countries had their African colonies. France, Germany, Great Britain, and Portugal were the countries that obtained the lion share. King Leopold of Belgium claimed the biggest territory known to belong to a single individual. He appropriated for himself the territory that constitutes today's Democratic Republic of Congo. France snatched a large territory in West Africa from Mauritania to Chad (French West Africa), and Gabon and Congo (French Equatorial Africa), as well as the Island of Madagascar. Germany took Namibia and Tanzania. Great Britain seized Egypt, Sudan, Uganda, Kenya, South Africa, Zambia, Zimbabwe, Botswana, Nigeria, and Ghana. Spain grabbed Equatorial Guinea. The European powers saw the territories that they claimed in Africa and elsewhere as extensions of their countries. They became empire-building nations. France's empire comprised the territories of present day Mauritania, Senegal, Mali, Burkina Faso, Benin, Guinea, Côte d'Ivoire, Niger, Togo, Gabon, Republic of the Congo, Central African Republic, Cameroon, Algeria, Tunisia, Morocco, the Islands of Mauritius, Reunion, Seychelles, Madagascar, Comoros, and Mayotte.

The French territories did not all have the same status. They were slave colonies, exploitation colonies, settlers' colonies, or protectorates; and France ruled them accordingly. Most French colonies in the Caribbean were slave colonies, whereas in Sub-Saharan Africa they were principally exploitation colonies. In exploitation colonies, France's goal was to run away with most of the resources the colonies could yield (coffee, cocoa, lumber, palm oil, rubber, tropical fruits and nuts, and various minerals) for the benefit of the metropolitan state. Also, Africans from exploitation colonies were not on the same footing as those living in settlers' colonies or protectorates. Settlers' colonies and protectorates had local rulers collaborating with a French appointed consul. The protectorate of Tunisia had a local sovereign, the Bey. In the Settlers' colony of Algeria, it was the Dey. Elsewhere, in the Americas, there had even been proposition of French citizenship for the people of the colonies at one time. For the people of the French colonies of Africa south of the Sahara, the question of equality or autonomy was hardly considered.

Indeed, the 1789 rebellion known as the French Revolution, and which was led by highly taxed peasants and bourgeois Republicans resentful of the rigid French monarchy, resulted in the fall of King Louis XVI, the replacement of the monarchy by a National Assembly (composed of the majority of French, rich merchants, and poor peasants), and the declaration of France as a Republic. The driving principle of the Revolution was the belief in the idea that all men are born free and equal in rights. This principle was drawn upon the French Enlightenment ideals as well as the English Bill of Rights of 1688 and the Virginia Bill of Rights of 1776. So, in the aftermath of the Revolution, the National Assembly adopted a document called The Declaration of the Rights of Man and of the Citizen, which was to be the blueprint of the new convention. Hardly had the Declaration been adopted that started a passionate debate about its implication for the people living in the old French colonies. Some proponents of equal rights argued that the philosophy of the Declaration should be extended to all the people living on French soil, including those living in the colonies. Consequently, in 1794, the elected National

Convention, which in 1792 had replaced the dissolved National Assembly, voted to abolish slavery in all French colonies. The French planters of Saint Domingue (today's Haiti), France's richest American colony, protested this decision. These planters were white and people of color slave owners for whom slaves constituted a much-needed cheap labor in the large coffee and sugar cane plantations of Saint Domingue. Around the time of the French Revolution, Saint Domingue had about 500,000 slaves, 30,000 free people of color, half of whom were Mulattoes, and about 20,000 whites planters, shopkeepers or paid workers (referred to as "*petits Blancs*").

These various populations with competing interests, who hardly got along, had anecdotal reactions to the Convention's 1794 decision to abolish slavery and extend French citizenship to people in the colonies. Many of the free people of color, who had, at one time, bought themselves from their former masters, were small plantation owners. They usually owned small numbers of slaves that they treated very cruelly, as they intended to draw the distinction and show that, as free men, they were closer to the whites than to their slaves. The Mulattoes, children of slave owners and slave women set free by their remorseful fathers, were resentful of blacks, whether free or slaves. The Mulattoes were usually overseers on large plantations when they were not planters themselves, and they would not miss an opportunity to take their frustration on the slaves since they had no authority over the free blacks. Among the whites, the paid workers, such as, merchants, shopkeepers, and teachers ("*petits Blancs*") hated the blacks — be they slaves or free — out of pure racism, and they resented both the black planters and the Mulattoes against whom they had to compete for social status. By all indications, the white planters, who relied heavily on slaves, would be opposed to setting them free. The Mulattoes, who were resentful of their black heritage, would welcome the possibility of being French citizens with much exultation. The poor whites' social position would not change. On the contrary, they would henceforth have, not just the free blacks, but also, the former slaves to compete against for social standing. As for the black planters, even though they would gain French citizenship, the end of slavery would also bring the ending of free labor and the vanishing of the class of blacks that have helped sustain any little sense of superiority they *had*.

The reality was even thornier. While the law that abolished slavery in the French colonies was passed in 1794, four years earlier, in 1790, amidst discussions about the status of the people in the colonies, the French National Assembly passed a piece of legislation that was particularly aimed at reassuring the opponents of abolition of slavery. That legislation stipulated that *only* owners of property would have the same rights as French citizens. The problem with that legislation was that, by trying to prevent slaves from becoming

French citizens, it also kept the *petits Blancs*, who were not landowners, from aspiring to French citizenship. Whites (planters and *petits Blancs*) created an alliance to fight this law that would give blacks French citizenship and refuse it to non–slave-owning whites. However, this alliance between white planters and poor whites to defeat a legislation that could enfranchise people of color was a fraught pact built on duplicity. The white planters were not really fighting so that the *petits Blancs* would become their equal. What the white planters really wanted was that which their people of color counterparts also wanted: a politically and economically autonomous Saint Domingue free from France's control. Neither the planters nor the free people of color had any desire to lose their slaves (free labor force) by pledging total allegiance to France. Planters (whites and free people of color) wanted Saint Domingue to remain an independent slave state, especially in light of the *Exclusif*, this French law that forced planters from the French colonies to sell their goods only to France and to buy their necessary supplies from France only. So, white planters united with free people of color to fight France's political and economic tyranny. The *petits Blancs*, who were not really affected by the *Exclusif*, wanted no part of this new alliance, especially as it included blacks, whom they hated viscerally.

Meanwhile, plantation slaves were also establishing alliances with runaway slaves (Maroons) who had retreated into the mountains. The Maroons, who had no intention of falling back into slavery, should the independent movement succeed, collaborated with black slaves to organize sporadic raids on plantations, ransacking and burning farms, and killing planters. As the raids on planters intensified, the planters' alliance for political independence became also a defense coalition against Maroon and slave rebellions. Once again, the *petits Blancs*, who were not plantation owners, saw no reason to join the alliance. The coalitions between free people of color, white planters, and *petits Blancs* were very versatile and volatile. They changed according to decisions taken in Paris. The only stable alliance was the pact between the Maroons and the slaves whose determination for freedom was inflexible. So the 1789 spirit of equality and citizenship for all people living in France and in the French overseas colonies never fully materialized. Blacks in the slave colony of Saint Domingue seized their independence by force, after very violent encounters with antagonistic interests both within and without the Island. On January 1, 1804, two years after the capture of their leader, Toussaint Louverture, and one year after his death in a French jail, the slaves declared Saint Domingue a free state and reclaimed the Island's former Creole name of Haiti, meaning land of mountains.

In the French exploitation colonies of Africa, France never attempted the Haitian experience. Instead, there, the policies of Assimilation and Association became the order of the day. Assimilation was a politics that sought to make the people of the French colonies in the likeness of French people in the motherland. The idea was that French civilization was the ideal civilization, and therefore French people had the divine duty of instilling French values in the Africans, thus considered uncivilized. This idea was proudly termed by the French as *mission civilisatrice* (civilizing mission), the true motivation of which, as has been discussed earlier, lies more in economics and self-image. However, Assimilation had its detractors. Many French did not like the idea that blacks should be placed on the same footing as whites. The celebrated French anthropologist, Gustave LeBon, for instance, was one of the passionate defenders of whites' superiority and an untiring opponent of Assimilation.[11] Also, in the colonies, many blacks resisted Assimilation because of its veiled notion of French superiority. Ultimately, Assimilation failed and was replaced by the less intrusive policy of Association. Faced with the Africans' refusal to assimilate, French administrators had no other choice but to come to terms with the fact that Africans felt a strong attachment to ways of living that they were not prepared to replace by anything foreign; ways of living that some scientists, such as the German ethnologist Leo Frobenius, have wished to theorize in not so pleasing terms as "the civilization of the person-plant."[12] So, Association was based on the recognition of an African civilization different from French civilization. From this perspective, the idea was to gently lead Africans toward an appreciation and a love of French culture and civilization without asking them to surrender their own cultures and civilizations. For that to happen, French administrators in the French colonies of Africa were asked to rule with much flexibility by relying on local chiefs as intermediaries between the people and them. These first French attempts at globalization were, like the ones that preceded them, devoid of any real reciprocity. The native populations of the colonies resisted them ferociously; and whatever justification France gave for its retreat from the colonies, it did not leave on its own good will. The cost in human and financial capital was too high for France to sustain, the determination of the colonized too strong to break. Imperialist France left because it was simply and purely beaten and forced to recognize the autonomy of its colonies.

However, the Hexagonal compulsion for takings was so imperative that France devised a number of "cooperation" schemes to remain the privileged speculator in the newly independent countries of Africa. French-speaking Africa's independences in the 1960s did not prevent France from seeking to exploit its former colonies. Responding to its protectionist itch, France tried numerous alternative schemes to keep the gaze of Africans turned toward France as the Promised Land, French language as the quintessential language, French culture as the exemplary culture, so that economic resources could continue to be transferred from Africa to France as natural and expected facts.

Previously, during the colonial system, protectionist France had mandated free entry of French goods in the French African colonies and imposed tariffs on colonial goods entering France.[13] This decision had the obvious consequence of impoverishing the colonies while enriching the metropolis. However, the 1930s recession made it crucial, for France's economic survival, to transform the African colonies into consumer markets. France thus eased tariffs on its colonies in order to allow them to sell more easily on French markets, earn money, buy French manufactured goods, and also pay interests on their debts. At the same time, in order to avoid competition from other powers, France imposed quotas on some foreign imports to France and to French colonies. France also forbade its colonies to export certain products to foreign markets, thus forcing those foreign countries to purchase only from France products that would otherwise be available in the colonies. In addition, France placed duties on some foreign imports competing with colonial goods entering France. These duties ranged from 11 percent on non-colonial bananas to 110 percent on cocoa, passing through 34 percent on peanuts and palm kernels and 91 percent on non-colonial coffee. Although many have argued that this pre-independence "preferential system" accorded to the colonies has greatly contributed to keeping French Africa afloat during the 1930s economic slump and is partly the source of what came to be known in the 1980s as the economic miracle of Côte d'Ivoire.[14] In fact, the market-driven economy that this colonial system fostered provided the colonies with some money, only to be returned tenfold to France. Furthermore, this market economy, which France managed to keep alive long after the African independences, was the source of many economic shocks, as it put French-speaking African nations at the mercy of international speculators.

In fact, the Hexagonal protectionist measures of colonial times continued through various appellations in post-independence Francophone Africa. Under the sly excuse of insuring the economic safety of the ex-colonies, the various preferential economic system put in place by France on its own, and later with the cooperation of the E.C. and the E.E.C., actually sought to maximize France's profits by curbing France's dwindling returns in the colonies. In 1959, the French commercial system made it possible for France's African colonies to consume 28.2 percent of French exports while contributing to 20 percent of French imports. These numbers dropped to 7.8 percent of French exports used by Francophone Africa against 5.9 percent of French imports coming from Africa. The various conventions (Lomé, Yaoundé, Lomé 2), which reinforced France's economic "cooperation" with its former colonies and later with Anglophone Africa and the ACP states, did little to create real conditions of development for non–European countries. In fact, France maneuvered to exclude "Asian ex-colonies from the ACP states on the ground that they would prove dangerous competitors in a range of industrial products," and the tiny country of Mauritius, a potential competitor in textiles was asked by the E.C. to voluntarily restrain from the ACP.[15] The E.C. states, and particularly France, its most aggressive member did nothing to foster manufactures in Africa. As far as the E.C. was concerned, Africa was to remain an eternal supplier of raw materials; and the late 1980s Washington Consensus, with its menu of one-sided de-politicization of the state that opposes social public sector investment in welfare, job creation, environmental protection, healthcare, education, and poverty reduction,[16] offered France the blessing of the Bretton Woods institutions to carry on a game that it had been perfecting for so long: that of draining off wealth from Africa under the semblance of reciprocal improvement.

From Colonization to Globalization

Globalization, this dogma implemented primarily under the impulsion of the financial institutions of Bretton Woods, presupposes an international violence. Globalization assumes, often on the ground of mere bureaucratic sixth sense and no scientifically dependable instance, that, in order to improve the welfare of human populations, the prescription is to oblige developing countries to fine-tune their economies according to the requirements of Euro-American multinational corporations by way of liberalizations of local markets. The result of this philosophical-economic exercise is that, as was the case in the days of the colonization of Africa, it effectively relocates crises of economic deterioration from North to South. The World Bank and the IMF's persistence that developing countries open their economies to Foreign Direct Investments has enabled the scheme of neocolonization of the countries that have resolved, half a century ago, to determine the course of their particular developments away from the imperial ambitions of Europe. In most cases, globalization has succeeded in reinstating European — and American — imperialism by allowing First World capitalists quasi-ownership of Third World countries through purchases of strategic government-owned enterprises, such as, power, water, and communication companies. As Petras and Veltmeyer note, the scheme works when "the imperial state bails out banks, investors and speculators and provides political pressure to open markets, sends military expeditions to eliminate alternatives."[17] In this grand design of recolonization disguised as globalization, resistance is ruthlessly squashed by a variety of coercive methods. For the Third World leaders who, against the First World's schema, try to pursue a populist agenda that advocates national control of their country's resources and benefits, and who, true to their people, refuse to fall prey to the trap of corruption and the promise of First World lifestyle, "[T]he EHM [Economic Hit Men] game plan includes a full menu of oppositions to ensure compliance, whether willing or not."[18]

Rich, indeed, is the list of options at the disposal of the EHM, which includes subversion of the political process, contact with and corruption of administration and business leaders, corruption of the military, of the media, of trade unions, and of academics, and the stirring of ethnic and religious divergences; a menu that seems to come directly from the handbook of the colonial era, and which begs to be verified against the inventory of treatments that countries like Congo, Côte d'Ivoire, and Haiti, to cite only these few, have endured for daring to stand against the tripartite collusion of the northern countries, the United Nations and the financial institutions, and their corrupt local political puppets. In Côte d'Ivoire, this threefold conspiracy functioned along the axis of an African IMF executive, Alassane Dramane Ouattara, who doubled as a shady native informant, during his years as prime minister of Côte d'Ivoire, his direct association with French multinationals, Bouygues and Bolloré, and his ties with the Chirac government in France. This web of international relationships is essential for understanding the current situation in Côte d'Ivoire, a situation that emerged as the result of Côte d'Ivoire's resistance to globalization *à la française.*

Côte d'Ivoire, 1970–1990: From Economic Prosperity to Scarcity

The 1970s were an age of prosperity in Côte d'Ivoire. The skyrocketing prices on international markets of cocoa and coffee, the country's main export commodities, had created an astonishing economic boom and established Côte d'Ivoire as the preeminent economic power in West Africa. Signs of development were visible in all sectors; and economic observers were not shy to compare the Ivorian economic sensation to the Japanese miracle. They were right to a certain extent: The Ivorian growth rate was only second to Japan's. However, this economic boom was heavily dependent on foreign capitals, as it was tied to international speculators' willingness to pay high prices for coffee and cocoa, which, unlike oil, for instance, were not products of crucial necessity. Attempts to diversify the economy and launch development programs led the country to borrow external capitals, which were not always judiciously managed. Furthermore, the falling prices of coffee and cocoa in the late 1970s and early 1980s amplified the country's external debt and led Houphouët to turn to the World Bank and the IMF for loans to stabilize his country's economy. The period spanning from the mid–1980s to early 1990s

was a time of mixed blessings for Côte d'Ivoire's economy. The exploitation
of newly discovered offshore oil reserves had helped alleviate some of the
country's hardships; however, the economic storm was not totally weathered.
Amidst rumors of government layouts, people took massively to the streets
to protest what they interpreted as the results of the grab for power of the
PDCI (party in power). To save his presidency, Houphouët bent to the conditions of the Bretton Woods institutions and invited the economist Alassane
Ouattara in April 1990 to chair the *Comité Interministériel de Coordination
du Programme de Stabilisation et de Relance Économique* (Interministerial Committee for Coordination of the Stabilization and Economic Recovery Program), a committee in charge of reflecting on ways to tackle the economic
crisis and find adequate solutions. Five months later, an ailing Houphouët
appointed Alassane Ouattara prime minister. What happened from April 1990
onward is a series of events that read like a novel.

Dominique Nouvian Folleroux: Femme Fatale

Ouattara's proximity to Houphouët had allowed him greater closeness
to Ms. Nouvian Folleroux, the woman that would become his wife and most
trusted associate in the most *rocambolesque* financial intrigues to define the
political future of Côte d'Ivoire. The circumstances in which Dominique
Nouvian was introduced to the epicenter of power in Abidjan are still not
very clear today. According to some reports, the late governor of BCEAO,
Abdoulaye Fadiga, Ouattara's former boss, presented her to Houphouët. Other
reports credit the late minister of construction, Bamba Vamoussa, of intro-
ducing her to the first president of Côte d'Ivoire. In any case, she had been
intimately close to both men, and her affairs with key figures of Houphouët's
powerful circle had unquestionably been opportune in occasioning her meeting with the Old Man of Abidjan. She became Houphouët's mistress and a
few months later, to the shock of the Ivorians, this angelic blond became the
exclusive administrator of Houphouët's huge estate and part of the country's
estate. Her heartbroken and powerless husband, a French expatriate, committed suicide — though many Ivorians, known for their fertile imagination,
would suggest that it was a case of euthanasia. Dominique Nouvian Folleroux' new title of executor of Houphouët's domain gave her tremendous name
recognition and financial power, even as her benefactor's popularity at home
was declining.
    In the early 1990s Houphouët was ailing and also assailed by a fierce polit-
ical opposition. For the first time, the "Old Man," as he was affectionately
called in Africa, released his grip on power. Under the pressure of the Bret-

ton Woods institutions and the French government, he legalized opposition parties and promised multiparty presidential and legislative elections in Côte d'Ivoire. The October 28 multi-candidate presidential election confirmed the strength of opposition forces, and especially the political weight of Houphouët's old political rival, Laurent Gbgagbo, leader of the socialist Ivorian Popular Front (FPI). According to international observers Gbagbo garnered more than 30 percent of the votes — though the official ballot count conceded him only 18.3 percent against 81.7 percent for the sitting president. On November 26, 1990, eighteen opposition parties competed against Houphouët's PDCI during the parliamentary elections. Houphouët's PDCI retained 163 of the 175 parliamentary seats. If anything, the contestation of the Old Man's hitherto absolute power ushered in a new era. Houphouët was a diminished man.

Nevertheless, Mrs. Dominique Nouvian Folleroux's business seemed to suffer no setback at all from Houphouët's trouble at home. On the contrary, her dealings were prospering. She made good use of Houphouët's one-of-a-kind address book and entered financial transactions with his exceptionally influential friends. Among other things, she sold some of Houphouët's real estates in France for the amount of 19 million Euros, a business deal that apprehensive Ivorian authorities had vouched to look into. She acquired Jacques Dessange's hair saloons in the United States. AICI (*Agence Internationale de la Commercialisation Immobilière*), the real estate office that she opened in Abidjan was attracting big clients. Her regulars were Martin Bouygues, the French king of concrete, owner at 42.9 percent of TF1 (the first French TV station drawing 31.6 percent of French TV audiences in 2006), owner of LCI, another French TV channel, special guest to Nicolas and Cécilia Sarkozy's wedding, and godfather of their son Louis Sarkozy; Vincent Bolloré (business partner of Bouygues) king of cigarette paper and media — it was Bolloré who paid the new French president a vacation trip to Malta on his luxurious boat as a congratulation present after the 2006 French presidential election; it was he again who lent his private Falcon 900 to Sarkozy and his then new girlfriend Carla Bruni for their December 25, 2007 vacation trip to Egypt; Dominique Strauss-Khan, former minister of finance of President Mitterrand and IMF president since 2007, Bongo, president of Gabon who, like Houphouët before him, has been so close to Dominique Nouvian Folleroux as to now entrust the administration of his real estate and part of his country's property to the Gabon branch of Mrs. Folleroux's AICI, run by her brother Philippe Nouvian.

Other patrons of Mrs. Dominique Nouvian Folleroux are Blaise Compaoré, president of Burkina Faso, and Kaddafi of Libya. Hers was a network of powerful financial friends; the same network that Ségolène Royal, the

Socialist candidate to the French presidential election accused on May 4, 2007, of trying to influence French elections by manipulating the news. Ségolène especially attacked the relations between Sarkozy, Bouygues, Vincent Lagardère (first world magazine publisher and owner of *Paris Match*, *Elle*, and Radio Europe 1). She charged them of working together to rig the electoral process.[19] Such is the association of powerful financial interests that Mrs. Dominique Nouvian Folleroux has been able to weave since she first entered Houphouët's bedroom in Abidjan. Dominique Nouvian Folleroux was the powerful woman that Alassane Ouattara declared to have fallen in love with, as he responded to President Houphouët's IMF-coerced call for help.

"Ouattara, Ouattara! He's Our Man. He Can't Do It, Nobody Can!"

"Ouattara, Ouattara! He's Our Man. He Can't Do It, Nobody Can!" Such seemed to be the mindset of the Bretton Woods institutions and big international corporations with financial stakes in Côte d'Ivoire since about the death of Félix Houphouët Boigny, in December 1993. An excellent student of the IMF, where he first worked from 1968 to 1973 before assuming various positions at the BCEAO, Ouattara was very receptive to the International Monetary Fund's prescription of Structural Adjustment Programs in Africa despite the burden that these programs put on local populations. As prime minister of Côte d'Ivoire, his solutions for redressing the country's economy did more harm than good: He cut subsidies to farmers, as recommended by the WTO, while the European Union and the United States were, at the same time, heavily backing their own farmers financially; he dismissed more than 10,000 employees from the state payroll. Those who were lucky to keep their jobs saw their salaries reduced by 40 percent or were forced to accept an early retirement package. He reduced access to early education by freezing the recruitment of new teachers. He closed students' subsidized restaurants. He eliminated transportation and basic healthcare services for students. He imposed fees on the masses for basic healthcare services. He initiated the devaluation of the CFA at the rate of 100 CFA francs for 1 French franc. He instituted the highly controversial resident cards for foreigners, which was the source of much harassment toward foreign nationals coming from neighboring African countries, and he aggressively pursued Mauritanian and Lebanese merchants for so-called back taxes in the upward of millions of CFA francs. These measures, as it was to be expected, frustrated the masses even further, and workers and students' demonstrations intensified; which, under his orders, were repressed in blood. Many students were killed

Abidjan, the economic capital of Côte d'Ivoire, was the playground of predatory French multinationals during Alassane Ouattara's tenure as prime minister (photograph by Julia Dresen-Coulibaly).

and student, union, and opposition leaders, among whom the current president, Laurent Gbagbo and the leader of higher education teachers' union, Marcel Etté, were jailed and tortured amidst international outcries and unsuccessful calls for an independent investigation. Undeniably, Ouattara was a good student of the IMF. In Côte d'Ivoire, Ouattara was the praiseworthy son of a powerful institution that had reared him to serve the father unreservedly. The question was whether he was really a son of Côte d'Ivoire, concerned with the interests of his fellow citizens.

As far as the World Bank and the IMF were concerned, this question had no bearing so long as the Washington Consensus had a powerful spokesperson in the country that would guarantee the interests of its shareholders. So, under further pressure, the ailing president Houphouët had Ouattara cumulate the portfolios of prime minister, minister of finance, and interim president. During Houphouët's long ailment and his medical treatment in Europe in 1993, Ouattara ordered that all public receipts (collection of taxes, debts, and returns from the customs, the ports, and even the treasury) be directly deposited in a special account at the office of the prime minister rather than at the treasury, as it was customarily the case. This atypical management style, to say the least, quickly mixed individual assets with state property, and millions of dollars from the public treasury remained unaccounted for, while Ouattara, taking as much as two flights a week to Europe, officially to visit his sick boss — but unofficially on capital flight missions — was tucking millions of dollars away in personal foreign bank accounts, making him one of the richest men on earth. Ouattara's mysterious fortune raised some eyebrows, even among those who supported his bid for presidency. Ahmadou Kourouma, the late Ivorian writer, once suggested that the origin of Ouattara's huge fortune ought to be investigated, because such wealth could not originate exclusively from his regular salary as Deputy Director of the International Monetary Fund. Kourouma hinted that the source of Ouattara's wealth might not be honest at all. *"Il a été Premier ministre quand Houphouët était malade. Peut-être que cela donne un début d'explication. L'histoire, un jour, nous le dira."*[20] (He was prime minister when Houphouët was ill. Perhaps, this is a beginning of explanation. History will tell us someday.) Likewise, Emile Constant Bombet, who was Ouattara's minister of interior in the 1990s, speaking in

1999 as Bédie's minister of interior, had promised to look into the source of Ouattara's fortune just a few days before his boss was toppled by a coup d'état: *"Je suis surpris de la partialité des journalistes ... personne ne s'est posé de questions sur l'origine de la fortune de monsieur Ouattara. Croyez-moi, nous en parlerons le moment venu...."*[21] (I am dumbfounded by the partiality of the journalists ... nobody has questioned the origin of Mister Ouattara's wealth. Believe me; we will look into that at the proper time.) There exists a consensus that during Ouattara's tenure as prime minister and interim president of Côte d'Ivoire — a period during which he took an extraordinary number of flights to Europe during Houphouët's illness — he has accumulated an astonishingly immense fortune. During his term as prime minister, Ouattara became one of the biggest actors of capital flight from Côte d'Ivoire toward European banks, thus depleting Africa of much needed resources, as he raided the country's coffers.

Alassane Dramane Ouattara, former IMF employee and first prime Minister of Houphouët Boigny, had been very receptive to the IMF's recipe of structural adjustment and unusually generous to predatory French multinationals (photograph by Alain Tieffi for FratMat).

Capital flight, the bulk of the private assets that are legally or illegally held in foreign countries outside Africa, is one of the continent's biggest impoverishers. Capital flight, reported to amount to about U.S.$ 22 billions, is as much as half of the aid that Africa needs for its development programs. Were this money brought back to Africa, it would constitute 64 percent of Africa's private capital stock.[22] As one of Africa's biggest capital jetsetters, Ouattara is, without doubt, and in proportion to the short time he spent as prime minister of Côte d'Ivoire (three years and one month), among the leaders who have economically siphoned the continent the most. As the prime minister was busy outsourcing his public function to the businessman in him, thus mixing state capitals with private capitals, Dominique Folleroux — whom Alassane Ouattara had by then married during a 1991 ceremony officiated by the former mayor of Neuilly, currently president of the French Republic, Nicolas Sarkozy — was now, against all ethical propriety, lobbying for Bouygues and Bolloré to acquire state-owned EECI (*Énergie Électrique de Côte d'Ivoire*) and SODECI (*Société de Distribution d'Eau de Côte d'Ivoire*), respectively power and water companies. It did not take long for her clients to obtain satisfaction. These strategic Ivorian state companies and others were sold off to Mrs. Dominique Nouvian Folleroux Ouattara's clients and friends, usually under their market values, sometimes for just one symbolic franc, all against the objection of opposition leaders and even leaders of his own party (the PDCI), such as Henri Konan Bédié, who was at the time president of the National Assembly. As a result, 27 percent of the assets of Ivorian enterprises are French-owned; 240 subsidiaries and more than 600 companies belong to French businessmen; which represented 68 percent of direct foreign investments in Côte d'Ivoire. Alassane and Dominique Ouattara's shady deals with their cronies, which have mortgaged the economic and political future of Côte d'Ivoire, have been widely reported.

> Mr. Michel Camdessus, a Frenchman who was the president of the IMF during the last term, when Alassane Ouattara was vice-president of the IMF, is currently serving as adviser to the French president Jacques Chirac. Of the members of the political parties and groups in Côte d'Ivoire, Alassane Ouattara, an unabashed advocate of IMF policies and an ideologue of the theology of neo-liberalism, and his current wife, a French businesswoman solidly connected with business lobbies, offer the best guarantee to satisfy the conditions for security and profit for the French government, corporations, settlers, and small-enterprise owners who can have a lifestyle of comfort they cannot afford or even imagine to have in France.[23]

This lack of probity on the part of Africa's most influential economists and leaders ought to be examined in relation to the dire future that their selfish proclivities set up for the continent. Between 1985 and 1998, the net outflows from Africa to developed countries have risen from of U.S.$ 3.6 billion to the alarming amount of U.S.$ 12.5 billion.[24] Capital flight by native pillagers has contributed enormously to these outflows. This, of course, has profound depressing incidences on progress. As a result, Africa continues to service huge debts and remains unable to invest in public and private sectors; which in turn erodes, not just poverty reduction projects, but also, serious foreign investors' confidence in the continent; and the cycle of poverty linked to debt servicing and fiscal deficit goes on until the corrupt agents' facility to plunder is short-circuited. It is Henri Konan Bédié, the institutional heir to the presidency, who put an end to Ouattara's capital flight activities.

Henri Konan Bédié: Not Exactly the Man Paris Had Dreamed Of

On December 7, 1993, Houphouët, who for three years had been sidelined by his illness from participating actively in Ivorian politics, passed away in his native village of Yamoussoukro. The Ivorian constitution had a provision for replacing a deceased head of state. Article 11 of the constitution stipulated that in such a vacancy of power, the president of the National Assembly was to assume the duties of head of state until the outcome of new elections. Bédié was therefore the constitutional heir to Houphouët. However, bypassing the legal process, Ouattara proclaimed himself legitimate successor to the presidency. This obvious constitutional hold up provoked uproar at the National Assembly, and during an unscheduled appearance on RTI, the national TV, Bédié announced his intent to carry out his constitutional duty by finishing Houphouët's remaining two years.

In the past, during his years as president of the National Assembly, Bédié had been openly critical of Ouattara's complacent economic liberalism that widely opened the doors to foreign buyouts of strategic companies with very little regard for the country's security. At the time when French politicians, led by then Minister of finance Nicolas Sarkozy, were hammering at employees gatherings and at the French national Assembly that EDF (French state-owned power company) and GDF (French state-owned gas company) were never going to be privatized because of their strategic importance to the French economy, Ouattara, the prime minister of Côte d'Ivoire, was selling his country's power and water companies to the closest friends of the French government.[25] What made Sarkozy's position so tenable in France and so untenable in Côte d'Ivoire? Could it be for the simple reason that one was dealing in one case with a country located in Europe, and in another case of a country located in Africa? It is this lack of moral reciprocity that the movement of *patriotes* in Côte d'Ivoire has taken to task. In so doing, their demonstration was also aimed at denouncing the collaborators from within who have betrayed their people for the promise of *economic lactification*. For, the waves of coups d'état and political instabilities that have succeeded one another in Côte d'Ivoire since 1999 are also strangely laden with odors of organic betrayals. Each time Côte d'Ivoire was affected by shockwaves of military blows, Ouattara was the insider that, for the promise of a Firstworldist enjoyment, betrayed the loyalty of a country he claimed to love. The precedents to this proclivity are bloodcurdling. One shall recall how in the Leopoldian system of the Congo Free State, King Leopold's auxiliaries were rewarded with free looting and raping in Congolese villages for increasing the king's rubber output (see chapter 9 in this book). The Consequences, as in the days of Ouattara's administration, proved disastrous for women and children.

Bédié, like Ouattara, believed in economic liberalism. Only insofar as one can speak in relative terms, Bédié's liberalism, however, was one that was committed to ensuring that his country would not lose total sovereignty to wealthy investors from Europe or from anywhere else for that matter; and he was working at it by making a number of reforms. Some of the measures that Bédié took in that direction were to thoroughly identify the populations living on the Ivorian soil through a systematic census program, clean up the prevalent anarchical land exploitation, and regulate landownership. Indeed, in the mid to the late 1990s, Côte d'Ivoire was the second immigration destination in Sub-Saharan Africa, right behind South Africa, with an unusually high immigrant population rate of 27 percent for 13 million Ivorians. The largest foreign communities were from Mali (2 millions), Burkina Faso (2 millions), Ghana (1.5 millions), Nigeria (500,000), and in smaller numbers from Benin and Togo. Though an agreement among the countries of ECOWAS (Economic Community of West African States) allowed free circulation and settlement of populations from any member state, the migration to Côte d'Ivoire was almost unidirectional. The important immigrant populations from neighboring Mali and Burkina Faso, whose main purpose for coming to Côte d'Ivoire was to work the fertile land of the country or to cut and burn trees for the very lucrative charcoal business toward drier countries (Mali or Burkina Faso) had clashed several times with local populations over issues of landownership, forest fires, and severe national reserve deforestation. In 1999, a land dispute between settlers from Burkina Faso and locals from the region of Tabou (South-West of Côte d'Ivoire) had caused about 12,000 Burkinabé to flee their fields. This event, which took place a year after the National Assembly adopted a law that would prevent the sale of land to foreigners, invited even harsher criticisms towards Bédié's reform. Bédié's land reform did not sit well with his Malians and Burkinabé counterparts. The governments of Mali and Burkina Faso relied heavily for their national incomes on the money that their expatriates sent from Côte d'Ivoire. They perceived in Bédie's reform a pretext to dispossess their compatriots of lands they had been exploiting for years, and they also found objectionable the reform's obvious consequence of depleting their countries of much-needed revenues. In their grievance, the Malians and Burkinabé could find stronger allies in the French. "The old class of French landlords who acquired large portions of land in the southern part of the country often in obscure contexts, with no proper or convincing legal papers stipulating, for instance, the duration of the lease ... oppose any form of land reform, as it could jeopardize transfer of these lands to their descendants."[26]

These French landlords and businessmen had seen their privileges increased and consolidated with Ouattara. Under the administration of Houphouët's prime minister, the nature of the state had shifted from that of a governmental institution to that of a non-governmental organization (NGO) — to use this term by James Ferguson[27] — whereby the prime minister had lost interest in state affairs and had, instead, become a businessman, increasingly drawn to establishing personal business deals and building private wealth to the detriment of public welfare. In the context of Bédie's reform, the question then was whether, after having had a taste of the state of Côte d'Ivoire as a non-governmental institution, with all the advantages that it entailed, France and the neighboring countries of Côte d'Ivoire, notably, Burkina Faso and Mali, were still disposed to see the administration of Côte d'Ivoire return to being a governmental institution. This was the challenge that confronted the Bédié government in the mid– to late 1990s.

Against this sociological background, it becomes clear that Bédie's demise — for he was to fall soon — was not the result of mismanagement or hostility to openness. In fact, Bédié was as open to FDIs as Ouattara had been; he was just a little more conscious of the governmental role of the state. The fact that, for the most part, Africa's openness to international trade and finance has left it at the mercy of insatiable First World capitalists and corrupt Third World collaborators should be less imputable to globalization itself than to the probity of the protagonists in the globalizing enterprise. Globalization has succeeded in places where the actors involved have shown a minimum of moral decency. Available data for Africa in the 1990s shows that countries in North Africa, and South Africa and Côte d'Ivoire had managed a low level of poverty with high level of openness. Côte d'Ivoire's numbers are 20 percent of poverty incidence for 40 percent of openness. Incidentally the data is not distributed on specific years of the 1990s, but it is easy to surmise that the incidence of lower poverty occurred during the Bédié years. Even Bédie's detractors acknowledged that between 1995 and 1999, Côte d'Ivoire had known economic growth and increase in individual wealth — though some cynics are quick to attribute this expansion to capital inflow from war-torn Liberia and Sierra Leone. Furthermore, a Trade Policy Review of Côte d'Ivoire's trade policies conducted by the World Trade Organization (WTO) on July 4 and 5, 1995, concluded with high praise for Bédie's government open trade policies and expressed optimism for Côte d'Ivoire's future.[28]

Bédie's demise is just one more evidence that Foreign Direct Investments or private capital flows are not that private after all; Foreign Direct Investments often unleash state intervention, with all its military shock and awe. Whenever a powerful state intervenes to invade a weak state, one can be sure that some private investors from the powerful state, unhappy about their returns in the weak state, have directly or indirectly triggered the military intervention. History is littered with examples where private investors have sent

Henri Konan Bédié, former president of Côte d'Ivoire (1993–1999), angered Paris with his land reform and his more cautious liberalization. He was deposed in December 1999 by General Robert Guéï (photograph by Alain Tieffi for FratMat).

their countries to war to protect or simply to increase their dividends. Bédie's lukewarm support for French interests was not what France had hoped for. Bédié was a man of France's, but not their number one man. His zeal for reforms could hurt French interests in Côte d'Ivoire. Ouattara had been more generous to French business with his unchecked liberalization and his *gré à gré* surrender of public corporations to French investors and to his French partners. With Ouattara in power, France was sure to regain its slippery grip on Côte d'Ivoire by continuing to buy under their market values state-owned enterprises and get government contracts by bypassing any calls for bids that would put them in competition with investors from the United States, Canada, Japan, South African, China, among others. For the sake of French interests, Bédié had to be deposed.

Meanwhile, Ouattara, who had returned to the IMF in 1993 upon the Ivorian Supreme Court's confirmation of Bédié as legitimate head of state, had been appointed by Michel Camdessus to serve as his deputy chairman of the institution one year later. Though at the IMF, Ouattara had not given up his presidential ambitions; neither was he willing to wait for regular elections to have his chance. The massive foreign electorate constituted by undocu-

mented immigrants from Mali and Burkina Faso, many who had voted before
in the one-party system farcical elections that had confirmed and reconfirmed
Houphouët by acclamation, and on which Ouattara, too, was relying to win
the 1995 presidential race, had been compromised by Bédie's identification
program. Bédie's identification program required that only established Ivorians should vote in presidential elections, though established foreign residents
were still allowed to vote in legislative and municipal elections. Bédie's land
reform as well as his census and civic formation projects fell under the umbrella
of what he had termed *Ivoirité*. This notion, whose origin had misleadingly
been attributed to Bédié, and which had even more deceitfully been translated as Ivorianness, rather than simply Ivority — as one had spoken of Africanity, Americanity, and Francity elsewhere — was said to have first appeared in
1945 in Dakar at a black students' conference. Later, and Ivorian writer and
poet, Niangoran Porquet, used it in an article entitled "*Ivoirité et authentic-
ité*," in 1974, and an Ivorian scholar, Kanvaly Fadiga, used it in 1997 to mean
the national consciousness, the common will of brotherly people who have
chosen to live together on the Ivorian soil, and together share the same sufferings, the same joys, and the same hopes.

Why Francité but Not of Ivoirité?

Ivoirité, as Bédié had recuperated it, was first intended to represent, for
the more than sixty ethnic communities of Côte d'Ivoire, a signifier of
identification, the social glue that would bond them together by instilling in
them a stronger patriotic fiber, and consequently a stronger attachment to the
state and its institutions as embodying the sum total of all individual nationalistic expressions. This was an essential societal project given the lack of
enthusiasm that the Ivorian populations had hitherto expressed for the state
and state institutions. In most foreigners' eyes Côte d'Ivoire stood as a state-
ECOWAS, a sort of Deadwood, but a rich one nonetheless, where any opportunistic member of the 15 ECOWAS states, and even beyond, would come to
seek fortune by all means necessary, with no sincere attachment to the land,
but a lucrative one. The people of Côte d'Ivoire had lost faith in their successive governments which they hardly saw as really concerned with safeguard-
ing the welfare of the nationals. Ivorians accused their successive governments
of rather bending over backward to live up to an image of sanctuary country
by satisfying the caprices of ECOWAS. This situation was exacerbated by
Houphouët's choice, throughout his presidency, of foreign nationals as cabinet members. For instance, Raphaël Saller (France) had been minister of
finance and development; Mohamed Diawara (Mali) had been minister of

development; Abdoulaye Sawadogo (Burkina Faso) had served as minister of agriculture; Hamadou Thiam (Senegal) had served as minister of information. To better understand this level of governmental openness and the resulting mass frustration that ensued, Americans would only have to imagine Canadian, Mexican, Columbian or Antiguan nationals (who have never been naturalized or who do not even intend to apply for American citizenship) occupy posts in the United Sates government, as treasury secretary, HUD secretary, or secretary of health. In the 1980s-1990s a phrase that illustrated the Ivorian distrust in their government and their detachment from public property was the infamous "*Tant pis! Ça appartient à l'État*" (who cares? It belongs to the state), a phrase that would justify any act of vandalism or spoliation of state property.

Bédie's *Ivoirité* was determined to rectify this mass cynicism. It intended to create the conditions for an allegiance that would no longer be based on ethnic background — as had until then been the case in the context of the aloof and impersonal state — but rather an allegiance that would be grounded in identification with the nation-state created on Independence Day, August 7, 1960. This was nothing novel. In the sphere of cultural contestations, coinages in -ité suggesting allegiance to geographical, national, racial or linguistic origins have abounded. Senghor, the only black consecrated by France — this France so reactive to *Ivoirité*— in its so elitist French Academy for being so French, thus "so righteous," said in his December 11, 1974 course at the Sorbonne that it was important to struggle, to suffer, and to die, "*plus volontiers pour une-ité ou une-itude que pour un-isme*" (more readily for an-ity or an-itude than for an-ism)? Curiously, however, it seems that African heads of state have been more willing to struggle, suffer, and die for France's specificity than their own. An illustrative example is Francophone African presidents' unashamed gathering around the theme of *Francophonie*, which, as we learn again from Senghor, is no more no less than a synonym of *Francité*. In May 1968, during a conference at the University of Beirut, while defending the so-called peaceful and non-imperialistic nature of *Francophonie* or *Francité*, Senghor insisted that *Francophonie* was not a war machine constructed by European imperialism, but a mode of thinking a certain way, a mode of approaching issues and seeking solutions, a spirit of French civilization or *Francité*.

Francophonie, Senghor declared, is *Francité*; and *Francité*, he swore had not the slightest imperialistic bent in it, but was merely the expression of French civilization and culture devoid of any political agenda; and while most African leaders accepted the word of Senghor, this griot of things French, that *Francité* would not harm a fly, yet, the same leaders were quick to condemn *Ivoirité* as a genocidal war machine. Today, as in 1968, the most passionate defender of *Francité* is an African, an ex-Senegalese president, Abdou Diouf. He is the current secretary general of *Francophonie*. He goes around world capitals selling French culture and civilization and promoting the expansion of French business and policy; and wherever he convenes his annual gathering, a plethora of African leaders follow him — among whom Bongo of Gabon, Wade of Senegal, Toumani of Mali, and Compaoré of Burkina Faso have the privileged front row seats. Lately, however, the Proselytizer-in-Chief of French language, wine, and *fromage*, the new griot of French culture and rectitude, Abdou Diouf, got a blunt reminder that, despite his professed worship of things French, he was specifically an African, and African he would remain. On May 13, 2006, as he was responding to the Canadian government's invitation to speak in Winnipeg on matters relating to the pseudo-apolitical *Francophonie*, Abdou Diouf, this easily recognizable towering political figure who travels with a diplomatic passport and a strong following, was stopped and body searched at Toronto Airport like a vulgar suspect. What? Had Diouf really believed that chanting the beauty of French culture around the world suddenly shook his black soul into a dew of milk and conferred him special regards in the eyes of the white world? Perhaps so, for the diplomatic reactions that followed this humiliation of an African noted former head of state proved beyond all doubts that *Francité*, or *Francophonie* as it is often referred to, was more political than its supporters knew or would admit to know.

President Diouf's humiliation at Toronto Airport was only symptomatic of the duplicitous nature of the North/South encounter, a reality to which Africans have never been able to respond in a coordinated way because of the North's successful politics of *Divide and Rule*, and most importantly, because of most African leaders' big complex of inferiority. While Senegalese, the most fervent believers of *Francité* in Africa, were protesting their ex-president's treatment at Toronto Airport, many Ivorians were chuckling at what they perceived as a fair shock therapy to all the French-African puppets who, like the Senegalese sharpshooters of World War II, were busy fighting France's war while the French populations were hiding in their basements,[29] or the modern native Africans Economic Hit Men who were starving their peoples by selling off their countries' resources to international multinational corporations in order to enjoy a little bit of white dreams. Ivorians had trouble understanding why, at the same time as Paris, with the support of some African leaders, was prosecuting Abidjan's successive governments in the media for a so-called maintenance of *Ivoirité*; the same African leaders were touring the world to promote *Francité*. As if *Francité* were the natural expression of their own salvation, Francophone African leaders like Bongo of Gabon, Abdoulaye Wade of Senegal, Compaoré of Burkina Faso, and Toumani of Mali, had been more vociferous about French nationalistic interests than they had been supportive of their own national interests. So, Toronto Airport reconfirmed, against the Senghorian denial, that neologisms of cultural renaissance have always had ideological/political dimensions; Toronto Airport only re-confirmed it, for many had known this fact long before Diouf's discomfiture.

At least, President Bédié was aware of the cultural-ideological nature of the concept. Having sensed France's undeclared support for Ouattara just before the 1995 presidential election, Bédié activated against the latter the ideological political dimension of *Ivoirité*. A modification of the electoral code of Côte d'Ivoire, adopted on November 23, 1994, stipulated that only Ivorians whose parents were both Ivorian-born could run for the presidency. Bédié took this new measure not out of the blue, but precisely because he knew Ouattara. They were from the same generation. They knew where each other came from. They had followed each other's formation and evolution. They had served for the same international financial institutions, and they knew how and why each one of them was appointed at the various posts they held. Bédié knew Ouattara as much as Ouattara knew him. Bédié knew — and Ouattara had admitted this in a signed correspondence to the Supreme Court of Côte d'Ivoire — that after his high school studies in Bobo Dioulasso (Burkina Faso) and Ouagadougou (Burkina Faso), Ouattara had benefited from an American scholarship to study in the United States of America as a student from Upper Volta (now Burkina Faso). Bédié knew that after his studies in the U.S., Ouattara first entered the IMF in 1968 under Upper Volta quotas. Bédié knew that Ouattara had obtained his first job at the BECEAO as an Upper Volta representative, and later served as vice-governor of the same institution between 1982 and 1984 as a functionary of Upper Volta (Burkina Faso). Apparently, Bédié was not the only one in the secret; for on August 8, 1984, on page 21 of an article entitled "Monsieur FMI," Béchir Ben Yamhed, the editorial manager of *Jeune Afrique*, reported that, starting November 1, 1984, the Africa Department of the IMF was going to have a new director; and that Dr. Ouattara, from Upper Volta, would be serving in replacement of Zambian Justin B. Zulu. The *Jeune Afrique* article even specified that Ouattara was born in Côte d'Ivoire of immigrant parents from neighboring Upper Volta.[31] Alassane Ouattara's Voltaic nationality was no secret to anyone, especially as he exhibited it whenever it served his purpose.

Having evolved in the same professional space as Ouattara, the sphere of international financial institutions, Bédié was well positioned to know, as *Jeune Afrique* had reported, the nationality of Ouattara. He was an Upper Volta citizen, who took advantage of an American scholarship as an Upper Volta student. He was first recruited at the IMF under the quota reserved for Upper Volta citizens, and later, he served as vice-governor of the BCEAO as a representative of Upper Volta, with an Upper Volta diplomatic passport. In

1985, After his military coup in Upper Volta, Thomas Sankara, the new strongman of Burkina Faso — a country that, unlike Houphouët's Côte d'Ivoire, was not in the business of appointing foreign citizens as cabinet ministers — offered Ouattara to enter his government as minister of economy and finances, a post that Ouattara, utterly resentful of Sankara's revolution, disdainfully rejected, preferring to remain at his more prominent and lucrative international position at the BCEAO. Sankara then asked him to resign as the Upper Volta representative. It is at that time that Houphouët, who had a profound antipathy for military regimes, especially the ones operating too close to his borders, intervened, and in a taunting gesture toward Sankara's junta, offered Ouattara an Ivorian diplomatic passport that would keep him at his post. As wrote Bédié, "*Le président Houphouët lui avait accordé un passeport diplomatique quand il avait des difficultés avec les autorités du Burkina Faso. Il servait alors à la Banque centrale, commune aux sept États d'Afrique de l'Ouest. Un passeport diplomatique, vous savez, n'est pas une pièce d'état civil.*"[32] (President Houphouët gave him a diplomatic passport when he was in trouble with the authorities of Burkina Faso. He then served at the Central Bank, common to the seven states of West Africa. A diplomatic passport is hardly proof of civil status, you know.)

In 1988, upon the death of Abdoulaye Fadiga, then BCEAO director, Houphouët twisted the arms of the member heads of state and imposed Ouattara as the new governor of the institution. Bédié knew, as another journalist of *Jeune Afrique* had also reported, that from the time he finished his studies, thanks to an American scholarship awarded to him as a Voltaic student, and for the many years to come, Ouattara served in many capacities, in several places (Washington, Paris, Dakar), at several financial institutions (BCEAO, WAMU [West African Monetary Union], ADB [African Development Bank], UNCTAD [United Nations Conference on Trade and Development]) and took part in many general assemblies as a Voltaic citizen, equipped with a Voltaic diplomatic passport.[33] So, Bédié knew that Ouattara had claimed Voltaic status each time he needed a scholarship or a job, simply because he was a Voltaic, like his father. "*[Alassane Dramane Ouattara] était burkinabé par son père et il possédait toujours la nationalité du Burkina Faso, il n'avait donc pas à se mêler de nos affaires de succession.*"[34] ([Alassane Dramane Ouattara] was a Burkinabé by his father. He had no right to involve himself into our debate of succession.) Bédié knew that by modifying the electoral code to request that both parents of any presidential candidate be Ivorian-born he was arresting Ouattara's presidential ambition; which he did.

Bédié was a cunningly shrewd politician for changing the electoral rules in the middle of the political process. Ouattara was right to have protested Bédié's unfair electoral practices. However, he challenged them on the wrong ground. It would have been more honorable of Ouattara to admit that, indeed, he had claimed Voltaic nationality to obtain a scholarship from the U.S. and later to take advantage of an IMF quota system that favored Voltaic nationals; but that he had changed his nationality since then; and he could have provided documentation to that effect. He could also have maintained that, though his parents were Voltaic, *he* was born on Ivorian soil; and he could have challenged the Ivorian electoral rule on the ground of his birthplace. Instead, he told two momentous untruths that were totally undeserving of any prospective president. First, he denied, in the face of accumulating evidence that he had ever been a Voltaic national; he maintained that as far as he could remember, he had always had the Ivorian nationality. Secondly he denied that his parents were Voltaic, while his father had been a well-known village chief in Upper Volta. These two fabrications alone were good enough to disqualify any presidential candidate. As Bédie's operatives started to produce proofs of Ouattara's deceptions, Ouattara left Abidjan for Paris under the pretext that his life was in danger. Bédie's Justice Department launched against him an international warrant for forgery. Just immediately, there started a vast media campaign that sought to legitimate any unconstitutional blow against the Bédie regime; a media campaign that resuscitated some of Bédie's formerly ignored shortcomings or simply invented him new ones.

How Does One Rationalize a Coup d'État? By Conducting It the Name of Globalization

In Côte d'Ivoire, the first coup d'état started with demonizing the Bédie regime on two levels. Socially and politically Bédie was to be presented as an insufficient leader who could not be the unifier that his predecessor, Houphouët, was. Economically, he was to be proven a reckless manager and an embezzler of public funds whose misconduct was hurting the masses. So, Bédie's notion of *Ivoirité* served to demonize him as a divider and a xenophobic. *Ivoirité*, as Bédie had explained, was a formulae meant to synthesize the aspirations of the multiple ethnic groups living within the borders of Côte d'Ivoire. As such, the concept was to encompass not only the autochthonous people of Côte d'Ivoire, but also, the people from all over the world who lived and worked in the country, insofar as they, too, shared and respected the values of the nationals. For Bédie, *Ivoirité* "...*la synthèse culturelle entre les ethnies habitant la Côte d'Ivoire ... concerne en premier les peuples enracinés en Côte d'Ivoire mais aussi ceux qui y vivent et y travaillent en partageant nos valeurs.*"[35] (...the cultural synthesis of the ethnic groups living in Côte d'Ivoire ... is primarily about the peoples rooted in Côte d'Ivoire but also those who live in the country and share our values.) Nothing in these words could hint to some official anti-immigrant or xenophobic stance, despite the fact that — and it has historically tended to be the case more in France than in Côte d'Ivoire — some frustrated fringes of the populations usually displace the inadequacies of their societies on the presence of foreigners.

Nevertheless, a powerful media campaign led by Ouattara's operatives successfully disseminated the idea that Bédie's *Ivoirité* was a recipe to repatriate immigrants from neighboring Mali and Burkina Faso; and an apparently "credible" French press went so far as to link minor occasional conflicts opposing locals to immigrants as direct consequences of *Ivoirité*, thus further exacerbating limited clashes by politicizing them. It did not take long for a country with a 27 percent immigrant population to be indexed as xenophobic. However, the French Press' real motive for demonizing Bédie's regime was elsewhere: Alassane Ouattara, France's ideal candidate, could not run for the Ivorian presidency on account of his doubtful nationality.

Bédié is no saint, one must admit. He is only a politician, and every act he posited was politically calculated. *Ivoirité* in its political reach could serve, not only to eliminate Ouattara's chances at the presidency, but also, to contain the massive electorate from Burkina Faso and Mali on which Ouattara was counting to this effect, and which, fitted with Ivorian national ID cards since the 1970s, had hitherto voted in every election. This electorate was geographically from countries north of Côte d'Ivoire, and religiously more than 90 percent Muslim. Ouattara wasted no time to coalesce topography and faith to his advantage, launching this designed sentence from his self-imposed Parisian exile, "*On ne veut pas que je sois président parce que je suis musulman et nordiste*" [They do not want me to be president because I am a Muslim and a Northerner], thus instigating an interethnic and interreligious pandemonium.

There was no reason to link Ouattara's disqualification to the fate of the five million immigrants that lived in Côte d'Ivoire. Yet, this is exactly what a corrupt and irresponsible national and international media did. For the purpose of the denigration campaign that Bédié was to undergo under the hostile media, Ouattara suddenly condensed all that was foreign and Muslim; and any wrong done to him — either proven or unproven — became automatically a wrong done to any of the five million immigrants or the northern Muslims living in Côte d'Ivoire. Equally, any justice rendered him could be interpreted as justice rendered to the immigrants or northern Muslim populations of the country. Curiously, however, the self-professed certified media that supported Ouattara's messianic campaign and was eager to impose him to Ivorians as legitimate president glossed over his own admission that he studied with an American scholarship reserved to Voltaic students and carried a Voltaic passport until the age of 42 with a disconcerting carelessness and an unforeseen lack of journalistic rigor. As one could read in *L'Express*,

> *A Paris, dans ce bureau de l'agence immobilière que dirige son épouse française, Alassane Ouattara, qui admet avoir été boursier du gouvernement de Haute-Volta et détenteur d'un passeport voltaïque, étale sur une tablette les copies des documents censés confondre ses détracteurs: cartes d'identité parentales, acte de naissance, certificat de nationalité.*[36]
>
> [In Paris, in the office of the real estate agency that his French wife manages, Alassane Ouattara, who admits to have held a scholarship from the government of Upper Volta and a Voltaic passport, displays on a little table copies of documents that are meant to prove his critics wrong: parents identity cards, birth certificate, certificate of nationality.]

Only journalists with premeditated purposes could be so blind as to pass over facts that begged so deafeningly for a minimum of objectivity.

Objectivity, however, was far from being the primary concern in the design to topple Bédié. Whoever has closely followed African politics, on the other hand, will know that African leaders are, in their great majority, corrupt officials, strongly encouraged by greedy Western political and business operatives to steal from their peoples or to embezzle foreign aids with impunity, insofar as these Western officials can be secured enormous benefits. One will recall how former French president Valérie Giscard d'Estaing and his cronies allowed former Central African Republic's Emperor Jean Bedel Bokassa to remain in power for many years so long as he permitted them to plunder the uranium and diamond mines of his country. One will also recall how successive French presidents, from Giscard d'Estaing to Jacques Chirac closed their eyes on the financial follies of dictators like Mobutu from Zaire, Bongo from Gabon, Eyadema from Togo, Papa and Baby Doc from Haiti, as long as these corrupt leaders made their countries the economic playgrounds of French multinational corporations. The rulers of Côte d'Ivoire, from Houphouët to Bédié, passing through Ouattara and Gueï, have all treaded in the muddy waters of France's organized crime, whereby they would cede their countries' resources to France under their market values in return for huge commissions that often came in the form of freedom to embezzle with assurance of no audits; this is, until the crooked leaders start acting like renegades. Bédié offers an interesting case study to this paradigm. Of all the misappropriations of funds in which Bédié and his close associates were involved, there is one that he would always remember the most as the scandal that helped kill his presidency.

Between 1992 and 1997, the European Union approved several grants to Côte d'Ivoire; which were earmarked to improving the healthcare system and supporting the country's decentralization program. Most of the aid vanished in government members' personal bank accounts. Between 1992 and 1997,

two different governments had been in control in Côte d'Ivoire, the all-powerful government of Prime Minister Ouattara (1990–93)—which, under an
ailing Houphouët, saw the prime minister cumulate the portfolios of interim
president and finance minister with that of prime minister—and the Kablan
Duncan government under Bédié's presidency (1993–99). Though the member states of the European Union acknowledged that the misappropriation of
the European Union's grants spanned over a five-year period, which should
include at least one year of Ouattara's administration, curiously, no mismanagement was imputed to the Ouattara government. The reason for this was
quite simple. Ouattara had been good to French business in particular and
to European interests in general, though at home much had been said and
written on the illicit source of his huge personal fortune, on his elitist style,
and on his arrogance toward the middle class that his blind support for the
IMF and the World Bank's forced structural adjustment was exponentially
pauperizing. Bédié, on the other hand, was becoming an annoyance to France
and to the European Union in general. His much-heralded reforms were not
to the liking of France. Land reform threatened big French landowners, especially many who acquired their lands in shady deals reminiscent of the dis-
honest treaties George Goldie, founder of the African National Company,
signed with African chiefs along the Congo River in the 1800s (see chapter 9
in this book). Bédié's project of identification, by regulating the flow of immigration along the borders of Côte d'Ivoire, threatened France's own politics
of immigration, which sought to keep West Africans away from French borders in particular, and from European coasts in general. For a long time, Côte
d'Ivoire had been the basin of African immigration. Many West Africans with
dreams of better lives away from home—who could have tried their luck in
Europe—had settled in Côte d'Ivoire, and had found in the Ivorian social
and economic haven, not only more than the economic prospects they could
envisage in France, but also, better social political and religious integration
than could be imagined in Europe. So long as these African immigrants could
remain in Côte d'Ivoire, they were millions less souls for the European Union's
immigration systems to worry about. Furthermore, Bédié's identification policy—termed *Ivoirité*—was susceptible of disqualifying France's greatest ally,
Alassane Ouattara, and thus killing France's hope of returning the state of
Côte d'Ivoire to the status of non-governmental organization (NGO), a status which though disadvantageous to the Ivorian masses, has made so many
French businesses wealthy and France's balance of payments affirmative. So,
five years after passively watching successive Ivorian governments indulge,
among others, in the spoliation of the European Union's grants, France was
suddenly struck by some pang of conscience and decided to act on behalf of
the oppressed masses that were being shortchanged by their leaders.

So, France, leading the European Union, ordered an audit of the management of the grants during 1995 and 1997, which was coincidentally the period concerning only the Bédié government, despite the fact that it was widely reported that the scandal went back to 1992, that is, as far back as the Ouattara administration.

> *Où ont disparu les 180 millions de francs que l'Union européenne a versés à la Côte d'Ivoire? Cette aide, destinée essentiellement au programme de santé, a été systématiquement détournée entre 1992 et 1997, comme l'attestent plusieurs audits récents de la Commission européenne et un rapport accablant de l'Inspection des finances ivoirienne, dont L'Express a pris connaissance.*[37]
>
> [What happened to the 180 million francs that the European Union disbursed to Côte d'Ivoire? This money especially earmarked for healthcare has been systematically diverted between 1992 and 1997 as indicated by several recent audits by the European Commission and a report of the Ivorian finance inspection obtained by L'Express.]

The audit of very limited scope undertaken by the European Union, though it appeared somehow commendable, was in fact one more artifice in a series of carefully choreographed ruses meant to sully Bédié's government and justify any military blow to come. The audit, conducted in November and December 1998 by the audit firm 2AC, uncovered that more than $30 millions, of an $88 million package, have gone missing. The assessment indexed Bédié, his family, and his close collaborators, especially his health minister, Maurice Guikahué, as economic criminals. This revelation coincided with the Cologne (Germany) announcement of debt reduction for heavily indebted poor countries (HIPC) and caused the European Union to freeze its budgetary help to Côte d'Ivoire. The story of embezzlement of international aid by the Bédié government made a big splash in Europe and was disseminated by all the conceivable French major TV networks and newspapers. Nevertheless, some voices in Europe expressed suspicion about the timing of this revelation. According to a French member of parliament Thierry Jean-Pierre,

> *Il est scandaleux que les députés européens n'aient pas été informés de ces détournements, qui concernent des secteurs aussi sensibles que la santé. Je ne comprends pas que la délégation sur place et les quatre experts du Fonds européen de développement détachés auprès de l'administration ivoirienne n'aient rien vu. Cela pose un problème de compétence. A moins qu'il n'y ait d'autres explications.*[38]
>
> [It is outrageous that the members of the European Parliament had not been informed of these embezzlements that touch such sensitive sectors as health. I cannot understand how the delegation on the ground and the four experts of the European Development Fund assigned to the Ivorian administration did not detect anything. This raises a question of competence. Unless some other explanations exist.]

Clearly, the French MP was not blaming this delayed assessment on ineptitude from the European Union's delegation in Côte d'Ivoire nor on incompetence from the four experts of the European Development Fund assigned to Côte d'Ivoire to monitor the use of the aid. If they had really wanted to, the European experts would have easily found out that, as early as the first years of the grants, monies were being diverted in private accounts; that programs targeted by the fund were never announced nor initiated; that medical materials, when they were effectively acquired, were being outrageously overpriced, and that some materials supposedly purchased were never delivered to their final destinations or simply ended up in the private homes of government officials. The experts of the European Union could not have been blind to the embezzlement going on for five years. They were well aware of the misuse of the funds. They just chose to ignore it because the time was not right yet to blow the whistle. That time came under the Bédié administration. Bédié's misappropriation of international development aid from the European Union became public only when the moment to justify a coup against him became opportune. The revelation of the scandal coincided with the time when the question of Ouattara's nationality became a burning issue in Ivorian politics, culminating with Ouattara's self-imposed exile in France. Thenceforth, Bédié had on his hands, not only multiple not-so-peaceful demonstrations organized by Ouattara's followers, the ire of the World Bank, the IMF, and the European Union, but also, the incensed populations of Côte d'Ivoire prompted daily by a hostile national media and a French gregarious media that has always mechanically aligned itself with the international policy of French politicians.

A few weeks after Ouattara turned up on the doorsteps of his Parisian friends and partners, on December 24, 1999, Bédié was deposed by the Ivorian military. On January 3, 2000, Bédié went in exile in Paris via Lomé and went to live in his private apartments on rue Beethoven, in the luxurious 16th arrondissement. Ouattara, as for him, returned to Abidjan triumphantly, persuaded that Robert Gueï, the new strongman of Abidjan, who had been his army Chief-of-Staff during his days as prime minister, was warming up the presidential seat for him. Ouattara was widely mistaken.

Robert Gueï: The House Sweeper Who Would Not Leave

Judging by his body language as well as the statements that General Robert Gueï made as he appeared on Ivorian national TV on the evening of December 24, 1999, to announce the successful putsch that had led to Bédié's fall, he was a terrified and unsure man; a man as surprised as the rest of the Ivorian population about the great burden that had suddenly befallen him. He was to lead a coup that he had not prepared and for which he was not prepared. He was peacefully getting ready to celebrate Christmas in his village, he told the viewers, when some young recruits came to him, weapons drawn, demanding that he be their leader and spokesman following a coup that they had just successfully undertaken against Bédié's regime after President Bédié had refused to meet with them and discuss their claims for better wages. The recruits, he said, had taken his wife hostage, and unless he cooperated, they would execute her. So, he accepted their demand to avoid any bloodshed in the country. He seemed believable. He was disheveled and shaking, and his words were hesitant. He looked pitiful. He must have loved his wife to take on such a huge responsibility. Like everyone else, he was taken aback by this unforeseen event; or was he? For those who knew that Gueï had an ax to grind with Bédié, his revelation seemed very improbable.

General Gueï was born on March 16, 1941, in Kabakouma, a Western village of Côte d'Ivoire. As a teenager, he attended the military schools of Ouagadougou, in Burkina Faso, and Saint Louis, in Senegal. Later, in 1963, he went to the military school of St-Cyr, in France. Back to Côte d'Ivoire, he was promoted to the rank of lieutenant in 1967, captain in 1971. In 1990, as a colonel and Army Chief-of-Staff under Houphouët, he was ordered to squash a revolt of young soldiers claiming back salaries. In 1991, under the Ouattara government, Colonel Gueï served his master with a loyalty that almost landed him in hot waters. It was General Gueï who, under Ouattara's administration, planned the bloody crush of student protest organized against the fallouts of structural adjustments in Côte d'Ivoire, and which resulted in the arrest, torture, rape and death of several students. In spite of an investigation that yielded damning allegations against Gueï, he was promoted general rather than being dismissed.

General Robert Gueï inaugurated the first successful coup d'état in Côte d'Ivoire. Alassane Ouattara came back from exile, convinced that Gueï was warming up the presidential seat for him. He was mistaken (photograph by Alain Tieffi for FratMat).

In 1995, Robert Gueï, henceforth a declared member of Ouattara's opposition party, the RDR, ignored President Bédie's order to repress a demon-stration by the RDR that turned into a violent and disorderly pillaging rev-elry. Gueï refused Bédié's orders less because he had come to good senses than because, that time, had he followed the orders, his party would be on the receiving hand of the brutal military machinery. For his insubordination and professed appurtenance to a party opposed to Bédie's PDCI, General Gueï was removed from his post of Army Chief-of-Staff and appointed minister of civic service, and later minister of sports. In 1996 Gueï, accused of coup d'é-tat, was removed from his post. Granted amnesty in 1999 Gueï withdrew to Kabakouma, ruminating his revenge until the famous night of December 24, 1999, when he appeared, scruffy, on national TV, claiming that he was forced, under the threat of never seeing his wife alive another day, to assume the coup that toppled Bédié. A few days later, soon after he had regained a little bit of self-assurance and had come to terms with the blessed hand that fate had just dealt him, Gueï reappeared on national TV, this time, a little more radiant, a little more tidy and soldierly, a little less cowardly than he looked during his previous appearance, and cockier, too, mocking Bédié and unveiling his program or lack thereof. Bédié, he snickered, was no real man for fleeing, for real men stay on the front line to face adversity. Bédié was free to flee like a coward if that was his choice. As for him, he planned to maintain excellent relationship with France, honor Côte d'Ivoire's financial obligations toward the Bretton Woods institutions, and return power to civilians as soon as he had swept the house and put things in order.

Gueï must have been very reassuring and unthreatening, for not a sin-gle time were there talks of French citizens being in danger in Côte d'Ivoire. None of the 20,000 French nationals living in the country was asked to leave by the French authorities. How could they be in danger? After all, was not Gueï close, very close, to Ouattara? Was not Ouattara himself the man of the IMF and the World Bank, thus the man of France and of the West in gen-eral? In fact, French newspapers, like *Le Monde* and French radio stations, like RFI, were literally dispatching Gueï's version of the coup, presenting the despot as a hero who was forced by moral imperatives to take power in order to rectify injustices caused by Bédié; and these injustices, as the French media were relaying Gueï's narratives, amounted first and foremost to Bédie's November 1999 jailing of RDR leaders for organizing violent demonstrations to protest the dismissal of Ouattara's candidacy. Powerful African leaders like Obasandjo of Nigeria and Mbeki of South Africa saw no reason to justify Gueï's military coup, and while they were strongly condemning the military overthrow in Côte d'Ivoire as illegitimate and were calling for the restoration of Bédie's power, France wasted no time, through its minister of coopera-tion, Mr. Charles Josselin, to recognize the new praetorian regime and to announce its willingness to work with Guëi. In the meantime Guëi dissolved the National Assembly and formed a so-called government of national unity constituted by ministers from all the political parties, except Bédie's PDCI. However, Guëi's government was filled in great part with Ouattara's collaborators. All signs seemed to indicate that at the end of Guëi's ostentatiously heralded "housecleaning" operation Alassane Ouattara would be the civilian leader to take over the presidency. Everything in Ouattara's demeanor indicated that a deal in that effect had been reached with Guëi. In July 2000, Guëi organized a constitutional referendum that though overwhelmingly approved by the population and even by Ouattara's party, failed to resolve Ouattara's eligibility question. Indeed, in the process of "cleaning" house Côte d'Ivoire, Guëi grew fonder and fonder of presidential perks and discovered for himself a presidential destiny. In August 2000, Guëi announced his intention to run as the candidate of the PDCI, the very party whose president he overthrew a few months earlier. Guëi's decision caused a rift in the PDCI between Bédié loyalists and those who had lost faith in any return to power of the deposed president. More importantly, it became henceforth clear that Guëi had no intention of passing the baton to Ouattara who, tired of waiting in the isle for the General to make his dream of becoming president of Côte d'Ivoire come true, had allegedly commissioned several coups against Guëi by the northern militaries. Mysteriously, the question of Alassane Ouattara's nationality, which had been a sticking point during the Bédié administration, resulting in Ouattara being disqualified from the 1995 presidential race, and which according to Guëi was at the foundation of the December 1999 coup against Bédié, resurfaced on the occasion of Guëi's presidential ambition. Like his predecessor, General Guëi pressed Ouattara to settle the issue of his doubtful Ivorian citizenship. On September 12, 2000, Guëi's lawyers produced some papers intended to disprove Ouattara's assertion that he had never availed himself of another nationality. Among the papers exhibited were Ouattara's marriage certificate to an American woman named Barbara Davis, in which he declared himself a citizen of Upper Volta and stated at the time of marriage, in 1966, that his mother was no longer living; a fact that contradicted his earlier declaration that his mother was a living eighty-year-old Ivorian woman by the name of Hadja Nabintou Cissé. There were also a 1978 bank account document and a 1980 property sale certificate in which Ouattara declared himself to be a citizen of Upper Volta. For Guëi, all these discrepancies spoke more of Ouattara's immorality and criminal mind than they could shed light on his honesty. Guëi threatened to charge Ouattara with falsification, and once again, the Supreme Court of Côte d'Ivoire rejected Ouattara's candidacy to the presidential election on the ground of suspicious nationality. The foreign press did not remain silent to this *nth*

injustice perpetrated against the misunderstood Savior of the Ivorian flock
and took it upon itself to lecture the Ivorian people about what great opportunity they were missing by persecuting the great messiah come from the
IMF. May the reader be patient with this long but instructive lament served
them by *Jeune Afrique*, in its May 23–29, 2000 issue (issue 2054), which is
only meant to shed some light on the way a corrupt media has tried to confuse the political issues in Côte d'Ivoire by manipulating information.

> *Le pays est de nouveau en situation de blocage et l'on craint qu'il ne soit entré le
> 18 mai dans une période d'agitation et de troubles. L'incertitude du lendemain
> avait déjà tari l'investissement intérieur et extérieur, contraint la Côte d'Ivoire à
> vivoter dans une économie anémiée. Le blocage actuel aggrave les choses, inquiète
> les Ivoiriens, leurs amis et leurs partenaires. Pourquoi ce blocage? En un mot
> comme en cent, une partie de la classe politique ivoirienne en est revenue, en mai
> 2000, au Bédié de novembre-décembre 1999. Sans Bédié et avec plus d'habileté.
> Si ses vœux sont exaucés, Alassane Dramane Ouattara, président du RDR (Rassem-
> blement des Républicains), leader incontesté du Nord musulman et candidat
> déclaré à l'élection présidentielle, n'aura pas la possibilité de s'y présenter! Non
> pas, cette fois, parce que son père et/ou sa mère ne sont pas ivoiriens ou parce que
> lui ne le serait pas, mais parce que — clause spécialement inventée pour lui bar-
> rer la route et en faire un inéligible — il a pu se prévaloir, il y a quinze ou vingt
> ans, de la nationalité burkinabè, ce qui n'est pas contestable et qu'il ne conteste
> pas, je crois. Il n'est pas nécessaire d'être l'ami d'Alassane Ouattara, il suffit d'être
> celui de la Côte d'Ivoire pour articuler que cette attitude politicienne dessert la
> Côte d'Ivoire, hypothèque son avenir.*

[Once again the country finds itself in a thorny position, as many believe
that May 18 has started a period of trouble and confrontation. The uncertain
future had already withered home and foreign investments and forced Ivorians to endure an anemic economy. The present obstruction disrupts things
even further, worries Ivorians, their friends, and their partners. Why this
blockade? To put it plainly, a fringe of the Ivorian political elite has returned,
in May 2000, to the Bédié philosophy of November-December 1999, this time
without Bédié, but with more tact nevertheless. If their wish comes true, Alassane Dramane Ouattara, chairman of the RDR (Rally of the Republican
Party), unchallenged leader of the Muslin North and declared candidate to
the presidential race, will not be allowed to compete! This time not because
his father and/or mother are not Ivorian nor because he allegedly is not Ivorian, but because — and this clause was especially invented to make him inel-
igible — he had adopted, fifteen or twenty years ago, Burkinabé nationality,
which is neither debatable nor disputed by him, I believe. One needs not be
a friend of Alassane Ouattara, one has only to be a friend of Côte d'Ivoire to
recognize that this political attitude does the country no good; it mortgages
its future.]

Was it not the same *Jeune Afrique* that reported on August 1, 1984, under
the penmanship of Béchir Ben Yamhed, that Zambian Justin B. Zulu was
being replaced at the head of the IMF Africa Department by Dr. Ouattara,
from Upper Volta, Born in Côte d'Ivoire, of immigrant parents from Upper

Volta? What had happened between 1981 and 2000 for *Jeune Afrique* to suddenly want to convince its audience that Ouattara adopted Burkinabé citizenship in his late thirties? What had happened for this magazine to want — by a lexical manipulation, the use of the conditional of allegation — to put the burden of proof of Ouattara's nationality on the Ivorian authorities? Now, thanks to *Jeune Afrique*, one was learning some new facts; but still faithful to its style of versatility and sudden change of direction, even these facts were being deliberately distorted by the periodical. Ouattara, *Jeune Afrique* announced, adopted Burkinabé nationality in his late thirties, before regaining his original — understood, Ivorian — citizenship. What had suddenly caused this magazine with important circulation to become amnesic to the point of disregarding the widely reported and documented facts that Ouattara studied the in the U.S. with an American scholarship earmarked for Upper Volta students? Is one then to understand that Ouattara got that scholarship to study in his late thirties? Furthermore, nowhere had Ouattara admitted to be a Burkinabé citizen at one time or another in his life, as the magazine stated. *Jeune Afrique* went further into its *grioticization* of Ouattara by anointing him the natural and unchallenged leader of the Muslim North. What a lack of basic journalistic rigor! Has the magazine really acquainted itself with the geopolitical landscape of Côte d'Ivoire before writing such irrationality? What then of this list of Northern sons, all precociously dead, who at one time or another had challenged Ouattara's leadership? What of Abdoulaye Fadiga (former governor of BCEAO, and former director of the CAISTAB), Boubacar Diaby Ouattara (Deputy Director of BIAO, former Secretary General of ECOWAS, a brilliant graduate of HEC in Paris and Harvard University), Vamoussa Bamba (former minister of technical education, then of construction and urbanism), Lamine Fadiga (former president of the Chamber of Commerce of Bouaké and vice president of the Chamber of Commerce of Abidjan), Balla Keita (former Minister of Education)? What of this list compiled by Ben Soumahoro, one of Ouattara's most vehement Northern and Muslim critics alive today, and a brilliant member of the Ivorian parliament? Is Ouattara the undisputed leader of the Muslim North that *Jeune Afrique* would like him to be? The cherry on top of the farce is *Jeune Afrique*'s bold assertion that to prevent Ouattara from running is to mortgage the country's future. Could the startling loss of memory, the distortion of facts, and the gloomy predictions augured for Côte d'Ivoire in the absence of a "Ouattara presidency" by the editorial board of *Jeune Afrique* have at their source some financial spur? After all, *Jeune Afrique* and Radio France International (RFI), this public French radio, so loyal to the Ouattaras, are illustrious for their ability to harvest some very lucrative promotional contracts from Mrs. Ouattara's numerous businesses. So, a legitimate question in trying to understand

Jeune Afrique's selective amnesia and fabrication of facts could be whether or not this magazine was in bed with the Ouattaras, whether or not this periodical, like many others, which pretends to be a friend of Côte d'Ivoire, has actually no friends but only its financial interests to care for. The hypothesis that the international media — for in Côte d'Ivoire such media as the newspaper *Le Patriote* or *Radio Nostalgie* had already lost all sense of journalistic deontology and had chosen to barefacedly eulogize Ouattara — could be financially coerced by Ouattara to write deceptive articles had been ventured in several places already. As noted *L'Inter*, an Ivorian paper, on March 9, 2003, *"Tout en vilipendant le couple Gbagbo, ces journaux français faisaient pratiquement l'éloge de Dominique et d'Alassane Ouattara qu'ils présentent comme des victimes de la politique 'ivoiritaire' du pouvoir FPI. ADO et sa femme ont-ils vraiment payé la presse étrangère et française en particulier pour quelle serve leur cause?"* (While bashing Mr. And Mrs. Gbagbo, these French papers were practically eulogizing Dominique and Alassane Ouattara, whom they presented as victims of the *Ivoirité* identity politics of the FPI. Did ADO and his wife really bribe the French media so they can serve them?)

Nevertheless, unencumbered by the criticisms of international media organizations that have lost all credibility even in the rare cases where they happen to get the news right, General Gueï barred Ouattara from the October 22, 2000, presidential election. As a result, five contenders vied for the presidential seat, General Robert Gueï for the military junta, Laurent Gbagbo for the socialist party FPI, Francis Wodié for the PIT, Mel Théodore for the UDCI, and the independent Nicolas Dioulo. Halfway through the ballot counting, Gueï attempted to load the dice to his advantage by stopping the count and declaring himself the winner while, the early returns had Gbagbo leading the race. Gbagbo's supporters took to the street to protest Gueï's *coup de force*, and with the support of the Defense and Security Forces of Côte d'Ivoire, they drove Gueï to hiding. A few days later, the Supreme Court declared Gbagbo the winner of the presidential race with 59.36 percent of the votes, against 32.7 percent for Gueï, 5.7 percent for Wodié, 1.5 percent for Mel, and .8 percent for Dioulo. Ouattara's RDR contested the results, demanding that the election, which saw only 37 percent participation and did not include Ouattara, be redone, this time with Ouattara's participation. This protest by the RDR remains the Damocles Sword hovering over Gbagbo's presidency that would be used to rationalize all the conceivable *coups bas*. Laurent Gbagbo, the saying goes, was elected in calamitous conditions — 59 percent of the votes with a participation rate of only 37 percent, and above all without Ouattara, the darling candidate of France and of the Bretton Woods institutions, he who, more than anyone else before, made French multinationals in Côte d'Ivoire so wealthy by selling them the country's strategic companies under the excuse of satisfying a World Bank/IMF program called the Washington Consensus. Therefore, against Gbagbo, all blows were permitted, even the most contemptible ones. The notion that Gbagbo was ill elected became the subject of a derisory gesture among the *patriotes*. Mahan Gahé Basile, a young Ivorian protestor intimated at a rally that with 59 percent of the votes, Gbagbo was not worse off than Chirac who only had 19 percent of the votes in France. He thus suggested that, before forcing Gbagbo to include rebels in his government, Chirac should live up to his own principle of democracy and appoint Jean-Marie Lepen and Bin Laden, respectively, as prime minister and interior minister.[39]

Hardly had Gbagbo been sworn into office than the "crimes" once imputed to Bédié and Gueï became his daily lot. Gbagbo had announced a program that disturbed French interests: *Refondation* (Reconstruction). It is true that the greatest distinguishing feature between imperial rule and independent government is the externality of the former. In colonial societies, the power to rule was taken away from local populations and entrusted to another state with which these populations had absolutely nothing in common. All happened as if "the ability to decide a country's destiny, its collective mind, had been cut out surgically and transplanted into another mind in London, Paris, Brussels, The Haye or Washington;"[40] a fact which in the France-Africa relationship, and for what concerns us here, in the France-Côte d'Ivoire relationship, had persisted throughout all the governments that had preceded the Gbagbo administration. Gbagbo had decided that the transfer of power, thought, and responsibility from Côte d'Ivoire to the *métropole* that had hitherto defined the France-Africa relation and made French African governments non–governmental organizations at the sole service of France's interests with no regard for the interests of the African people had to come to an end through political, economic, and social purgative *Refondation*. *Refondation* was meant to dig into the foundation of the Ivorian society in order to correct the structural flaws that were slowing or impeding progress and, thus, undermining the social growth of the Ivorian people.[41] Economically, among other resolutions, *Refondation* wanted to review the terms of renewal of a number of conventions ceded to France multinationals under their market values by the Ouattara government, conventions the clauses of which French firms had hardly abided by, and which were to fortunately come to expiration around 2004. Among these were the exploitation of Côte d'Ivoire Telecom conceded to France Telecom, the exploitation of Côte d'Ivoire's power (EECI) and water (SODECI) companies conceded to the Ouattaras' friends Bouygues, the exploitation of the Abidjan-Niger railway system conceded to the Ouattaras' friend Bolloré, and which, in violation of the terms of the contract, was in dire need of modernization. *Refondation* also meant reassessing some construction contracts by which French firms were fleecing the Ivorian economy by overpricing their services. For instance, the contract of a third bridge to be built in Abidjan was ceded to the French Bouygues, although a Chinese company (COVEC) would build the same bridge for ⅓ of what the French asked for, and would even accept part of payment as exchange in coffee and cocoa.

In short, Economically speaking, *Refondation* was to liberate the Ivorian economy by doing away with France's exploitative and manipulative "friendship," which had not changed since the days of the colonial *Exclusif*—this French policy whereby French colonies could only buy from France and sell to France at prices fixed by France — in order to stretch a hand to all those who were willing to be partners of good faith rather than abusing speculators, as has usually been the case with France. It was obvious that if such reassessing was to happen, the pressure exerted by France on Côte d'Ivoire to cede all its development deals to French multinationals without any bid for contracts would be fruitless; and French firms would henceforth have to openly compete with other multinationals (American, British, Canadian, Chinese, Japanese, South African, etc.) for a chance to obtain contracts in Côte d'Ivoire. This could be economically hazardous for France, especially as 2005 was announcing new privatizations, such as the privatization of the Ivorian oil refining company (SIR) and number two Ivorian cellular phone company TELECEL. In an open competition, French multinationals, which have proven in the past to be driven by no other concerns but exponential returns at all cost, would have very little chance of securing further contracts in Côte d'Ivoire, a country sitting on relatively immense oil and natural gas fields. Actually, in an open competition, French multinationals risked losing everything to Americans, British, Canadians, South African, Japanese or Chinese.

Perhaps, after all, *Refondation*'s pretensions were only a tale, the bluff of a nostalgic socialist out of touch with the realities of the moment. Perhaps, France had nothing to fear from *Refondation*, as Gbagbo had practically inherited a country on its knees, a country that, because of the disastrous politics of the PDCI in the previous forty years, was more dependent than ever on international aid, and especially on France. Without France, its colonial and post-colonial guarantor, where could *Refondation* get the money it needed for its program of development? After all, the devaluation of the CFA, the depreciation of coffee and cocoa, the country's two major exports, the European Union's and the World Bank/IMF's refusal to lend any more money to Côte d'Ivoire after the Bédié administration's much-publicized financial scandal had left Côte d'Ivoire no other alternative than to be on the good side of France, which could then intercede with international financial institutions to garner some much-needed loans and grants on behalf of Abidjan. Gbagbo

Laurent Koudou Gbagbo, president of the Côte d'Ivoire since 2000, has so far resisted all attempts at destabilization by France (photograph by Alain Tieffi for FratMat).

could not be serious. He could not run the risk of losing France's support at such a crucial moment by threatening French multinationals' monopoly in Côte d'Ivoire.

Yet, Gbagbo was not bluffing. Gbagbo had anticipated the difficulty of receiving any external financial funding for his development and poverty reduction programs. To remedy it, he initiated a measure of austerity that consisted in working at eradicating poverty with a secured budget, a budget that could not rely on any external resources, and which he appropriately named *le budget sécurisé*. Also, he undertook to fight corruption and tax evasion at the customs. Gbagbo's determination, his earnestness, and visible success were indisputable and to ignore them or to treat them as failures would have been highly disingenuous. Faced with the irrefutability of such a measured management, the World Bank had no other choice but to join the bandwagon of triumph by unconditionally returning to doing business with Côte d'Ivoire. In 2002, the IMF, the European Union, and the African Development Bank followed suit.

Paris's apprehensions started to materialize, especially as to signal France's loss of esteem in Côte d'Ivoire and *Refondation*'s resolve to rectify its cooperation with the Hexagon, and with all partners for that matter, a South African Company had just beaten French Bolloré at a bid for the construction of a new airport in San Pédro, in South-west Côte d'Ivoire. French multinationals had no intention of competing fairly with other countries. In the past, it had been easy for France to buy influences in French Africa by financing the campaigns of politicians sensitive to French interests or by bribing local officials. *Refondation* was undercutting this practice and leaving French multinationals, which hitherto garnered enormous dividends for France's economy, at the mercy of other international competitors. France had no intention of loosening its grip on Côte d'Ivoire, the wealthiest former French colony in Sub-Saharan Africa. Furthermore, Côte d'Ivoire's stance, if left unchallenged, could be infectious. Other French-speaking African nations could start questioning the validity of their "cooperation" with France; and should they, like Côte d'Ivoire, have the audacity to voice the anomalous makeup of that cooperation, France-Africa relations could be in great danger of vanishing for ever. This was not about to happen, for, as Koureyssi Bâ observed so fittingly, the French policy in Africa, characterized by deceit, lawlessness and violence, remains unchanged no matter which party is in power in Paris. Furthermore, France can always rely on the servile devotion of its puppets and its docile locals informants who do not care about their legacy in history, and who are ready to draw a dagger into the back of any brother who dares to say *no* to the master.[42] Ouattara, who had dreamed of being president of Côte d'Ivoire at all cost, had no problem driving the dagger in the back of Laurent Gbagbo, Paris's most annoying killjoy in French Africa. Convinced that France would back any subversive coup against Gbagbo, this is what Ouattara had to say in 2001 to a freshly elected group of mayors from his party.

> *Nous n'attendrons pas 5 ans pour aller aux élections. Après tout, dans certains pays, il y a des coups d'Etat et les gens s'accomodent bien de ces personnes pendant*

une certaine période. Nous avons des monarchies dans le monde et les gens acceptent bien qu'une personne non élue représente le peuple dans sa totalité. Pourquoi devrions-nous attendre 5 ans pour que vous ayez ce à quoi vous avez droit et surtout ce que les populations réclament? Nous avons certaines relations extérieures. Nous avons commencé à les actionner. J'aimerais vous dire aussi que nous avions convenu avec le maire Adama que nous aurons des réunions périodiques pour qu'ensemble, nous puissions développer assez rapidement une stratégie pour la conquête du pouvoir.[43]

[We will not wait 5 years to go to the elections. After all, in some countries, there are coups d'état, and people get used to the situation after a while. We have monarchies in the world, and people accept that a person who has not been elected represent the country in its totality. Why should we wait 5 years before you get what you deserve, especially when the populations are asking for it? We have external contacts. We have started to activate them. I would also like to tell you that with Mayor Adama we have agreed to have periodic meetings so that, very quickly, we can all develop a strategy for the conquest of power.]

So, in the night of September 19, 2002, France triggered one of the bloodiest punitive campaigns against Côte d'Ivoire. A group of deserters from the Ivorian army, who had been training in neighboring Burkina Faso, simultaneously hit the cities of Bouaké and Abidjan with a brutality never experienced in the country. More than 100 unsuspecting members of the Ivorian defense forces in Bouaké were executed in their sleep along with their families. Scores of wandering civilians were shot. Emile Boga Doudou, the Ivorian minister of interior who had just returned from a visit to his French homologue Sarkozy a day earlier, a visit during which he had raised the question of Ivorian deserters being trained in neighboring Burkina Faso, was executed in his bed, along with members of his family and his domestics. General Gueï, the former president and his wife were assassinated. In Bouaké, where the rebels had taken their quarters, an amateur video caught French paratroopers participating in the ceremonial slaughter of a captured Ivorian defense troop. Seated in the first row of the official guests to the ceremony, among whom the rebel leader Chérif Ousmane, French soldiers in their official uniforms, watched a traditional *dozo* hunter slit the throat of the frightened barechested soldier still wearing his camouflage pants. Then, the high priests of this gruesome ritual invited the French soldiers to dip their hands in a boiling pot of human blood and body parts to be later consumed. When given the floor, after their participation in the macabre feast, one of the French soldiers had these words of praise for the organizers of the rituals: "We are extremely proud to be welcomed here by out friend Chérif and to share this ritual with you. We thank you for making us feel as Ivorian as you."[44] After this well-inspired speech, the French soldiers joined their rebel brothers in a triumphant sacrificial dance. It was a night of carnage. Gary K. Busch has

French tanks and machine guns against bare-handed young Ivorian protesters in Abidjan (photograph Ayala Bakaba).

detailed the operational organization of that atrocious nightly attack on Côte d'Ivoire.

   In September 2002, about 650 rebels loyal to General Robert Gueï attacked both Bouaké and Abidjan from neighboring Burkina Faso while Gbagbo was in Rome to meet the Pope. Gbagbo refused a curiously precipitous French offer for political asylum in Paris, shortened his Vatican visit, and returned to his country to organize a response to the attack. The rebels' operation was supposed to last five days maximum. They had hoped to seize power in a matter of minutes with shock and awe, force Gbagbo to exile, and put in place a new government. Indeed, their approach was awful and bloody. However, they were ill armed and disorganized. Furthermore, they had misjudged the strength of mind of the Ivorian defense forces and their determination to safeguard the republican institutions embodied in the democratically elected head of state. The Ivorian National Defense Forces (FANCI) opposed a fierce and disciplined counter-offensive to the rebels. In a matter of hours, after the initial effects of surprise passed, the FANCI cornered the rebels and reduced them to half. It was then that the commander of the French army in Côte d'Ivoire requested a cease-fire so that he could evacuate the French citizens and a few American nationals living in Bouaké.

   During the 48 hours allotted the French army, three Antonov-12 flew from Franceville (Gabon) to supply the rebels in armaments. Other planes and truck brought in weapons and mercenaries from Liberia and Sierra Leone, and the rebel force, which was previously estimated at a little over 600 troops, grew to 2500 mercenaries armed with Kalashnikovs and other weapons that had never been part of the Ivorian armory. The French army also supplied the mercenaries with sophisticated logistic and communication equipments that kept the insurgents always aware of the movements of the Ivorian defense troops. The French then retreated gradually leaving the rebels in charge with Eastern Europeans mercenaries as technical advisers. Once the rebels were well positioned, Paris then activated the international pressure machinery through the United Nations to obtain a resolution entrusting France with a peace-keeping mission in Côte d'Ivoire.[45]

While tergiversations were taking more time than needed at the United Nations, the rebels were multiplying their fronts not just in the Northern part of the country (Bouaké, Korhogo, Katiola, Odienné), but also in the Western part (Man), recruiting more mercenaries from Samuel Doe's civil war troops as well as mercenaries from the RUF in Sierra Leone. The rebels' indiscriminate killing and raping of thousands of children, elderly, and women led to mass exodus toward Yamoussoukro (the political capital in central Côte d'Ivoire) and Abidjan (in the South). After much groping and stuttering to explain the real object of the failed coup that they transformed into a protracted rebellion, the rebels finally, through the voice of a former mediocre

Bare-handed young Ivorian protesters carrying the body of a fallen comrade shot by French soldiers in Abidjan (photograph Ayala Bakaba).

student, former student association leader, Soro Guillaume, settled on accusations of ethnocentrism and xenophobia against the Gbagbo regime, charges that have become so common since Ouattara's bid for the presidency, and which have been the burden of all those who have stood in the way of his political ambition. Ouattara's supporters, led by France, were principally accusing Gbagbo, as they did Gueï and Bédié before him, of hating foreigners in general, and Muslim Northerners in particular; as if, in Paris's political imaginary, Ouattara condensed all that was Northern and Muslim in Côte d'Ivoire.

As the accusations of ethnocentrism have persisted from the Bédié regime to the Gbgagbo administration passing through Robert Gueï's military junta, and seemed to have legitimated all the *coups de force* supported by Paris, would it not be fair to examine which ethnic, geographic, or religious groups have been persecuted and kept apart from the political process, and which ones have benefited from it? This is what a French mathematics teacher, a long time resident of Côte d'Ivoire, exceeded by the intoxication campaign organized in France about the Ivorian crisis, had to say to his misinformed compatriots beaten every day by a lazy French press and deceptive government officials.

> *Un peu d'histoire alors? (Que les Ivoiriens m'excusent pour les considérations « ethnographiques » suivantes, qu'ils ne prennent même pas la peine d'opposer aux classifications françaises, mais qui peuvent aider les Français à enfin s'interroger sur le fameux découpage « ethnique » qui fonde leur compréhension de l' « Ivoirité »!) Trois présidents successifs sont censés avoir été « ivoiristes » : Bédié, mais il est Baoulé (du Centre), Gueï, mais il était Guéré (de l'Ouest), Gbagbo, mais il est Bété (de l'Ouest aussi, mais un peu plus au Sud), sa femme (une « dure »), mais elle est Abouré (de l'Est), le « dur » du Régime, Mamadou Koulibaly (mais il est Sénoufo, « musulman du Nord »). Qu'ont de commun ces trois présidents (et pour Gbagbo les « durs » qui l'entourent) réputés « ivoiristes »? Apparemment, rien sur le plan ethnique! Mais qu'ont-ils donc de commun? Une seule chose : ils ont à un moment ou à un autre été opposés à Alassane Ouattara. D'où la définition provisoire suivante que l'on pourrait proposer (en l'absence de toute autre) : l' "Ivoirité" est un concept français qui désigne le fait, pour un Ivoirien, de n'être pas Alassane Ouattara ».[46]*

[Should we indulge in a little bit of history, then? (I hope that the people of Côte d'Ivoire will forgive me for the following "ethnographic considerations," which could help the French people to finally start questioning the so much rehearsed "ethnic" categorizations upon which their understanding of "*Ivoirité*" is based). Three successive presidents are said to be "ivorist": Bédié, but he is Baoulé from the Center; Gueï, but he is Guéré from the West; Gbagbo, but he is Bété from the West, too (but a little more to the South); his wife (a "radical"), but she is Abouré from the East; the most "radical" of the regime, Mamadou Koulibaly, but he is Sénoufo, a "Muslim Northerner." What do these three presidents have in common (and for Gbagbo, what do the "radical" figures that surround him have in common with the other notorious "ivorists")? Apparently, nothing from an ethnic viewpoint! What then do they have in common? Only one thing: They have, at one point, been opposed to Alassane Ouattara. Hence the following provisional definition could be put forth (in the absence of any other definition): "*Ivoirité* is a French concept that describes the condition of any Ivorian who is not Alassane Ouattara."]

In other words, *Ivoirité* is that which has helped Paris rationalize all its military actions in Côte d'Ivoire since the death of President Houphouët and the continued decline of France's influence in its richest ex-colony. Of all the regimes that had dared questioned France's manipulative practices in Côte d'Ivoire, Gbagbo's Socialist government was the most unbendable. It was only by breaking it that Paris could submit Gbagbo's administration and could hope to recover its monopoly in the country. So, France launched against Gbagbo the biggest firepower ever delivered on Côte d'Ivoire. Now the United Nations, through the Security Council, could play its partition by blessing France's direct intrusion in the country and by consecrating Paris's overseeing of Côte d'Ivoire's resources, and, perhaps, the coronation of Ouattara, and thus the putting in place of a puppet regime more amenable to France's interests; for, indeed, ethnocentrism and xenophobia had nothing to do with it. The acclaimed Ivorian writer Ahmadou Kourouma, who had never been known to have great esteem for Gbagbo, and who, like many observers, has been led to read more than he should have in the concept of *Ivoirité*, nonetheless acknowledged that the question of the injustice of *Ivoirité*, which after much searching became the central pillar of the rebellion, was almost solved by Gbagbo, until "these people"—referring certainly to the rebels—arrived.[47] Yet Some self-styled expert Africanists, speaking on the antennas of such hostile French radios like RFI, are still maintaining that *Ivoirité*, was not only practiced by Gbagbo, but also constituted the major cause of the rebellion, an assertion that either was the result of incompetence or bad faith;[48] an incompetence or a bad faith that have enabled the French military's constitutional holdup in Côte d'Ivoire to go unquestioned by the international community. The deafening silence of the international community in the midst of what is taking place in Côte d'Ivoire, the utter indifference that greeted the French massacre of the Ivorian youth determined to stand up for their rights against French imperial compulsions, and who had no other weapons than their voices to chant freedom and their bare fists raised in the air against the French war machine, is a *failure of the international community's duty of consciousness.*

Yet, Gbagbo's *Refondation* was not merely a rumination posture against France. Evidently it intended to rectify Côte d'Ivoire's uncharacteristic relationship with France. The rosy economic definition of liberalization that treats

Foreign Direct Investment as "...a decentralized process wherein each foreign company takes the investment decisions of the others as beyond its control..."[49] is exploded in French Africa. There, nothing is meant to remain beyond the control of French multinationals whose barons have vouched to filter all non–French multinational investments' access to the continent to the point of reducing them to nothing. "Exploding" is not just a figure of speech, as the daily conflagrations caused by heavy French artillery and the frequent turning out of black corpses scare Anglo-Saxon and Asian investments out of French Africa, while France remains curiously present before, during, and after the cannon roars. From the perspective of most French investors in Africa, Foreign Direct Investment should have nothing to do with each firm forming "...an expectation about the host country's eventual trade policy and [evaluating] the profitability of its own potential foreign investment accordingly."[50] Instead, the host country should be bomb-pressured to accepting the level of protection and the terms of profitability dictated by France.

It is unfortunate that, in economic circles, the kinds of *quid pro quo foreign investments* that have made French multinationals and a few corrupt nationals wealthy while impoverishing most Africans by a relocation of their economic resources are still treated as epiphenomenal or isolated episodes involving a small number of disreputable industrialists. French multinationals' brutal practices in Africa are systemic, and they ought to be examined as such. The much-publicized Elf-Aquitaine affair has now shown that French multinationals' dirty economic practices run deep into the French government no matter which party is in power. As Bro Grébé, the leader of the women section of the PDCI explained, Gbagbo's *Refondation* was principally a program of poverty reduction through education of the young, distribution of supplies, creation of universal healthcare for the masses, and creation of jobs;[51] a program that fell well within the United Nations Millennium Development Goal (MDG) for Africa. The French-supported rebellion put Gbagbo's poverty reduction program at a standstill, and the passion with which Koffi Anan's United Nations defended the French actions and supported France's subsequent direct intervention in Côte d'Ivoire was mind-boggling. The victim was presented as the victimizer, and the victimizer was made both judge and Jury of the victim. This collaboration of African leaders such as Ouattara and Koffi Anan with a brutal European force against their people, though revolting, nevertheless has an explanation. In all times, Africa has had local collaborators who enabled the exploitation and impoverishment of the continent by Western powers, so long as these local informants could be left to collect a few morsels alongside their plundering Western masters. At the time of the question of Côte d'Ivoire, Koffi Anan had his own scandals at the United Nations hovering over his head, and the *oil-for-food* humiliation in which his son, using Daddy's influence, was deeply involved, and for which Anan needed France more than ever to testify on his behalf. This could only happen if he took care of France's interests in Africa, no matter what the consequence could be for the African people. Anan and Ouattara were only repeating an ancient gesture called North/South collaboration. Unfortunately, this African managerial style, which tends to place personal gain over any ethical consideration, is a proclivity derived from the old partnership of Africans with Europeans in the Trans-Atlantic Slave Trade, and which has greatly contributed to Africa's underdevelopment by preventing African so-called leaders from perceiving any alternative for growth other than their participation in dirty trades.

> The old staple of foreign trade in West Africa, namely slave trading, had been very intimately bound up with the rise of new monarchical governments and societies ... [that] could not readily or quickly change the nature of their activities ... the replacement of slave as an export staple by other commodities did not really enter at all into the thinking of the men who governed or managed these African societies.[52]

Here is a proposition for which one only has to substitute a few contemporaneous signifiers to appreciate how true it rings today for many African elites. For the Ivorian youth, this paradigm of collaboration, which carried all the signs of neocolonialism, was to be conquered. The *Galexie Patriotique* developed as a response to this need. In fact, at the Linas Marcoussis roundtable — where after successfully sabotaging any African attempt to resolve the conflict, Paris proclaimed itself the mediator between the fighting parties — Gbagbo was firmly urged to share his power with the rebels and officials from other opposition parties. Subsequent to the Marcoussis meeting, Mr. Affi N'Guessan, Gbagbo's prime minister was replaced by a "prime minister of consensus," in the person of Mr. Seydou Diarra. Guillaume Soro, the rebels' spokesman, became minister of communication. Yet, still holding on to the North, the rebel forces henceforth legitimized by Paris, which at Marcoussis insisted that the signifier "rebel" be scratched from the Ivorian political lexicon, continued to show no regard for the Republic. As if to mock all principles of democracy, the rebel leaders kept their quarters in Bouaké and never showed up at government meetings. They cut the North from national TV coverage and instituted their own television and radio stations, diffusing propagandist programs around the clock. They established their own police and treasury. Assisted by French soldiers, they regularly raided the local agencies of the BCEAO (Central Bank of the West African States) in Bouaké, Korhogo, Katiola, and Man; and they engaged in the most appalling acts of human rights abuses. On November 6, 2004, Gbagbo finally warned Paris that the loyalist forces had decided to free the North from the rebels and reunify the country. Ivorian defense planes taking off from Yamoussoukro executed two successful rounds in Bouaké, weakening the rebel positions. On the third round, the French military claimed that a bomb fell on their position and killed nine French soldiers and one American civilian. In retaliation, the same day, and before any investigation in the matter could even be set up, the French army destroyed all the Ivorian army air force planes. For the Ivorian populations committed to the republican institutions, this French open attack made it clear that Paris, which had until then supported the rebels indirectly, was now in a direct confrontation with the Republic of Côte d'Ivoire. That night, responding to a call for protest by their leader, thousands of Ivorian young men and women decided to march to the 43rd BIMA (the French military base in Port-Bouët) to mark their indignation and free Côte d'Ivoire from this French mindset that has not yet understood that Côte d'Ivoire "is not a district of Paris." On their way, as members of the foreign press were able to witness, barehanded Ivorian young men and women became the targets of French helicopters armed with machine guns that shot at them for four hours, massacring scores and wounding hundreds. This event hardly created a quiver in the international community. From her Parisian office, Michelle Alliot-Marie, the French minister of defense's explanation for this savage act was that the French army responded to the provocations of Gbagbo's armed militias. This is what a French reporter, who had managed to keep his head above the swirl of French propaganda, had to report about that night of butchery.

> From our windows, we can see the protesters. It is 11:00 P.M. We can hear helicopters above the roof of our hotel. From the sky, the helicopters of the French army are shooting at the protesters. They are civilians. We can hear tracing bullets, loud grenades, and persistent machine gun blasts, causing panic in the crowd and forcing the protesters to retreat from the bridge. A few minutes later, the protesters return, but the helicopters are now positioned ahead of them and are shooting directly at the protesters again to cut their advance. Even isolated protesters are targeted. The few cars going south of the town are also shot at. As you can see the first car manages to get away, but the one following is not that lucky. The French helicopters made about thirty passages. For the four hours that the attack lasted, we did not witness a single protester shoot back at the French helicopters. Silence returned at about 3:00 A.M.[53]

The politics of France in Côte d'Ivoire runs counter the very notion of globalization. The moral bankers of the IMF and the World Bank, those who have become adept at moralizing the world about openness, transparency, and good governance, have lost all credibility, not just in Côte d'Ivoire, but in most of the Third World, for they are the very ones who, through the backdoors of the institutions that employ them and pay them inexcusably aberrant salaries, have legalized corruption, nepotism, and coups d'état as the order of the day in the Third World. Often, the discourse on good governance promoted by the World Bank and the IMF is travestied as a discourse for direct intervention into Africa.

It would be utterly hypocritical for anyone who unreservedly condemns the resistance organized by the *Galexie Patriotique* to pretend to speak in favor of poverty reduction and growth in the Third World, and especially in Côte d'Ivoire. It is obvious that France's gangster-like intervention in Côte d'Ivoire has undermined progress by any theory of economics. Let us only point to some of the consequences of France's disquieting intrusion in Côte d'Ivoire as they relate to the armoring of the most pessimistic economics theories for the Third World and the undercutting of all development theories ever to cast any promising outlooks on poor countries.[54]

To proponents of *dependency theory*— the theory that winners and losers are two inevitable sides of the same coin of development[55]— the Chiraquian martial incursion in Côte d'Ivoire to protect lamenting French multinationals terrified of international competitions makes factual the hypothesis that as economic trade grows between rich and poor nations, global income inequality grows, too. In the kind of liberal commerce that, in the wake of the Washington Consensus, has characterized the "exchanges" between Côte d'Ivoire and France, and in which the French government and the French army, following an age-old tradition, have figured more like bullying middlemen than state institutions, profits have been unashamedly unidirectional. So, this explaining that, the *convergence theory*— the theory claiming that someday, in a happy future, *the last shall meet the first*, and that rich countries will experience dwindling returns and be caught up by poor countries — is belied. If the economic trends, as we observe them today, keep up, convergence theory becomes, for the proponents of global equality, wishful thinking, an unrealizable fancy. The impossible possibilization of convergence theory is pushed even further back into the dominion of bleakness by the doing of rich countries that have specialized in altering, in poor countries, all the control variables in which advocates of *endogenous growth* have invested so much optimism. How so?

Indeed, against convergence theorists' pessimistic outlooks for rich countries and optimistic perspectives for poor countries, proponents of *endogenous theory* would argue that humanity is only at the beginning of useful discoveries, and therefore, rich countries will always be able to subvert the menace of diminishing resources and remain dominant just by the significance of the scientific, technological innovations that they make at home. This is possible because rich countries have traditionally been able to control certain variables, such as, fertility rate, level of human capital (education), and government spending. These controlled variables are referred to as *conditional factors*.

Traditionally, the control for these variables has been absent in poor countries. So then, the factors that come to be known in rich countries as conditional convergence factors (insofar as the conditions for their control are present) become unconditional convergence factors in the Third World (insofar as the condition for their control are absent). No one, however, would dispute the fact that conditional and unconditional convergence factors are not natural occurrences. They do not respectively appear in rich and poor countries by Devine design. They are not the making of an omnipotent *Big-Other* who assigns them, in that order, to civilized capitalist societies on the one hand, and to primitive territorial populations on the other hand. Conditional and unconditional convergence factors are not inherently attributed to one group of people who are in control of all their intellectual faculties as opposed to another group subjected to lobotomy. Conditional and unconditional convergence factors are created and manipulated by greed, ruthlessness, and brutality, which are not necessarily signs of intelligence. Therefore, before proponents of endogenous theory rest assured that any responsibility for failure and economic decline is *entirely* organic, perhaps, it would be wise to situate responsibility. On the levels of human capital and government spending, the multiple muscled interventions of France in West Africa have always, intentionally, turned conditional and unconditional factors on their heads in a theatrical diagram that made perfect sense for France while disturbing any prospect of planned development for the African nations. This viciously masterful manipulation made conditional factors unconditional for national social engineers while at the same time keeping them conditional for French business. *Bare Hands Victory* becomes enlightening in disclosing France's responsibility in that regard; but Bakaba's documentary can only expose the symptoms of a bigger infection in Africa. In *Bare Hands Victory*, Côte d'Ivoire is but a case study of a more pervasive Hexagonal will to power determined to make profits *by all means necessary*. In the early morning of November 7, 2007, a young *patriote*, laying on a stretcher, his face and body drenched in blood, but who had still enough humor left in him despite the killing night he had just survived, had this to say in the midst of the dead and the wounded that surrounded him in this Abidjan emergency room.

> We were at home in Abobo when we heard Blé Goudé's call for resistance. I decided to join my comrades in the march to Port-Bouët. Once on the bridge, we saw a helicopter shooting at us. Some people would say that the bullets were not real. But I am here to tell you that they were very real. We saw people fall next to us. Three young women were hit in the heads and collapsed in front of us. I am among the lucky ones. Right now, the march is still on. And the French army continues to shoot without any consideration for human lives. And that is revolting.[56]

Revolting, indeed! Is it only by killing Africa's human capital that the rest of the world could give the black continent a chance of turning the tides of global inequality? France seems resolved to spin the grim images of Ivorian youth falling under French multinationals' hired guns into a neo-classical resolution of income inequality; one which would eerily assert, on account of *the role of population growth* in the race for development, "We are saving them from themselves." If growth is a race between increases in population and capital stock, this pessimistic-optimist argument would thus go, then, wars — which have been more exogenous than endogenous in French Africa — by their ensuing effects of population decrease, will lead to better distribution of wealth in Africa. How depressing! And how disingenuous, too, to link the slaughter of the dynamic and educated force of a country to its chances for progress!

In fact, until an international outcry puts an end to the incendiary practices of the hired armies of imperial nations, the butchering of the young brains of Africa will continue to widen the technological gaps between North and South — one of the major causes of global inequality — and maintain an East-West-West-East-bound spread of technology and industrialization. It is not by accident that most Third World countries, claim appurtenance to the Orient when they cannot establish their belonging to the Occident.[57] Have not theorists of *economic geography* told us that the Occident, with its temperate climate and smoother terrains, is blessed by the gods and has all the best prospects for development? Nevertheless, has African geography really

A memorial to the scores of young protestors who fell under the bullets of the French Army in Abidjan (photograph by Julia Dresen-Coulibaly).

been a problem at any time in history for opportunists resolute to plunder the riches of the African continent? Have not European explorers, as far back as the sixteenth century, defied the negative endowments of Africa and pushed deep into the *heart of darkness* to dig up Africa's iron ores, its gold, and its diamond, to cut its timber, to bleed its rubber trees, to remove its elephants' defenses, to practice their shooting ability on its game? Have not European speculators designed ingenious methods to transfer Africa's human capital and riches to the Occident despite Africa's much-heralded negative endowments? Why has Europe become so paradoxically impotent when it came to developing infrastructures in the continent that would benefit African populations? And what to say of this so-called poor continent that yet continues to stir up so much interest in greedy multinationals? Geography and poverty have nothing to do with the underdevelopment of Africa. In fact, to be fair, Africa is only victim of its wealth.

9

"There Is No Trade Going on There"

Tales from the Killing Fields of the Congo

What of ... the burden which others are bearing now because of us?
Where are they whose shoulders have bent beneath its weight in the
dim valleys of the centuries? Vanished into nothingness, pressed and
stamped into that earth on which we set our conquering seal. How is
it with those who but yesterday lived free lives beneath the sun and
stars, and to-day totter to oblivion?

— E.D. Morel,
The Black Man's Burden

"[T]he creation and transmission of ideas," Rivera-Batiz and Romer suggest, "have been extremely important in the development of modern standards of living." Most economists and social engineers would not dispute the truthfulness of this proposition. Yet, the world seems to watch, immobilized in stupor, the creation and transmission of ideas scurry back and forth on a latitudinal artery. Technological innovations and exchanges propagate between Western and Asian nations while Africa, though a reservoir of natural resources and a gorge of ingenious brains, remains, once again, through some ingenious *racialogical* propaganda, the West's testing field, its supplier of raw materials, and its source of human guinea pigs for technological developments that seem to benefit Africans only by accident. The Republic of the Congo has come to epitomize the injured party of the non-reciprocal exchanges between northern and southern nations. Perhaps, no other African country has ever paid so high a price, in human and material capitals as well as in duration, for Europe's proclivity for wealth accumulation as the Congo has.

Covetous Europe Meets the Congo

Until 1876, the Congo was little known by European speculators. Much of the economic activities in Africa — which essentially amounted to the Trans-Atlantic Slave Trade — happened on the western coasts of the continent. Though as early as 1482 a Portuguese explorer by the name of Diogo Cão, upon landing on the shore of the Congo River by chance, had erected a cross there and claimed the region for his sovereign, King João II of Portugal, the Portuguese exploration and exploitation of the Congo remained at best external and spasmodic. The more than thirty unforgiving cataracts along the Congo River made it practically impossible to navigate. Moreover, tropical diseases like malaria and yellow fever against which Europeans had no protection at all kept the interior of the Congo impenetrable. The Portuguese stayed in the coastal regions of the Congo whence they sent daring slave hunters to catch slaves and fill their boats to Brazil, which they had also discovered by accident in 1500. So, for almost four hundred years, Europeans barely ventured in the interior of the Congo nor did they recognize the Congo's full potentials in natural resources. Like much of Africa, apart from the slaves and elephant tusks it supplied Europe, the Congo was perceived as "faceless, blank, empty, a place on the map waiting to be explored, one ever more frequently described by the phrase that says more about the seer than the seen: the Dark Continent;"[1] and explorers, there were several, who, like David Livingstone, Lovett Cameron, Henry Morton Stanley, and Savorgnan de Brazza battered torrential tropical rains, merciless landscapes, unknown diseases, and often apprehensive native populations to unveil and tame the great mystery that the Congo was. It was only by default that the Congo became the object of desire of Leopold II, the excessive sovereign of the tiny European kingdom of Belgium.

King Leopold's Tour De Main

By most accounts, Leopold was an ugly duckling. His excessive nose and tall, thin, idle body was much emotional burden to his mother, who showed him less affection than his two younger siblings, a brother and a sister. His cold and distant father, whom he could see or communicate with only through a swarm of secretaries and official go-betweens, did not show him much love either. To add to his mother's anguish, Young Leopold was almost good at nothing; that is, nothing except geography, a subject in which he dove with uncommon passion. Leopold had very little interest in the opposite sex, and especially in his bride, Archduchess Marie-Henriette, in whose arms he was thrown at age eighteen by his father who wanted to establish stronger political ties between Belgium and the Austro-Hungarian Empire. To escape his conjugal duties, Leopold found himself a second passion in matters of trade. Nevertheless, a prince had to leave his country an heir. So, after some royal tutorials on matters of sexuality, Leopold and Marie-Henriette were able to have a child, before going back to their separate interests; hers being horseback riding, and his being discovering the world, exploring trade possibilities and ways of aggrandizing the tiny kingdom that he was soon to inherit. Before setting his eyes on the Congo, Leopold II of Belgium had caressed the possibilities of annexing the Philippines, China, Borneo, New Guinea, Formosa, Tonkin, Sumatra, Java, and Japan.[2] As reports Wesseling, Leopold II had displayed his yearn for overseas treasures in ways that were unbecoming of a king. Like a vulgar housebreaker, he once emitted the wish of stealing the "poorly guarded" treasure of the Japanese Emperor. "[Leopold's] mentality was more that of a buccaneer and a mafioso than of a king," we are told.[3] Leopold longed for properties abroad, and he was ready to use any means to that end.

However, the Belgium that Leopold II inherited upon the death of his father, in 1865, had no desire for colonial expansion. Memories of Belgium's own fight for freedom were still fresh in the collective imaginary of the Belgian people, and it inhibited in them any violence against another people. In fact, thirty-five years earlier, on October 4, 1830, Belgium had proclaimed its independence after a seemingly insignificant riot developed into a fierce revolution. From 1814 to 1830, Belgium was part of the Kingdom of the Netherlands. French-speaking Roman Catholic Walloons occupied that part of the kingdom. For various reasons, the Walloons felt disenfranchised. Politically, their small number gave them little representation at the Assembly. Economically, their less developed industries and their agricultural activities suffered greatly from the prevailing free trade spirit of their Dutch counterparts. Religiously, they had little affinity with their Calvinist sovereign, William I. The French-speaking Walloons' sentiment of independence got a boost of audacity thanks to the July 1830 French Revolution, which resulted in the overthrow of King Charles X. So, on August 25, 1830, following a patriotic opera performance in Brussels, some energized proponents of self-government took to the streets, chanting disloyal slogans against their king, William I. Slowly, the crowd grew in size. The rioters occupied government buildings and within a few days, with King William I's inability to squash them, the revolutionaries announced the creation of a provisional government. On October 4, 1830, Belgium declared its independence from the Kingdom of the Netherlands. Though most European powers recognized the nation of Belgium after two months' hesitation, until 1839, King William I of the

Kingdom of the Netherlands made several unsuccessful attempts to recapture Belgium. Finally, in 1839 the Treaty of London, signed among the belligerents, recognized Belgium's independence under conditions that, as a buffer zone between the European continent and Great Britain, it should remain a neutral country in Europe, and that it should rely on Great Britain for its defense against eventual external aggressions. King Leopold I became the first sovereign of independent Belgium, which he ruled from 1831 to 1865. When at his death his son Leopold II acceded to the Belgian throne, Belgium was a thriving industrial and iron mining country with 5 million inhabitants. It was a country turned more within than without. Its fresh anti-imperialist experience gave it no invading inclination. Furthermore, had Belgium cherished imperial aspirations, its army was too small and its coffers not strong enough to support a colonial enterprise. Besides, Belgium also could run the risk of losing its neutrality and thus the protection of Britain against France's invading ambitions had it chosen to become a conquering empire. King Leopold II, whose exploitative drive preceded his accession to the Belgian throne, understood that to undertake a colonial venture meant doing so, not on behalf of Belgium, but rather, as a private entrepreneur, perhaps, backed by his family name and wealth. This he could; but a place to take over, he still had no precise idea of.

Around 1875, tales of great explorers such as Livingstone, Stanley, and Brazza were trickling down to Europe.[4] In 1875 Paris organized the Congress of the French Geographical Society, which showcased the reports of various "expert Africanists." The Paris Congress gave participants a cursory understanding of the interior of Africa. For King Leopold II, it was an opportunity to be educated about the heart of Africa and to appraise his chances for an African colony. Following the Paris Congress, Leopold II convened his own Brussels Geographical Conference in his palace on September 12, 1876. Scientists, explorers, and geographers from seven countries attended Leopold's symposium. From the various "expert" testimonies, he certainly learned of a thriving early commercial intercourse which, with the fading of the Slave Trade, had developed in the Congo between native Congolese and Europeans through a network of African go-betweens, some who, deep in the hinterland, had never seen the face of a white person at all. In fact, the Ba-Congo, from the lower parts of the Congo River, carried goods from European merchants (cloth, kettles, brass rods, cooking pots, looking glasses, pipes, knives, beads, muskets, and powder) up to the cataract areas. From there, they brought down products gathered by the Bateke people through various African intermediary sources as far as 2000 miles from the coasts. African products exchanged against European goods were red wood, cam wood powder, ivory, wax, copper, tin, lead, palm oil, and rubber;[5] all riches that titillated Leopold's pecuniary glands, and which he was determined to acquire at little or no cost.

Two days after it began, the Brussels Geographical Conference yielded the *Association Internationale Africaine* (AIA) with Leopold II as its first president. The advertized objectives of the AIA were to repress slavery in Central Africa and open the region to "civilization" by equipping it with communication and commercial and social infrastructures. The AIA was to be a nonpolitical body with national subcommittees in France, Germany (the two most enthusiastic participants), Holland, Austria, Hungary, Spain, Italy, Russia, and Switzerland. England refused to have a national subcommittee bound to any international authority. Leopold's International Association, supposedly created to bring civilization and compassion to the heart of Africa, was nothing else but a subterfuge to arrive at his personal pecuniary objective. Most European powers were not dupe. Some, like Britain, snubbed Leopold's Association out of cheer detestation of the over-ambitious king of a tiny, insignificant state acting like the authority on human rights. Others, like Germany and France, too busy searching for local responses to the 1870s widespread economic slump, signed on to Leopold's idea with feigned enthusiasm, only to let Leopold run it as he pleased. Somehow, this international detachment toward Leopold's Association, coupled with Britain's refusal to support Stanley's plan for the annexation of and economic investment in the Congo converged in Leopold's favor. In effect, in 1877 Stanley had returned from the Congo with a very wholehearted appeal to the powers (England, America, and France) to recognize the political and commercial import of the Congo, and especially of the Congo River, this waterway that, in his view, would become "the grand highway of commerce to West Central Africa."[6] Stanley proposed that Britain should build a railway that would connect the mouth of the Congo River to Stanley Pool around the waterfall areas, which were not navigable, and to build intermediate steamboat stations in the navigable sections of the river. Britain plainly rejected Stanley's plan as vague and legally too complex to implement.

Sensing gains to be made, Leopold II co-opted Stanley's blueprint and know-how. He convinced powerful business and princely figures to invest in the *Comité d'Études du Haut Congo* (CEHC), a company that would study the feasibility of Stanley's plan. Of the one million francs estimated for the project, Leopold II invested 260,000 francs loaned him by a banker friend; a sum that made him the major shareholder and president of the company, followed by a Dutch group with 130,000 francs. The stipulation of the CEHC was that if the venture were successful, subscribers would rip the benefits proportionally to their investments; but in case of failure, the residual money was to be returned to the shareholders. Providence came Leopold's way when the Dutch group went bankrupt and investors scurried to get out of the CEHC. Leopold announced to his partners who were too eager to remove the CEHC's albatross from around their necks that, though much of the one million francs had already been engulfed in the project, the plan could still be salvaged with extra funding. However, he proposed to dip into his own pockets in order to make the necessary supplemental investment for three stations to be built. If these stations yielded profits, he promised, he would reimburse the subscribers their investments with 5 percent interest. In case things did not turn out for the best, the assets would be sold and the investors could be refunded their shares. The only caveat was that, from then on, the CEHC would have to be dissolved; a suggestion that the subscribers, happy to get out of an apparently succumbing company, did not object to. Leopold, now sole steward of the Congo venture, entirely funded a new association of his creation, the *Association Internationale du Congo* (AIC). The phonemic similarity between the AIA and the AIC was purposely meant to confuse. Leopold wanted the public to not be able to tell apart the more or less *international* AIA and the very *private* AIC. Leopold was not successful in confusing the public only. By some linguistic manipulations that he, better than anyone, had mastered, Leopold fooled the powers, too. Soon, the United States, Britain, and France signed on to Leopold's AIC, presuming that they were giving their blessing to an association with the international and free trade dedication, and for some, the moral devotion of the AIA. In fact, the AIC was Leopold's private company, for which Leopold recruited Stanley as main agent and official land hunter.

As Stanley traveled through the Congo signing morally questionable treaties with local chiefs to secure territories for King Leopold II, he crossed path with Brazza, who was also engaged in his own unethical annexations on behalf of France, as well as the Portuguese, who claimed to hold the oldest exploitation rights in the Congo.[7] These various international posturings intensified the rush toward the Congo and added to the existing rivalries that the Berlin Conference was set to resolve. By the time the Berlin Conference was to take place, Stanley, armed with hundreds of blank treaty forms issued by Leopold on which local chiefs only had to appose a cross in guise of signature, had given Leopold II a huge advantage over the French and, of course, over the mollified Portuguese.[8] Thus well positioned before the Berlin Conference, Leopold II managed to be all things to everyone. To Britain's free trade's spirit, Leopold II made a touching plea for open commercial borders in the Congo. To France, his fiercest rival in the area, Leopold II offered priority rights in the Congo. The Americans, as for them, had little interest in Africa at the time. Finally, the Powers signed on to Leopold's *Association Internationale du Congo* and gave the King of the Belgians carte blanche to define the borders of his central African possession. As is well known, Leopold II, King of the Belgians, became the sole owner of an area ninety-five times the size of Belgium, a huge personal plantation on which he would use some of the most appalling exploitative methods known to have existed in post–Slave Trade Africa.

A Traiblazer of Hitlerian Cruelty

When on Christmas Eve 1907, almost a month after Leopold II was laid to rest in a crypt of the Church of Laeken, Cardinal Mercier, to whom Leopold had preferred a parish priest for his Extreme Unction, in an attempt to silence his beloved king's unrelenting critics, made a sermon that history would later come to belie, as more information on Leopold's government in the Congo Free State became available.

> You have taken part in the nation's recent mourning. The priest have cele-
> brated mass, the faithful have prayed, have taken communion for the repose
> of the soul of the great king that Belgium has just lost and whose glory, con-
> trary to the fate of most human reputations, will grow as years permit us to
> appreciate better the immense services rendered to the Christian civilization
> by his genius and perseverance.[9]

Not only has not history proven Leopold II to be the glorious and great king Cardinal Mercier has prophesied, but neither have Leopold's so-called "immense services" aggrandized Christian faith. In fact, Leopold and his missionaries have greatly stained both Christian civilization and human decency. This is why, in chronicling Leopoldian atrocities in the Congo in his *White King, Red Rubber, Black Death*, Peter Bate announced that long before the arrival of Hitler, a white crowned head had pushed brutality to its paroxysm when Leopold II made up his mind that he should capitalize on the advent of automobile and bicycle industries in Europe and the United States and their subsequent huge demand for pneumatics. Peter Bate's documentary about the atrocities that the King of the Belgians committed against the populations of the Congo between 1895 and 1908 is very factual. Adam Hochschild's *King Leopold's Ghost* inspired most of Bate's relations.[10] Hochschild's book itself relied heavily on contemporaneous eyewitness accounts consigned in diaries, on exchanged correspondences, on commercial record keeping of the period, on contrapuntal analyses of colonists' narratives as well as explorers and seamen's memoirs, and on documents smuggled out of the Congo by remorseful employees in the colonies. Yet, as a Belgian paper, *La Gauche*, reported, not only has Leopold received praises and honors in his country for his actions in the Congo, but also "the press did not treat Hitler with as much rage and virulence as they did Patrice Lumumba," who, as first prime minister of independent Congo, dared question the inhumane conditions that Congolese have suffered in the hands of Leopold and Belgium's later rulers of the Congo. What had Lumumba done to the world to be so detestable? What sins had he committed that in Belgian judgment could be so atrocious as to win him "honors" which would make Leopold II, the trailblazer of Hitlerian cruelty, as well as Hitler himself, turn green of jealousy in their graves? The answer to these questions indubitably calls up a contrastive examination of two collective mentalities; the first one is a slave and colonial mentality. It devalues any non-white or non-western human being and can only see the non-white as an exploitable and throwaway product. The second one is an emancipated mentality. It is inherently committed — even before it has had the opportunity to see it couched on the pages of any declaration — to the maxim that human beings are endowed with inalienable rights for which it is worthy to fight and die. Lumumba belonged to the second order of men. Leopold II, King of the Belgians, belonged to the former. For Leopold II, as has been denounced by many, among whom George Washington Williams and E.D. Morel, who, through his Congo Reform Association, crusaded against the atrocious government of the Congo Free State, Africans, and especially Congolese, were no more than workhorses. While Morel was castigated and almost driven to insanity by Leopold's apologists for this denunciation, Lumumba was purely and simply murdered by Belgium and its allies for it.

Indeed, Leopold II, King of the Belgians, deserves a seat in the company of Hitler. Leopold, who never set foot in the Congo, was yet very present there. He had a good sense of the geography and social makeup of his African empire. From a continent away, he administered the Congo with the heavy fist of an omnipotent master. By Morel's very conservative estimations, at the time of its formation, the Congo Free State had a population that varied between 20 millions and 30 millions. By 1911, a census published in Britain but not in Belgium reported that the Congo's population dropped to 8 millions. During the twenty years that Leopold's exploitation of the Congo lasted, an estimated 10 million men, women, and children died from direct or accidental result of abuses suffered in the hands of Leopold's agents. These numbers, of course, have been challenged by many among whom Belgian historian Jean Stengers of the University of Brussels. In fact, Stengers disputed many of the claims advanced by Morel, and he did so with a charge of fanaticism more creditable to Belgian chauvinism and to attempt to restore a Belgian disgraced monarchy than to commitment to scientific accuracy. Stengers's best sources for countering Morel are high Belgian officials in the Congo; and despite "the elaborate veil of secrecy with which the high officials of the Congo Free State in Brussels conducted their master's [Leopold's] business," it is highly incongruous that Stengers should rely on their words more than he did those of the people committed to unveiling Leopold's crimes.

Obviously, in Stengers's view, Morel was too interested a party to remain objective. What could be the stakes that so blinded Morel as to make him lose all sense of impartiality? Was it a personal blood feud against the King of the Belgians, a dislike of Leopold that drove Morel to forego a stable career with Elder Dempster, a career with evident opportunities for promotion, only to brave the "avalanche of abuse, ridicule, scepticism, and suspicion" that came his way? "My knowledge of French," Morel wrote, "caused my services [at Elder Dempster] to be in frequent requisition. I was gradually entrusted with the supervision of the whole work, with its manifold ramifications."[11] What could make an ambitious young man in his early twenties who, after having lived "a boyhood clouded with poverty and not free of sickness," was finally getting a foot in the door, leave such a promising career and take issue with one of the most powerful monarchs of the twentieth century backed by his appreciative Belgian people? Could it be a British aversion toward Belgians, through their monarch? It was none of these. Justice, it was; justice for the people of the Congo and for all human beings in general. Stengers seemed very cynical about Morel's sense of Justice, and he exhibited very little faith in Morel's data. Oddly enough, while admitting the high degree of uncertainty that characterized demographic data collection in the Congo Free State — and the bad faith of official data collectors, a fact to which Stengers seemed to accord little or no attention — and despite the fact that travelers, missionaries, and penitent agents of Leopold's administration widely reported innumerable cases of carnage undertaken by Leopoldian agents in the Congo, Stengers would only settle for the lowest possible of the most conservative casualty estimations, going so far as to fall prey to one of the most bigoted hypotheses against whose perils Morel had warned. In fact, as has argued Morel, it would be absurd to want to compare the death tolls that Africans, by their intertribal wars, inflicted on themselves, to the systematic slaughter that Europeans, armed with technologically advanced weapons, were able achieve in Africa. In fact, for Africans to attain the level of killings scored by Europeans, they would have nothing else to do but war. For that, Africans would have to give up all forms of commercial, cultural, and subsistence activities, and just kill one another, day in and day out. Stengers's plea in favor of the King of the Belgians is of the most unscholarly, as he seemed to subscribe to this macabre hypothesis. One of Stengers's choice quotations in support of this thesis is from Grenfell, "a missionary of the greatest integrity," as he called him, who in 1890 had this to say of the Bolobo people of the Congo:

> It is rare indeed for Bolobo, with its thirty or forty thousand people, divided into some dozen clans, to be at peace for any length of time together. The

loss of life from the petty wars, the number of those killed for witchcraft, and those who are buried alive with the dead, involve, even within our narrow limits here at Bolobo, an almost daily drain upon the vitality of the country, and an incalculable amount of sorry and suffering.[12]

So, here we have it. Blame not the white man for the population decrease in the Congo. Blame the bloodthirsty and cannibalistic Congolese for exterminating one another. Also, blame their weak defense against tropical and a few imported diseases — the latter which are the inevitable lot of human encounters; but above all, blame not the white man for the black man's burden, for all the white man's actions put together are merely epiphenomenal and, as Stengers earnestly quoted from the most authorized report by the 1904-5 Commission of Inquiry on the Congo, confined in page 238 of the most official *Bulletin Officiel de L'État indépendant du Congo*, "*Toutes ces causes de dépopulation sont secondaires. L'action de tous ces facteurs réunis disparait presque en présence des ravages exercés, durant ces dernières années, par la variole et par la maladie du sommeil*"[13] (All these causes of population decrease are secondary. The actions of all these factors put together almost disappear in comparison with the ravages done, during these past years, by smallpox and sleeping sickness.) Stengers's fancy for reducing contemporaneous figures, gathered with the best possible means of the period, to their lowest possible significance as well as his deliberate, or perhaps involuntary, trivializing of the sufferings of the Congolese undermines the historical scholarship of his claims and lends more credence to figures put forth by scores of contemporaneous eyewitnesses' accounts of the Leopoldian system. It is highly incongruous that such a covetous man as Leopold, whose correspondences indicate unambiguously that he spent years scheming to hide from other European rulers his intention to dispossess other sovereigns of their treasures and lands, should suddenly be struck with a sense of philanthropy as he got his hands on the Congo. This is yet how Stengers urges us to understand Leopol'd intervention in the Congo: a philanthropic gesture of which, ultimately, Leopold personally profited not a single dime. After quoting an article of the *Bulletin Officiel de L'État indépendant du Congo* that exonerated Leopold, and after much circumlocution of his own, Stengers arrived at this colorful conclusion.

What [historians] have discovered so far tends to confirm the truth of the King's denials. The King invested enormous sums drawn from the Congo — especially the greatest part of the capital of the Congo loan — into public works and into foundations, such as the *Fondation de la couronne* and the *Fondation de Niederfullbach* destined to subsidise public works. He also reimbursed himself of a large part of the expenses he incurred in the Congo at the beginning of his enterprise. But the general balance of his personal expenditure and revenue in relation with the Congo does not seem to have been in his advantage ... Morel could not have known all this. It was the King's secret. But not all of the King's secret was black.[14]

At least, Stengers could not deny that Leopold drew enormous sums from the Congo. That he invested them in building Belgium is irrefutable; that he disinterestedly developed the Congo with these sums is a voluminous deception. That the Congolese paid the price of this majestic deception is without a shred of doubt. Stengers's critical notes lack balance and seek to force compassion toward a man and his system widely denounced by a variety of people with unrelated interests or no interests at all in the Congo as sadistic. Stengers's numbers are purely rhetorical and his so-called evidence in defense of Leopold is a fabrication of his nationalistic imagination.

Justifiably brushing aside Stengers's ill-disguised plea in favor of Leopold II as affected and thus deserving of no objective label, one will heretofore agree with the scores of incriminating testimonies against the Belgian monarchy that the Congo Free State was a slave camp of 10,000 black souls continually working in rubber plantations all year round and 10,000 men, women, and children kept in hostage houses yearly. A local squad of auxiliaries under the command of a few European soldiers was trained to insured that the native Congolese had no other occupation but to toil for Leopold. In fact, in the five years following the Berlin Conference, Leopold was able to raise an army of natives (called *capitas*) 5,000 troop-strong; which he progressively increased to 20,000 men. Armed with rifles and "a plentiful supply of ball cartridge," the role of these local soldiers was to terrorize villagers and submit them to Leopold's rules. One such rule was that

> Native rights in land were ... confined to the actual sites of the town of village, and the areas under food cultivation around them. Beyond those areas no such rights would be admitted. The land was "vacant," *i.e.* without owners. Consequently, the "State" was owner. The "State" was Leopold II.... Native rights in nine-tenths of the Congo being thus declared non-existent, it followed that the native population had no proprietary right in the plants and trees growing upon that territory, and which yielded rubber, resins, oils, dyes, etc.[15]

To supply the labor force necessary to harvest latex from the rubber vines growing on the stolen lands, Leopold's soldiers would round up villagers at gunpoint and make them work for no pay. In fact, these soldiers were to insure that the villagers neither cultivated, nor fish or hunt, as these activities of subsistence would distract them from working on Leopold's plantations. As if they had to pay Leopold in order to live on their own lands, in their own villages, in their own country, on their own continent, the Congolese were forced to pay rubber taxes (for farmers) ivory taxes (for hunters), and all sorts of taxes in the form of products; which ultimately prevented them

from owning anything that their ancestral land, waters or sky could yield. As
lamented a resigning Governor-General fed up with Leopold's regime, "[T]o
deny the natives the right to sell ivory and rubber produced by their forests
and plains belonging to their tribes, which forests and plains form part of
their hereditary natal soil and which they have traded from time immemorial, is a veritable violation of natural rights."[16] The petitioner of this letter
could not be more right. As redundant as this might sound, the Congo was
the land of the Congolese, and a land whose yields they had bartered for generations before the arrival of the white men. For the Congolese to be told that
activities of farming, fishing, hunting and bartering they had been freely practicing since as far back as they could remember were henceforth to be forcefully undertaken for the benefit of an invisible king in a remote country
beyond the seas was not well received. Many Congolese people resisted Leopold's abusive administration. For instance, at one time the Budja people
refused to work under such excessive conditions and rebelled, killing thirty
of their guards. The subsequent punitive expeditions that Canisius and two
other white officers commanding fifty black troops led resulted in a frenzied
slaughter. As Canisius proudly recorded, "we had killed over 900 natives,
men, women, and children." This was killing at a genocidal proportion, even
though, as Hochschild perceptibly underscores, the intention of the Leopoldian system was not genocidal per se, but rather — and incoherently, one
might add — one of finding cheap labor.

The more the Congolese rebelled against Leopold's orders, the harsher
the punishments came. Leopold's soldiers and agents executed their master's
instructions as if he were constantly observing them. They applied themselves
with the zeal and malice they knew their employer to like and to reward. "The
terror in the Congo was sanctioned by [Leopold]. For a white man to rebel
meant challenging the system that provided you your livelihood. By going
along with the system, you were paid, promoted, awarded medals."[17] To go
along was to take part in the regime of terror that Leopold instituted in the
Congo, and whose ultimate objective was to yield him immense wealth. It
meant seizing vacant as well as occupied lands from the Congolese in order
to develop lucrative rubber plantations. It meant raiding natives' granaries to
feed Leopold's soldiers rather than supplying them food on Leopold's budget.
It meant recruiting Africans at gunpoint to work as porters for Leopold's
thousands of missions or to die as slaves on rubber plantations. While
Leopold's white agents were rewarded with medals and bonuses proportion-
ate to productivity, the *capitas* or native soldiers were rewarded with permission to loot villages and rape native women. Leopold's punitive measures were
done with little if not any common sense at all. One could be mutilated or
killed for refusing to work; Children could be mutilated of both hands and

feet to force their recalcitrant parents to go to work. In a letter home, Mr. Clark, an American missionary wrote that "it is bloodcurdling to see the soldiers returning with hands of slain, and to find the hands of young children amongst the biggest ones ... the rubber traffic is steeped in blood."[18] The most current punishment was the raiding and burning down of whole villages. In the report of the British vice consul, Wilfred Thesiger, who, at the greatest embarrassment of Belgian officials visited the Congo for three months, traveling on the steamboat of American Presbyterians, one could read how hitherto prosperous Congolese villages had been reduced to smoldering deserts by Leopold's agents.

> The rubber tax was so heavy that the villages had no time to attend even to the necessities of life ... the company's armed soldiers stationed in the villages told me they had orders not to allow the natives to clear the ground for cultivation, to hunt, or to fish, as it took up time which should be spent in making rubber.... In consequence, their huts are falling to ruin, their fields are uncultivated, and the people are short of food ... and dying off.... This district was formerly rich in corn, millet, and other foodstuffs ... now it is almost desert.[19]

The native Congolese died by the millions under Leopold's brutal regime; and what of their surviving children? In fact, what of the Congolese children *tout court*? Leopold would "nurture" them as replacement laborers for those that toiled to death making him rich. "I believe," Leopold once wrote, "we must set up children colonies [each capable of housing 1500 children]. One in the Upper Congo near the equator, specifically military, with the clergy for religious instruction and for vocational education. One at Leopoldville under clergy with a soldier for military training. One at Boma ... to furnish us with soldiers."[20]

Leopold's insistence on the role of the clergy for the instruction of these children was not fortuitous. The Belgian clergy had received strict orders from Leopold, and, like his administrative agents and his soldiers, the Belgian missionaries were in the Congo to serve Leopold first and God last. "Unlike the Congo Protestant missionaries, who were foreigners and beyond Leopold's control, the Catholics were mostly Belgian and loyal to the king and his regime. Leopold subsidized the Catholics lavishly and sometimes used his financial power to deploy priests almost as if they were militaries."[21] With Leopold, Fanon's allegation that during the days of colonization religious and military powers conspired to dispossess and enslave Africans cannot reverberate any truer.[22] The instructions that Leopold gave to Belgian missionaries as they embarked for their proselytizing mission in the Congo were very telling. In 1935, Moukouani Muikwani Bukoko, a native Congolese, purchased a used Bible from a Belgian priest. He discovered, tucked between the pages, and certainly forgotten there by the priest, a copy of Leopold's mandate to his corrupt missionaries.[23] While he had wished to reject any responsibility for the atrocities that were taking place in the Congo on his behalf, insinuating that he had no personal knowledge of them, Leopold's recommendation to his priests proved that not only was the Belgian sovereign *au fait* of his agents' brutal methods, but he even engineered these methods and expected their implementation. This is what Morel dedicated his energy and resources to proving.

Outcries Over the Congo Free State

Three years before the first European war, Morel urged the Powers to convene an international conference on Africa in order to "elaborate a native policy toward Africa worthy of civilization," a conference whose resolution would be profitable to both the North and the South, as it would be "ministering to the peaceful future of [the peoples of Europe] as to that of the peoples of Africa."[24] Morel's outlook on the world was interestingly global. He refused to see the question of the Congo as an isolated, localized evil with no repercussions on Europe. If only for its own survival, he warned, Europe had to attend the Congo problem and find it a "civilized" resolution, for the chickens might come home to roost; the racial divide designed by Europe might not hold for eternity; and soon, a coalition of the invaded could threaten Europe.

> To-day, after long years of furious struggle with some of its peoples, long years of rough insolence towards others, White imperialism finds itself confronted with a racial force in Asia, which it can neither intimidate nor trample underfoot.... Do we hope that the "colour line," we ourselves have drawn so rigidly and almost universally, may operate between brown and yellow?[25]

Morel's effort was part of a larger movement of denunciation that started in the early days of Leopold's assassin regime. It is Morel, however, who, through his Congo Reform Movement, internationalized the outrage against the treatment of the native Congolese by the King of the Belgians. For that, Morel relied strongly on such precursory revelations as proffered by James Washington Williams, William Henry Sheppard, and Roger Casement as well as on sporadic condemnatory reports with, alas, very fleeting successes. The failure of the first critical reports to catch fire with the "international opinion," if such a thing existed at all, had a number of explanations: A powerful press bureau established by Leopold was in the business of discounting any accusation against the King as unserious and of humiliating any accuser; a mystified Belgian public constantly fed with news of their altruistic monarch found little reason to react to spasmodic disclosures of horrors in the Congo; a British opinion focused on rationalizing its own commitment with the Boer War in South Africa had little interest in stirring mud in Belgium; The British Royal family's personal strong ties with Leopold stifled any official intervention in Leopold's handling of the Congo; and King Leopold and his secretaries' daily refutations had such a tone of "virtuous indignation" and his "protestations of philanthropic intent were so earnest" that they created doubt and hesitation in some of the people who had the power to intervene.[26] Morel was able to keep his head afloat in spite of the wicked attacks that came his way from Leopold and his apologists, because he, unlike Williams and Sheppard, had a good organizational infrastructure at the service of his fight against the Leopoldian system.

Morel was like Leopold in that he had never set foot in the Congo; a fact which the overall hostile Belgian press as well as an international press sympathetic to Leopold used in their attempt to discredit him. Then in 1903, Morel met with Casement on the urging of a common friend, Herbert Ward, who had forwarded him a letter he received from Casement, a man he described as "absolutely good and honest and noble-minded" for the unprejudiced views he expressed about the administration of the Congo Free State. Upon meeting with Casement, Morel realized that the latter had as much admiration for him as Ward for Casement. "[Casement] told me that he was amazed to find that I, five thousand miles away, had come to conclusions identical with his in every respect on fundamental issues."[27] Commissioned by the British government to go to the Upper Congo in order "to acquire, by personal inspection, knowledge of the conditions of the enormous territories forming his district," Casement had left the lower Congo, where he was stationed as the British Consul, for the Upper Congo on June 5, 1903. Upon returning to Britain, Casement wrote a scathing report against the administrators of the Congo Free State, whom he charged of "grave maladmistration and ill-treatment." Perhaps, because, as a diplomat, it would be unfeasible for him to be leading a protest movement against a foreign monarch or maybe because he sensed that Morel, by the work relative to the Congo that he had already undertaken and the passion with which he went about his denunciations of Leopoldianism, was more ready than he, Casement begged Morel to found a movement that would bring down Leopold's sadistic regime in the Congo. "His suggestions were concrete. If Leopoldianism was to be overthrown, an organisation would have to be created, and I must be its creator. He would help."[28] In 1904, one year after Leopold and Casement had met in Ward's empty house in Chester Square for a long discussion and comparison of notes on the Congo, Morel created the Congo Reform Movement. The heartless practices that Casement witnessed during his three-month inspection in the Upper Congo, and which prompted his scornful report, had been

documented and brought to the world's attention more than ten years earlier
by a maverick man-of-a-thousand-trades, George Washington Williams.

Born on October 16, 1849, in Bedford Springs, Pennsylvania, Williams
was the eldest son of Thomas Williams, a freed slave, son of a rich planter,
and of Ellen Rouse, daughter of a Mulatto barber. After Thomas took to
drinking and was unable to care for his family, Ellen took her four children
to Pittsburgh, at her mother's. Young George was a troubled teenager, and
attempts to teach him barbering and religious faith were unsuccessful. At the
age of fifteen, George left home to make it on his own. Passing for older than
he was, he enrolled in the army to fight in the civil war, probably under the
name of William Steward or Charles Steward.[29] By Williams's own account,
he crossed the Rio Grande to lend a hand to Mexican Republicans overthrow
Maximilian rule after his enlistment in the American Northern army was
over. He then returned to his country after the war to take up career in the
regular peace time army on August 29, 1867. His dedication and good work
in the army won him a series of promotions until his discharged in 1865. The
long years of fighting had convinced Williams of the absurdity of killing, and
upon his discharge from the army, he sought ways of doing God's work. Under
the guidance of Baptist Minister Henry White, Williams was initiated to
priesthood. However, it is at Newton Theological Institute, in Cambridge,
Massachusetts, that the semiliterate Williams obtained his formal minister
degree after enormous efforts to catch up with classmates who had previously
attended such prestigious schools as Harvard, Amherst, Brown, Washington
University, Colby College, and the University of Vermont. "When Williams
went to Newton in 1874, [he] was semiliterate at best. By the time he grad-
uated, he had fully caught up with his classmates."[30] Henceforth equipped
with the knowledge afforded him by his college education and the compassion gained through his strong religious training, Williams went on to become
a successful clergyman and an advocate of blacks' rights.

By 1889, Williams had seen the end of his career in the United States.
The publication of his *History of the Negro Race in America from 1619 to 1880:
Negroes as Slaves, as Soldiers, and as Citizens* brought him fame and recognition as a historian of his race, nevertheless one whose reputation was also tarnished by vindictive reviewers whose pens spewed more venom than objective
literary assessments. His religious ministry to black Americans and his struggles for their rights became often enmeshed in partisan political bickering.
He often found himself leading a camp of black intellectuals fighting a mud-
slinging battle against another camp of black elites led by Frederick Doug-
las. In this and almost every partisan battle he waged, Williams ended up on
the losing side. One of Williams's most humiliating defeats was his appointment in 1885 by President Chester Arthur to be the United States resident

minister to Haiti in the last days of President Arthur's presidency; an appointment that the following administration recalled even before Williams had served a single day, though the Senate had confirmed him. By late 1885, prospects for promotion at home seemed bleak for Williams. It was a somewhat disenchanted and sickly Williams, seeking other ways to recapture his reputation and regenerate his work for the advancement of the blacks, that sailed to Brussels, uninvited, to take part in the Antislavery Congress that was to be held there in 1889. Brussels was also a break in his journey toward the Congo, which he intended to visit "in order to further his notion that American blacks should help improve conditions there,"[31] as they would also improve their own conditions and gain leadership in ways that were impossible for them in the United States. Williams had shared that idea with Leopold II, who had found it excellent.

In Brussels, Williams was able to secure an audience with Leopold and interview him for the Associated Literary Press, whose founder, S.S. McClure, had commissioned Williams to write him a few articles relative to the Antislavery Congress in Brussels. From this interview, Williams retained a very affirmative impression of Leopold, whom he qualified in the most gratifying terms.[32] Williams's initial efforts to recruit Americans of African descent to work for Leopold in the Congo took place at Hampton Institute during a series of lectures. Soon, it became obvious from the audience's questions that Williams was lecturing about a place he knew almost nothing of. So, he set about to rectify this lacunae by visiting the Congo and by assessing the conditions there for himself before committing any American blacks to work for Leopold. In the meantime, he had also requested a meeting with American president Harrison, to whom he had disclosed his project and whose support he was wishing to obtain. However, for President Harrison to back such a project would imply that he should also ratify the Berlin Act that allowed Leopold to take possession of the Congo; President Harrison was not prepared to do that, and Williams hoped that were he to go to the Congo and bring back reassuring news, then perhaps President Harrison would reconsider his position. So, it was also with the hope of easing President Harrison's misgivings that Williams sailed back to Brussels, en route to Africa, on December 1889. Williams's plan to conduct an exploratory trip in the Congo met with strong opposition in Brussels. As long as Williams was writing Leopold's eulogies in the United States, he was royally tolerable; but Leopold could not bear that Williams should go to the Congo with the declared purpose of investigating treatments of natives by his agents. Leopold seemed to know what Williams would find in the Congo Free State and was not enthusiastic to see him undertake his trip. Williams was determined, and when Leopold failed to dissuade him, the King of the Belgians simply forbade him to use state steamboats.

Williams, Leopold suggested in no ambiguous terms, could only travel on missionary boats. Williams did go to the Congo, among other places in Africa, traveling on Dutch boats. Leopold insistence that he should avoid the Congo and the King's sudden irascibility toward Williams aroused the latter's suspicion that the King of the Belgians had something to hide to the world. Williams's intuition turned out true. What he saw in the Congo horrified him. What Williams wrote about natives' conditions in the Congo and the spirit of Leopold II was a far cry from his previous acclamation of the Congo as a thriving nation under the compassionate care of the King of the Belgians. The Congo that Williams visited was a huge slave camp, and Leopold II, King of the Belgians, was an enormous vampire feeding on the sweat and blood of the Congolese people. In *An Open Letter to His Majesty Leopold II, King of the Belgians and Sovereign of the Independent State of the Congo*, Williams indicted Leopold of "crimes against humanity," and demanded that he be brought before an international tribunal to answer for crimes.[33] After recalling all the "praiseful" things he had said and written about Leopold as based on his belief, at that time, that Leopold's "government was built upon the enduring foundation of *Truth, Liberty, Humanity* and *Justice*," Williams proffered twelve specific charges against Leopold and his "unwise, complicated and stupid dual Government of the State of Congo."

1. In the Congo, Leopold has bitten more than he could swallow. Leopold's claim on the vast territory of the Congo is too ambitious. He actually lacks the means to implement order and develop the region in such a way that would improve the lives of the natives.
2. Leopold's government has instituted lawlessness, arbitrariness, injustice and murder as State policy.
3. Leopold's government has persistently engaged in breach of contracts it signed with black soldiers and machine workers.
4. Leopold's legal system in the Congo was prejudiced, deceptive and corrupt.
5. Leopold's governments and agents were continually committing against the natives excessive acts of cruelty and inhumanity that would not be conceivable in Europe.
6. Leopold's government was guilty of promoting prostitution and sex slavery, whereby individuals were paid to capture indigenous women or incarcerate them under false charges just for the purpose of sexually gratifying Leopold's white agents. Whenever children were born from these forced rapports, they would be considered government properties and thus, later, forced to work for Leopold.

7. Leopold's government forbade natives to trade while his agents were encouraged and rewarded to raid villages and seize villagers' goods.

8. Leopold violated the fundamental terms of the Berlin Act by which the Powers permitted him to acquire the Congo.

9. Leopold's government would arm villages to fight one another so that war prisoners could be utilized as forced laborers for Leopold. In the process, Leopold's government encouraged mutilation and cannibalism of natives by Bangala soldiers.

10. Leopold's government bought, sold, and stole slaves.

11. Leopold armed Arabs in territories where he had no jurisdiction.

12. Leopold, Stanley, and his agents have alienated the natives, who would therefore not respond spontaneously to their authorities or to any program they could put forth. Leopold's sanctimonious claims of improving the lives of the natives constituted an outright fraud. "Trade in the Upper Congo consists only of ivory and rubber. The first is old, the latter is poor." There was no real development taking place in the Congo that would benefit the natives. Consequently, "Emigration [could not] be invited to this country for many years."

These charges, Williams assured, were not made frivolously. They were rather meticulously examined.

> [A] list of competent and veracious witnesses, documents, letters official records and data has been faithfully proposed, which will be deposited with her Brittanic [sic] Majesty's Secretary of State for Foreign Affairs, until such time as an International Commission can be created with power to send for persons and papers, to administer oaths, and attest the truth or falsity of these charges.[34]

As Leopold and his army of apologists braced themselves for a vigorous and merciless rebuttal of the charges proffered against the King, they could not know that the King's principal accuser did not have much longer time remaining. Williams's body had already started to wither under the effects of a lingering disease. In 1891, at age forty-one, Williams lost his last battle to tuberculosis.

However, his denunciations of Leopold's murderous regime in the Congo were by then widely read and reacted upon both in the United States and in Europe. From press rooms to the Belgian parliament, the effects of Williams's letter were felt. The barrage of insults and defamations that were launched against Williams, the "Colonel noir," the "so-called-'colonel,'" the "insolent and insulting," the "totally illiterate," who "has never held even the lowest rank in the United States Army," did little to keep Leopold's hitherto immaculate reputation intact. Leopold's image was stained, and his rule in the Congo became a matter of interrogations both at home and abroad. Williams's *Open Letter* had inspired many a crusader against Leopold's government. Yet no mention of it was ever made by those who would later come to fight the battle that Williams had initiated. Casement certainly had heard of Williams's report, read it, and used it as a roadmap in his own investigations, as he could not have ignored the firestorm that the report unleashed in Europe. If there is something depressing to be told about the collective outcry that Leopold's horrors in the Congo generated, it is that in all of the voices that worked in unison for justice, a great injustice was perpetrated, once again, against a black voice, one of the first voices to sound the alarm about the plight of their African brothers and sisters. Casement's acknowledgement of Williams's contribution to the fight against Leopoldianism came, perhaps, in this circumlocutory whim that he offered in a 1904 letter to Morel, when he wondered — in a moment of lament for his own health — whether there were not "some extraordinary Fate which seems to protect Leopold and ruin — or greatly injure those who are trying to expose him."[35] Had Williams been alive at the moment of the creation of the Congo Reform Movement, perhaps his greatest consolation would have been that finally, no matter what had become of his own name in history, the world was paying attention to what was going on in the Congo.

Upon meeting Casement, Morel became ever more obsessed with the Congo. "The Congo already lay like an incubus upon my path. It was invading my sources of livelihood.... It was seriously interfering with the conduct of the weekly newspaper.... I was raising up formidable enemies against the paper's prospects."[36] On the other hand, however, Morel was also rounding up prominent allies in his campaign against Leopoldianism. In the United States, his campaign was catching steam thanks to the devotion of American journalist Robert E. Park, who took upon himself to organize the Congo Reform Movement in the U.S. René Claparède successfully represented the movement in Switzerland; Pierre Mille and Emile Vandervelde respectively supervised the movement's actions in France and Belgium, and the Archbishop of Canterbury landed his visibility and authority. Though not so generous as Morel would have wished them to be, donors, too, were supporting the Congo Reform Movement. Morel's greatest allies were the eyewitnesses to the Congo horrors who contributed anecdotes to his campaign. Soon after he left Elder Dempster for their collusion with Leopold, and especially exceeded with their repeated attempts to bribe him, Morel created the *West African Mail*, a weekly paper, thanks to financial help from John Holt, a British businessman. The *West African Mail* became the principal outlet for Morel's campaign, but, also, it became the channel of grievances for people who had for long silenced their opinion of Leopoldianism in the Congo.

Soon, Morel's paper started receiving invaluable stories and pictures from repentant agents, traveling observers, missionaries in the Congo, and even Africans. One such African was a Nigerian shopkeeper Ezekiah Andrew Shanu born in Lagos in 1858. Shanu was a successful entrepreneur in Boma, patronized by mostly whites, he witnessed many abuses of Congolese and sent damning information to Morel. Betrayed by an informant, Shanu was ruined and driven to suicide in 1905.

A Disconsolate Monarch

Morel's publication of the stories and pictures he received from his many sources caused many people in Britain, both commoners and political figures, to start questioning Leopold's real motives in the Congo. The King's first response was reactive. His friends circled the wagons in his defense, launching attacks at Morel and at Great Britain, which they accused of trying to oust Belgium from the Congo in order to occupy its place. Nevertheless, the suspicion against Leopold was reaching home, too. Socialist deputies in the Belgian Chamber pressed Leopold to respond to the charges leveled against him by the Congo Reform Association by investigating the alleged crimes. On July 24, 1904, Leopold appointed a three-person commission by decree to look into the accusations. This was a gesture more intended to appease the critics than to find facts — or so Leopold had hoped. The Commission's report, which after much delay and doctoring was finally published in the Official Bulletin of the Congo Free State on October 1905, was, nevertheless, a disappointing blow to Leopold. The crimes uncovered, though not directly imputable to Leopold in person, were atrocious enough to stir some agitation in the Belgian Parliament and to give impetus to the question of Belgium's takeover of the Congo Free State from Leopold's private hands. On March 2, 1906, the Belgian Chamber voted to annex the Congo despite Prime Minister Smet de Maeyer's vigorous plea in favor of Leopold II. However, before the annexation of the Congo could be effective, an embittered Leopold rushed to create three monopolistic companies in the Congo, whose assets would directly go to the preservation of the *Domaine de la Couronne*, a vast territory totaling ⅓ of the Congo, which he had altered his will to keep as part of his private domain even in case of a takeover of the Congo by the Belgian government. One of these companies, the *Union Minière du Haut Katanga* will have a great role in changing the tides of the second European War by supplying the United States with the necessary uranium for the atomic bomb that destroyed the Japanese cities of Hiroshima and Nagasaki.[37] Leopold's desperate act of defiance against the Belgian government caused him to lose even some of his strongest supporters in the Chamber. Exasperated conservatives and Catholics finally joined Liberals and Socialists and defeated the pro-Leopold government. Parliament finally succeeded in suppressing the Crown Foundation. A disconsolate Leopold was paid fifty million francs by Belgium to give away the Congo Free State — more a consolation prize than "a token of the nation's gratitude"; for till then, Belgium was convinced that the Congo was a burden. On October 18, 1908, Belgium officially annexed the Congo.

The Last Shudders of Paternalism

Leopold's unenthusiastic betrothing of his Congolese empire to Belgium did not, however, put an end to the atrocities in the Congo, though it lessened them. Perhaps, the Congo was no longer at the mercy of a madman with genocidal impulses. Nevertheless, it was not paradise either. This is why Morel did not stop his anti–Congo campaign right after Leopold's death. For Morel, the fight had to be directed no longer at Leopold, but, henceforth, at the Belgian government for a betterment of the Congolese's conditions. By that time, however, many of Morel's supporters were willing to see in the annexation act the turning of the ugly page of the Congo's history, and they were less eager to continue Morel's battle. On December 17, 1909, King Leopold passed away. Morel's friends and supporters started pressuring him to stop beating a dead horse and to wind up his campaign. In June 1913, the Congo Reform Movement was dissolved over a self-congratulatory note. The Congolese, however, continued to endure atrocities under the new regime as the world gradually turned its gaze away from the Congo and little by little let the lingering Congolese tragedy slip into oblivion.

Leopold II's reign over the Congo should unquestionably make him the road companion of the most efficacious genocidal minds in history. Yet it is not to Leopold but, rather, to Lumumba that the majority of the Belgian media bestowed this somber tribute. Lumumba's most unpardonable sin, which caused the press to treat him with "more rage and virulence" than they did Hitler, which ultimately led to his assassination, was to have destroyed a Grand Belgian Imaginary-Ideal, but also, and more importantly, to have been in the way of Western financial interests. As is evidenced in the works of such scholars as Martelli and Stengers, for instance, long after the denunciations of the Williams, Sheppard, Shanu, Casement, and Morel, and despite the overwhelming substantiations that the crusaders for justice in the Congo proffered, and which demonstrated that Leopoldianism was a brutal and murderous system implanted in the Congo for the self-aggrandizement of the King of the Belgians, an image of Leopold as a saint still persists in the collective imaginary of Belgians to this day. In the early 1960s, the cult of Leopoldianism was still very fresh in the imaginary of the Belgians, and it found its strongest expression in the speech that Leopold's great grand-nephew, King Baudouin, delivered in Leopoldville on the occasion of the celebration of the Congo's independence. Baudouin's speech articulated the paternalism that had defined Belgium's policy in the Congo from the annexation to independence, and which was no more than the legacy of Leopoldianism.

In fact, as has been observably argued by many critics, the annexation of the Congo by Belgium did not necessarily usher in a peaceful era for the Congolese.[38] The colonial constitution pompously called *la Charte Coloniale*, which was created right after the Belgian government's annexation of the Congo, was publicized as a set of measures intended to do away with the atrocities suffered by the natives during the regime of Leopold and to introduce a kinder gentler government in the lives of the Congolese populations. Nevertheless, the Charter was no more than a carefully designed statement drafted by men many of whom were shareholders in Belgian companies with interests in the Congo. In fact, the Colonial Charter even kept the authority of the king intact; the king was able to appoint administrators to the Congo, albeit through parliamentary consent. Consequently, the charter was a mere smokescreen intended to continue Leopoldianism by just smoothing a few edges of the subjugation machinery. In fact the central pillars of Leopold's abusive system remained, which constituted the foundation upon which the administration of the Belgian Congo would function until 1960. Economically, as in the days of Leopoldianism, the Congo was to function as a source of wealth accumulation for Belgium. So, from 1906 onward most of the Congolese economy was transformed from a life sustaining system to an export economy. The Belgian government replaced Leopold's forced labor with a system of taxation and obligation to the state. The colonial administration required native populations to work at least 120 days for the state in various sectors. This scheme continued to supply the Belgian government with free labor, while, on the other hand, increasing the misery of the natives. Not having enough time to devote to their own subsistence activities, many families, once again, died of hunger and diseases, while the implantation of capitalist models with their focus on intense productivity continued to enrich the Belgian state and the capitalists associated with its ventures in the Congo.

Agriculture was transformed from the cultivation of small family plots to the exploitation of huge state or commercial plantations for cash crops or exports crops. The introduction of new farming methods and the training of native Congolese in the use of these new techniques helped intensify productivity while preserving soil quality. The Congolese forests and soil, too, were exploited to satisfy the profitable metropolitan commodity market. Timber was cut, and cobalt, copper, zinc, gold, iron, silver, and diamonds were mined at vertiginous industrial scales by such companies as the *Société Internationale Forestière et Minière (Forminière)* and Union *Minière du Haut Katanga*, both created by Leopold in 1906. The Congo was internationalized enough — or to put it in contemporary jargon, globalized enough — to profit many countries. Major economic powers (Great Britain, France, Germany, Australia) benefited from businesses in the Belgian Congo through the commercial interests that individual investors had with Belgian companies operating in the Congo. Some prominent names with ancient vested interests in the Congo were the Ryan and Guggenheim groups (involved in diamond mining) and the Rockefeller group (involved in industry, commerce, agriculture, and finance of public works).[39]

The intensive commercial exploitation of the Congo for Western capitalist nations and its consequent disruption of natives' ways did not always meet the agreement of local chiefs, who were more inclined to resist and sabotage the Belgian government's heavy demand of labor than to collaborate. In order to minimize disruption and insure maximum output, the colonial administration replaced many local chiefs with their own salaried appointees. These appointees had no real authority on the populations and were often unnecessarily discourteous and violent. They further estranged the natives and intensified resentment toward the colonial administration and especially toward the colonial paternalistic stance. It is on this resentment that future anti-colonial struggles led by young educated Congolese or *évolués* would draw. Colonial paternalism entailed that Africans were big children to be cared for by Europeans, as fathers would care for their offspring. In that perspective, Africans' needs, be they material, moral or spiritual needs, will be taught to them by state and parastatal organizations. Learning to produce in order to feed these needs are thus affirmative skills to possess; but these skills, Africans will acquire them by first producing for the benefit of the state rather than for their own benefit. By employing Africans as free labor, the thinking then goes, the state is not depriving them of any rights; on the contrary, the state is serving them; for eventually, the skills acquired will serve the Africans. However, to work for the state supposes that one produce at large scale and no longer at the indolent pace of subsistence economy that had maintained the natives in the primitive age. Of course, some old habits will have to be broken and new ones learned; and this is a violent process both figuratively, by the psychological distress it causes, and literally, by the muscled intervention of the *Force Publique* (colonial military force led by European officers) that it often unleashes. But this violence is necessary for the perfection of the native as a father's "tough love" is essential for the development of his child.

Laboring under difficult conditions will teach the natives work ethics and civism, which are civilized moral qualities. However, it is to the priests and the missionaries that the real spiritual education of the natives will be left; this explains the threefold requisite of state, military, and religious interventions in the colonial government.

On June 30, 1960, King Baudouin I, who was still trapped in the Belgian colonialist state of mind, tried to rationalize this paternalistic paradigm that his great grand-uncle Leopold II initiated in the Congo, appealing to the newly created Congolese independent government and the Congolese masses to work for its continuance. Baudouin's speech denoted either the monarch's utter loss of touch with Congolese reality or his sheer lack of knowledge of historical facts, and especially his lack of education about the empire that his great grand-uncle could have bequeathed him had it not been for the international outrage that forced Belgium to snatch the Congo from his deadly hands. Some of the many historical contradictions in Baudouin's speech ought to be unveiled here.[40]

Fiction: Baudouin praises Leopold II as a benefactor-genius who designed a great future for the people of Congo.

Fact: Leopold was indeed a genius for having engineered some of the most intelligent schemes to deceive the European powers at the Berlin Conference and take possession of more than 1 million square miles of territory in Africa. His genius, however, was never at the service of the Congolese. It served his aggrandizement and his country's prosperity. Never had Leopold envisaged the independence of the Congo. It is a forced act by Belgian Parliament that caused Leopold to release his clutches on his African empire.

Fiction: According to Baudouin, the greatest sacrifice was consented by Belgium for sending the best of its sons in the Congo to work on the betterment of the Congolese people.

Fact: This is a chilling statement on the moral fiber of the Belgians. If Leopold's government in the Congo was run by the most compassionate of Belgians, what is there to say, then, of the ordinary Belgians, when it is proven that under the ruthless rule of Belgium's "best sons," 10 million Congolese died of exhaustion in slave fields and of starvation and diseases from land dispossession? Indeed, Congolese, not Belgians, paid the heaviest price for Leopold's insatiability.

Fiction: According to Baudouin, his great grand-uncle freed the Congo Basin from slavery.

Fact: The Congo was Leopold's huge slave camp. In fact, in his open letter to Leopold, George Washington Williams accused Leopold of violation of the principle of the Berlin Act that permitted Leopold's occupation of the Congo. Some of the provisions of the Act were to work at eradicating slav-

ery, to establish free trade in the Congo, and to improve the conditions of
the natives. Leopold did none of these. Instead, he instituted his own brand
of slavery in the Congo; he forbade the natives from engaging in any kind of
intertribal commerce or from undertaking any kind of trade with the Europeans. Under Leopold's rule the living conditions of the native populations
of the Congo worsened.

Fiction: Leopold, Baudouin would have us believe, unified the diverse
ethnic groups of the Congo.

Fact: Leopold played the "ethnic card" very well. He used tribal differences to his advantage, arming one tribe against another. In fact, the fierce
Bangala people were preferred as *capitas,* and they were encouraged to rape,
torture, kill, and cannibalize recalcitrant Congolese's family members. This
was all part of the *Divide and Rule* policy, which persisted in the Belgian
Congo. "It was the policy of the Belgians to garrison the provinces with soldiers from another part of the Congo, who would not therefore have to take
action against their own tribesmen."[41] During the pre-independence moment,
this caused political parties to function less along nationalist lines than along
the axis of ethnic considerations as movements opposed to Belgians or to ethnic groups that, in particular regions, were auxiliaries of the central Belgian
power. In fact, the politics of *Divide and Rule* commenced in the Congo by
Leopold and continued by the Belgian government is greatly responsible for
the balkanization of the Congo that would take place in the post-independence era.

Fiction: Leopold, Baudouin asserts, has enriched the material and moral
heritage of the Congolese.

Fact: Leopold brought immorality, cupidity, and division to the Congo.
Nothing of his moral disposition is worth retaining as the measure of ethics.

Fiction: Belgium has modernized agriculture and exploited the Congo's
minerals for the betterment of the Congolese people's standard of leaving.

Fact: The modernization of Congolese agriculture was meant to change
agricultural methods so as to satisfy the European commodity market. The
transformation of the Congo's subsistence economy into export economy had
little to do with enriching the Congolese people. It was meant for Belgium's
development. Likewise, the intense exploitation of Congolese minerals benefited more Western countries than it did the Congo. In the 1940s, mining in
the Congo has largely contributed to sustaining the economies of Western
countries after the war.

Fiction: Baudouin affirms that the independence of the Congo was
greeted by Belgium with much enthusiasm.

Fact: Baudouin fails to mention the struggle for independence, the harassment, imprisonment, and torture of Congolese freedom fighters by Belgian

authorities. The truth of the matter is that Belgium never wanted the Congo to be an independent nation. The potato just got too hot to handle; and, as we shall see in this chapter, after the Congo's independence, Belgium continued to plot for the re-colonization of the Congo.

Fiction: For Baudouin, the Congolese's real friends are the Belgians. So, the Congolese, who are still inexperienced in self-government, should not hesitate to come to "Papa Belgium" for advice on how to govern their newly independent nation.

Fact: Congolese are not children, and Belgium is not their father. Congolese have the right to choose their friends. Furthermore, before the bloody rule of Leopoldianism, the Congo was a self-governed entity where various societies, with sophisticated economic, political and social organizations, lived in good intelligence for centuries. It is Leopold's centralized rule, and later the Belgian centralized administration of the Congo that disrupted the Congolese societal organizations.

Fiction: Baudouin warns that many European countries have their eyes on the Congo. So as not to fall in the trap of these countries, Congolese authorities should constantly consult with Belgian authorities.

Fact: Yes, the Congo is rich; and its wealth attracts much covetousness from Western countries. However, Belgium has shown that it cannot be trusted any more than these other Western countries. Congolese authorities will use their own judgment in deciding who to trust.

Fiction: Baudouin asserts that Belgium has trained sophisticated minds that are ready to assume the stewardship of the Congo.

Fact: "From the very days of Leopold's regime, Catholicism has been the predominant influence in Congolese education."[42] However, Catholic missionaries in the Congo were, in their great majority, corrupt clergymen, who had pledged total allegiance to Leopold. The missionaries' interpretation of Belgian patriotism clouded their sense of duty to the spiritual cause. As notes Hennessy, even in South Africa were all possible efforts were made to prevent blacks from having easy access to education and, thus, to emancipation, Catholic missionaries were providing intellectual training to blacks in ways that would be inconceivable by Catholic missionaries in the Congo. In South Africa, it is Catholic education that has produced the love of country and nationalism that ultimately led to emancipation.[43] On the other hand,

> [It] has been avowed very truthfully that the Catholic missionaries in the Congo were Belgians first and Catholics afterwards.... The Primary education system of the Belgians, and the technical training which accompanied it, created in the Congo a lower middle class, but no professional class which could have taken over the reins of government in a crisis. The limit to which this was carried can best be judged from the almost unbelievable fact that, at present moment, there is not a single trained Congolese lawyer."[44]

This was 1961, and though many of the factors that led to the failed Congolese independence were also ascribable to the unpreparedness of the Congolese leaders, to suggest that, the Congo, on account of the *naïveté* of its leaders,
was not yet ready for independence would lead one right into the trap of Belgian authorities. Congolese leaders' inexperience had been deliberately planned
by the educational system in Belgian Congo in order to delay the Congolese's
emancipation. In the end, that political immaturity played in favor of the Belgians' visceral resentment of the Congo's independence.

The hard facts of Congolese's daily lives from 1885 to 1960 were there
to be seen, which blatantly contradicted Baudouin's recollection of the Congo's
history. Perhaps — and this needs not be taken as an insinuation that it would
have doused Belgium's intent to see independence fail so that Belgians could
re-colonize the Congo under the pretext of rescuing the Congolese — on June
30, 1960, they needed not be thrown with so much bitterness at the face of
Belgium, and especially of Baudouin, who was after all, on that day, independent Congo's guest. Lumumba's impetuous rejoinder to Baudouin's distressed,
paternalistic lecture spoke more of the Congolese prime minister's political
immaturity. Baudouin's sermon was the last shudder of Belgium's dying colonialism. Lumumba did not have to retort with the hotheadedness of a rebel.
Yet, one of Lumumba's greatest imperfections, despite his many qualities, is
that he was always clothed in the garb of a rebel, even as the prime minister
of an independent country expected to establish diplomatic and economic
alliances.

In his film *Lumumba*, Raoul Peck clearly captured the leadership traits
of Lumumba and his unwavering passion for a free Congo; but Peck also projected the impulsive and, sometimes even, reckless side of Lumumba's character through the superb rendition of Congolese actor Eriq Ebouaney. Patrice
Emery Lumumba was born on July 2, 1925, in Eastern Kasai, at Katako
Kombe. At the age of twenty, Lumumba, who had dropped out of missionary schools, had only an elementary school education and was trying to teach
himself by reading extensively everything he could get his hands on, and by
joining many of Stanleyville's liberal discussion groups. From these discussion groups, Lumumba developed a sociable character, a keen sense of obser-
vation, and the early bearing of a leader. In Stanleyville, Lumumba was already
chairing as many as seven associations, but above all, he was the chairman of
the *Association des Évolués*, a group of Congolese middle-class civil servants.
As such, Lumumba visited Belgium for a month thanks to a government
sponsored tour. In Belgium, he had the opportunity to see another side of
Belgians and to understand that there was considerable support abroad for
Africa's autonomy. Lumumba's Belgian visit comforted his nationalistic views
upon his return to the Congo, and his greater-than-before activism won him

registration in the black book of the colonial administration. He was deemed "subversive," which at the time meant frequenting Liberals and Socialists. In fact, as a member of the *Cercle liberal de Stanleyville*, Lumumba had the opportunity of meeting the liberal Belgian minister to the colonies of the time, Auguste Buissert, who took him under his wing and even thought of appointing him as the first Congolese on his staff. Certainly frowned upon by the white elite of Stanleyville, Buissert's idea never materialized, and, instead, Lumumba accepted a job as a post-office clerk. In the introductory soliloquy that starts *Lumumba*, the film, Lumumba recognizes that Stanleyville holds no future for him, as he gets off a bus at Leopoldville. This is because, in 1957, accused of embezzling post office funds, Lumumba was arrested and jailed for a two-year sentence in Stanleyville, a prison term of which he only served a little over six months thanks to a campaign for his release organized by his liberal friends in Belgium as well as in the Congo. Upon his release from jail, Lumumba, seeing no prospect for a respectable career in Stanleyville, purchased a one-way bus ticket to Leopoldville. There, he took a job as a public relation man for Bracongo, a local brewery that was in a fierce competition with Bralima. His mission was to reverse the declining sale trend of *polar*, Bracongo's signature beer. *Primus*, the competition beer from Bralima, was waging a dirty war against *polar*, alleging that the consumption of the latter rendered consumers impotent. Lumumba was not only expected to erase that popular gossip from the imaginary of the Congolese masses, but his employers also expected him to establish the *polar* as the premier beer. With charisma and humor Lumumba succeeded.

Joseph-Désiré Mobutu (Alex Descas) meets Patrice Lumumba (Eriq Ebouaney) for the first time, as the latter is doing one of his promotion pitches for the polar beer. Bartender is unidentified (*Lumumba*, directed by Raoul Peck, Haiti, France, Belgium, 2000).

The days and nights Lumumba spent scouring the popular local bars and nightclubs of Leopoldville to sell his beer sharpened the social and oratory skills he had already developed in Stanleyville and brought him closer to the masses and the *évolués* of Leopoldville. In 1956, Lumumba founded the MNC (*Mouvement National Congolais*). Either for practical reasons or for his resolute belief in national imperatives, Lumumba envisioned his movement to go beyond ethnic and regional considerations. In fact, before the MNC, most political associations in the Congo functioned on the basis of cultural or ethnic appurtenance. For instance, Joseph Kasavubu's Abako (*Association pour la Sauvegarde de la culture et des intérêts des Bakongo*) founded in 1950 was primarily concerned with preserving the proud cultural and ethnic heritage of the prosperous agricultural and trading fifteenth century Kongo Kingdom that gave its name to the country. Moïse Tshombe's Conakat (*Confédération des Associations Tribales du Katanga*) drew its constituency from the tribes of the Katanga, and Jason Sendwe's Balubakat drew its membership from the Baluba people of Northern Katanga. By the late 1950s, however, a new consciousness had emerged in the Congo, especially in light of the wave of African independences and the Accra Pan-African Conference, which was more inclined to see the Congo as a nation than as an aggregate of tribes and ethnic groups. Many people belonging to this new spirit of political activism joined Lumumba's MNC and made it one of the most important parties, if not the major party, in the Congo. Soon, however, the MNC was going to fall prey to geopolitics.

Lumumba's popularity with the masses started to cause much jealousy among the other Congolese *évolués*, even among those leaders that were active members of the MNC, and before long, the MNC split along ethnic lines. In December 1958, Lumumba, along with two of his companions, Joseph Ngalula and Gaston Diomi, were allowed to attend the All-African People's Conference organized in Accra by Kwame Nkrumah, the leader of newly independent Ghana. At the Pan-African conference, Lumumba had the opportunity to rub elbows, not just with the Ghanaian leader, but also, with such prominent black political actors as Sékou Touré of Guinea and Frantz Fanon of Martinique/Algeria. Accra fortified Lumumba's standing at home and internationally, but also it brought him many foes that disliked his rising popularity and were suspicious of the special treatment the minister of the colonies seemed to give him. Why was Lumumba, as the leader of the MNC, allowed by the minister of the colonies to go to Accra while leaders of other political parties, such as Tshombe or Kasavubu were refused authorization to make the trip? In Peck's *Lumumba*, the suggestion is that the leader of the MNC got this preferential treatment for selling the beer of the minister of the colonies; a fact Lumumba did not seem to be aware of, as he appeared baffled by the allegation made by leaders of the other parties. While this could explain the choice of Lumumba for Accra, there could be a more strategic motive behind the Belgian administration's preference of Lumumba to represent the Congolese *évolués* at the Pan-African conference: the desire to have a moderate, rather than a radical anti-colonial, Congolese leader in Accra. From this perspective, it would be fair to say that Maurice van Hemelrijck, the Belgian minister to the colonies who signed Lumumba's authorization, was a very progressive man, though the Belgian administration that employed him could view him as a *saboteur* of Belgian interests in the Congo.

Hemelrijck was a convert of Joseph van Bilsen, a Belgian professor at the Institute for Colonial Studies of the University of Antwerp, who had published a thirty-year plan for the gradual emancipation of the Congo. Van Bilsen's thesis was that the Congo would need thirty years to create properly educated leaders capable of filling the void left by any eventual withdrawal of the colonial administration. Though criticized in Belgian radical milieus as being anti-colonial, van Bilsen's plan seduced Hemelrijck, who was a proponent of authorized, but controlled, nationalism for the Congolese. In fact, Hemelrijck's moderate administration of the Congo caused many Belgians to distrust him. Hemelrijck was heckled and called the unflattering sobriquet of *Momo la terreur,* "a nickname which was supposed to indicate that he was recklessly encouraging political advancement in the Congo."[45] Among the Congolese who endorsed van Bilsen's plan were leaders of the *Conscience Africaine,* a group of moderate Catholic liberals among whom Joseph Ngalula, who will later join Lumumba's MNC and accompany him to Accra. A more radical reception of van Bilsen's paper came from Abako leaders, and especially from Kasavubu, who on August 23, 1956, publicly rejoined with a more radical proposal of his own that fell short of asking full and immediate independence.

In fact, Peck's *Lumumba* does not do justice to Kasavubu. In the film Kasavubu, played by Congolese actor Maka Kotto, is an obese, amorphous character with no decision-making ability that seemed to agree with every proposition the colonial administration would put forth. In *Lumumba,* the movie, the first glance viewers get of Kasavubu is during the emergency Independence Political Roundtable that takes place in Brussels at the initiative of the Belgian government. The almost inattentive, soft-spoken, and idle Kasavubu could hardly be thought to have played an important role in the events that precipitated the Brussels independence negotiations that gathered Belgian authorities and more than forty Congolese party leaders. Yet it was Kasavubu, as leader of the Abako movement, who instigated the passing of Belgium's paternalism by calling for immediate independence for the Congo. Abako, founded in 1950 by Edmond Nzeza-Nlandu, was no more than a cultural movement until Kasavubu took over its leadership in 1956. It is Kasavubu's radical rejoinder to van Bilsen's pamphlet that put Abako on the map as a political party. In fact, in his written response to van Bilsen's plan Kasavubu did not ask for the Congo's independence but for Congolese's rights to create several political parties when it was obvious that the time called for a unified front against Belgium.

Actually, until the independence of the Congo, and even after independence, Kasavubu had not shaken Abako's initial ethnocentric aspirations, and he was dreaming of a balkanized Congo where he could be left to rule as the all-powerful king of the Kongo people. So, if Kasavubu was daydreaming in Brussels, as Peck's movie seems to indicate, perhaps was he only dreaming of his Kongo Dominion autonomous from the rest of the Congo. These deep-seated ethnocentric sentiments animated most political leaders, which Western powers, and especially Belgian authorities, would later use to undermine the Congo's independence. In any case, Kasavubu's insinuations of immediate and total independence came later at political rallies that he organized to protest Belgium's reluctance to grant self-determination to Congolese. It is his growing radicalism that lost Kasavubu an authorization to travel to the Pan-African Conference in Accra with Lumumba. Kasavubu's frustration for missing the Accra meeting did not douse his activism. He spent his time in Leopoldville infusing energy in his party and speaking at rallies.

On January 4, 1959, Belgian authorities issued an interdiction to Abako to hold a political gathering, because the leaders of the party had not followed the requisite procedure. Frustrated members of the party took to the streets in protest of the measure. The subsequent aggressive attempt by the

Kasavubu (Maka Kotto), Walter J. Ganshof Van der Meersch (André Debaar), and Lumumba (Eriq Ebouaney) announce that they have arrived at a consensus whereby Kasavubu would be president of the Congo, and Lumumba would be the prime minister in charge of forming a government of national unity (*Lumumba*, directed by Raoul Peck, Haiti, France, Belgium, 2000).

Force Publique to squash the demonstration generated widespread violence that resulted in many deaths among Congolese, 50 by official estimations, and several wounded. Belgian authorities arrested Kasavubu and jailed him for the tort caused by his followers. Nevertheless, the disaster convinced Belgium that independence was unavoidable in the Congo; that the Abako leaders would necessarily have to be consulted during the transition talks, and that delaying tactics could only amplify the mistrust between Congolese and Belgians. So, on January 13, King Baudouin announced Belgium's "firm intention without undesirable procrastination but also without undue haste to lead the Congolese populations forward to independence in prosperity and peace."[46] Belgium's plan was to grant independence to the Congo in 1964. Through a document called *Déclaration Gouvernementale*, Auguste de Schrijver, the minister to the Congo and Ruanda-Burundi, articulated Belgium's promise. Municipal elections would be held in October 1960; Congolese would have a dual chamber parliament for which they would elect provincial representatives. The Congolese would have until 1964 to seriously reflect on whether they desired complete and total independence from Belgium or a partial independence whereby Belgium would retain control of the Congo's currency, defense, and foreign policy. On March 13, 1959, Hemelrijck, certainly with the backing of the King of the Belgians, discreetly released all jailed Abako leaders and flew three of them, Kasavubu, Daniel Kanza, and Simon Nzeza, to Belgium on a military plane. As the families of the three leaders inquired about the fate of their relatives, they were assured by Hemelrijck that the Abako leaders were "released but deported with their consent for consultation with the Belgian government."[47] Apparently, Brussels had wished to have a privileged look at Abako's response to the *Déclaration* and thought that by having the Congolese leaders on Belgian soil Brussels would have a say on the final draft of the reply before it was divulged to the Congolese. So, for three days, from 13 to 16 March, Kasavubu and his collaborators were kept at a discreet location in Brussels and had secret meetings with Belgian authorities, and especially with Hemelrijck, to discuss their eventual official response to the *Déclaration Gouvernementale*. The final copy did not exclusively please the Belgian authorities, as it seemed to question Belgium's composure and sincerity. Back in the Congo, Kasavubu threatened to boycott the elections. For Kasavubu, Belgium's pledge of independence in five years was nothing more than a delaying tactic. The Abako leader requested immediate independence. Belgium's reticence in setting a definite date for the Congo's independence incited smoldering sentiments of balkanization, as insecure pro-federalist leaders prepared to declare autonomies based on ethnic and regional appurtenances. For instance, the kind of scenario that defined settlers' politics in the French colony of Haiti was also being played in the Congo.[48]

The rich mineral province of Katanga had a strong white population of 34,000 people. These white settlers, many of whom were involved in the prosperous mining business, had once dreamed of making Katanga an independent white colony escaping Belgian central authority; a colony where their social and economic privileges would be guaranteed. However, with the inevitability independence for native Congolese and the strong probability of a unified Congo under black leadership pointing on the horizon, the settlers' aspiration shifted from establishing a white colony to making Katanga an independent country separated from the rest of the Congo, where whites would still have considerable political influence. For that, the settlers turned to the leader of the Conakat party, Moïse Tshombe. The Conakat's constituency was mainly made up of the Luanda and Yeke people from southern Katanga. These populations who regarded themselves a "true" Katangese have for long been resentful of the economically successful Luba-Kasai people who immigrated from the Kasai province in the North to work in the Katangese mines. Since its inception, the binding glue of the Confederation of Tribal Associations from the Katanga (Conakat) was the logic of tribal purity that made them hate the Luba-Kasai; and were the province of Katanga to become independent, it is that idea that would also sustain its cohesion. In order to secure their privileges in the event of a Katangese secession and Conakat's dominance, the white settlers united with Tshombe in his hatred of Luba-Kasai. As a result, Luba people from Northern Katanga, gathered under the banner of Jason Sendwe's General Association of Baluba People from Katanga (Balubakat) were also threatening to secede from the province of Katanga, thus furthering the dismembering of the Congo. Belgium had not foreseen a parceling of the Congo escaping the control of Brussels.

With the intensification of intertribal clashes in the Congo and Belgium's gradual loss of authority in the colony, Brussels perceived no other sensible alternative than to yield, unless Belgium was willing to face an independence war in West-Central Africa comparable to the one that France was losing in Algeria. For what Belgian Parliament perceived as Hemelrijck's failed effort at securing Congolese's approval of the *Déclaration*, the minister was strongly criticized and by September 1959, he had to hand in his resignation. Hemelrijck was replaced in the Congo by two Belgian officials, Auguste de Schrijver for Congolese political and administrative affairs, and Raymond Scheyven, a rich Belgian businessman with stakes in the Congo, for economic and financial affairs. Hemelrijck had paid a price for his convictions. He was "one of the very few Belgian politicians able to keep a balance ... between the aspirations of the Congolese people and the financial interests of those who lived off the riches of the colony."[49] He had a genuine love for the Congolese, given the circumstances; for the Belgians, However, he was a "nigger-lover" that had to go unless Belgium was prepared to lose its colony. Nevertheless, placed before the *fait accompli*, the Belgian government convened a Political Round-table in Brussels in January 1960 to discuss conditions for the independence of the Congo. Forty-four Congolese political leaders, among whom Kasavubu and Lumumba were the most prominent, participated in the talks. The meek and lethargic Kasavubu that Peck's film features was in reality a fiery slayer of Belgian colonialism. Around 1958, Lumumba, and not Kasavubu, appeared more moderate.

So it is no surprise that in 1958, Hemelrijck should think that by author-izing Lumumba, Diomi, and Ngalula, rather than the radical Kasavubu, to go to the all African Congress in Accra, he was playing it safe, all in the logic of controlled nationalism. The fact is that Lumumba came back from Ghana more radicalized than ever, but more popular, too, multiplying political gath-erings and demands for the Congo's autonomy. In fact it was in response to one of Lumumba's very triumphant rallies held in Leopoldville on Decem-ber 28, 1958, that Kasavubu, who would not be overshadowed, scheduled his memorable January 4, 1959, gathering. Following Kasavubu's rally, Lumumba animated a MNC congress in Stanleyville from 23 to 28 October, 1959; which ended with a riot as violent as Abako's January 4 demonstration and regis-tered almost as many deaths. The colonial administration arrested Lumumba on November 1 and sentenced him for six-month jail time; a decision which had the unsought effect of increasing Lumumba's recognition among masses.

Lumumba needed that regained popularity in the face of so much eth-nic division plaguing any idea of unified Congolese nationalism. By 1959, save Lumumba's faction of the MNC and the state-controlled PNP [*Parti National du Progrès*], which the cynical Congolese masses had been deriding as the *Parti des Nègres Payés* (Party of Paid Negroes), because mostly staffed with Congolese collaborators of the colonial administration, all the other parties were "ethnically or regionally based."[50] In fact, in July 1959, the MNC under-went its own crisis of immaturity. Feeling somehow irrelevant because of Lumumba's increasing fame, three leaders of the MNC, Abert Kalonji, Joseph Ileo, and Cyrille Adouala split the movement and created their own branch of the MNC, which they named MNC-Kalonji or MNC-K, as opposed to the MNC-Lumumba or MNC-L; Kalonji's MNC-K became for the most part Luba-Kasai movement. Despite their dissensions based on ethnic and regional appurtenance, the more than forty leaders invited to the Brussels Political Roundtable acknowledged that without Lumumba, there could not be any strong and credible interlocutor to discuss the future of the Congo with Belgian authorities; so, the Congolese leaders insisted that the colonial administration should release Lumumba from prison and invite him to the Political Roundtable before any talks could proceed. On January 26, 1960, six days after the inauguration of the Political Roundtable, Lumumba, with bandages around his wrists from tortures he suffered in the hands of his jailers, was greeted at Brussels Airport by his friends among whom Joseph Mobutu and Albert Kalonji. In Brussels, Congolese leaders were able to snatch a firm date for the independence of the Congo from the Belgian authorities. Auguste de Schrijver, the minister of the Congo and Ruanda-Burundi, announced that independence would be granted on June 30, 1960, after legislative elections to be held in May of the same year. Independence was henceforth an attainable reality, and most Congolese leaders rushed back home to campaign for the legislative votes that would determine the leaders of independent Congo.

The legislative elections of May 30, 1960, gave Lumumba the largest number of votes. He captured 35 out of 137 seats; Abako gained 12 seats, the Conakat 8 seats, and the Balubakat seized 7 seats. However, because the MNC-L leader failed to capture the majority of votes and since the cumulative number of his opponent votes largely exceeded the MNC-L's, compromises had to be found to appoint the new leaders of the country. After discussions monitored by Resident Minister, Ganshof van der Meersch, a prominent lawyer expressly appointed to the Congo by Brussels to supervise the colony's transition to self-government, Lumumba was appointed Prime Minister in charge of constituting a new government for the new nation, and Kasavubu was chosen as President. This arrangement was fraught with the very tensions that had always defined political parties in the Congo as ethnocultural movements; and it would later serve to undermine the country's fragile independence. It was a testimony to their inexperience that the Congolese évolués' attention should be markedly focused on political positioning and nothing else, while the real future of the Congo was being decided elsewhere, in the economic arena, where Congolese leaders were so conspicuously not in attendance. The Congolese leaders who were present at the Brussels Political Roundtable made no objection at all to Belgian authorities' proposal that economic and financial issues should be discussed at another roundtable, called Economic and Financial Roundtable, to be held at a later date. The Belgian authorities were well aware of the under-the-surface brewing rivalry between the party leaders and the high price that they tended to put on what political position they would occupy in the eyes of their constituencies when all was said and done. In fact, Brussels had ensured that the atmosphere of the Roundtable would be propitious to massaging some egos and frustrating others. Peck's movie shows well all the dazzling that surrounded the conference, and which could be enchanting and distracting at the same time for those who were allowed to enjoy it, and create bitterness and suspicion in those who were not permitted to benefit from it. The hotel that hosted the

Congolese attendees was a carnival site. Belgian fine chefs hustling and bustling to wait on their African guests, young Belgian girls being ushered into the attendees' rooms, journalists and autograph seekers waiting in line to see the political leaders gave the Congolese *évolués* a false sense of importance and assurance. At least, for one month, Congolese leaders naively trusted the very Belgian administration that they had mistrusted for decades and all but gave Brussels *carte blanche* to determine the economic future of the Congo, as they rushed back home to campaign for the legislative elections. The Economic and Financial Roundtable that "sealed the fate of the country" finally took place in Brussels from April 26 to May 16. Most political leaders, except Tshombe, were absent. Belgian economic experts were left to discuss the economic prospect of the Congo with mere Congolese students who had very approximate understanding of the complex conventions they were agreeing to. "The Belgians laid the groundwork for transferring much of the enormous state portfolios in colonial companies to Belgium, through privatization, while leaving virtually all the public debt to [the Congo]."[51] On September 1, 1960, the Congolese realized the full consequence of this negligence when, in the chamber of representatives, Joseph Kasongo, the Congolese Speaker of the House, reported his last trip to United States in the following terms:

> We arrived in Washington where we were officially welcomed with a nineteen-gun salute; we were given rooms in the presidential guest house, where all important guests stay. On the day of our arrival we were received by the American secretary of state.... We took the opportunity of asking to become members of the World Bank and the International Monetary Fund.... We had also intended to choose this moment to ask for a loan. It was then that we discovered that Belgium had made a contract in the name of the Congo to borrow 120 million dollars.... We were told that of the 120 million dollars, Belgium had already received 79 million and was still to receive 41 million. We were told that we could not touch this remaining money, because Belgium had not yet given receipts to show how she had spent the 79 million she received. We were asked to pay back the advance. We replied that we had not had any of it, and were in serious financial difficulties which would make it impossible to do so. Belgium was supposed to have repaid 14½ million dollars at the beginning of the previous August, but had not done so.... Both our wealth and our hard work had been exploited.[52]

The Congolese leaders were victims of their overvaluation of political power and social prestige over economic independence. Obviously, if Congolese leaders like Lumumba were pleased to be in the company of leaders like Fanon, they had all the same given little consideration to this Fanonian proposition that decolonization had more to do with building a new society ridden of colonialism's moral vestiges than settling complacently on the throne of the former master. "While they neglected to protect the country's economic assets, the newly elected leaders were more concerned with enjoying the material benefits that colonialism and the colour bar had denied them than with a radical transformation of the inherited system for purposes of meeting the people's expectations of independence."[53] A clever synecdoche of the lack of sophistication of the new African leaders is offered by Peck in *Lumumba*, the film, when in the palace he has just occupied, Lumumba, the newly appointed prime minister of newly independent Congo, refuses to pick up his phone, complaining that since the departure of the Belgian administration, domestics are scarce, and the boss has to do everything himself. In this, Congolese *évolués* easily gave credence to apologists of Belgian colonialism in their claim that for most Congolese, independence "consisted of a common desire to take over the white man's job as a means of enjoying his higher standard of living."[54] For, indeed, many of the Congolese leaders displayed utter dereliction for the job at hand; which had a distressing effect on those who really took their post-independence mission at heart.

> The first meetings of our Council of Ministers were unforgettable. Our discussions were of the most desultory kind. All of us were happy, or at least cheerful and satisfied, at being ministers. It was play-acting; some of it pure comedy, some nearer to tragedy. We were ministers; we, the colonized, now had title and dignity; but we had no power at all about any of the instruments we needed to carry out the functions expected of us. We argued about offices, about suitable and available sites for them, and how they should be shared among us. We discussed the allocation of ministerial cars; the choosing and allotting of ministerial residences; arrangements for our families and their travel — some from the country into the capital; others from the African part of Leopoldville to what had been the European part. In short, we talked endlessly, laughed ourselves silly, and concluded by generally agreeing that the Belgian colonizers were to blame for all our troubles.[55]

Without excusing the reactionary and Machiavellian colonialist ethics that prepared and executed the assassination of Lumumba, it is nevertheless deplorable to realize how much the discourse of victimology had clouded the decision-making faculty of the new Congolese leaders and especially the judgment of Lumumba. The prime minister's impetuosity was self-destructive. His imprudent methods frightened Western powers. In the context of the Cold War, Lumumba's recklessness and undiplomatic stance signaled to the Western coalition that there was very little to no likelihood of ever arriving at conciliation with him. Lumumba terrified the Western powers so much that they plotted his death. The Elimination of Lumumba was horrendous as it was easy. Killing Lumumba did not prove a very complicated task given the antagonism that the first Congolese prime minister, by his eccentric methods, had managed to weave around his person. In fact, by June 1960, Lumumba had managed to alienate most of his true friends and to surround himself with individuals that were more plotting for his downfall than wishing his success. "His enemies were more numerous than he ever realized. Chief among them were those who were jealous, ambitious like himself, and vengeful."[56]

The negotiations that resulted in the choice of Kasavubu as President of independent Congo were full of maneuverings. Besides Kasavubu, another candidate, Jean Bolikango, a leader of the powerful Bangala tribe of the Upper Congo, was vying for the position. Bolikango had sought Lumumba's support for the presidency and had received a written promise from the latter in exchange for Bolikango's support for the government election. When it became clear to Lumumba that he could only become prime minister if, as Belgium wished, Kasavubu became head of state, he was ready to break his word on the promise made to Bolikango. Lumumba suddenly reversed his views on Bolikango, to the astonishment of some of his closest collaborators urging him to do good on his word, and he unexpectedly qualified the man he had hitherto praised as a man of his word and worthy of trust as a "pawn of Belgium and a protégé of the Catholics" for whom Lumumba had little consideration. So, Lumumba directed members of his party and other nationalist parties to vote for Kasavubu to whom he had also promised support. In the end, Kasavubu was elected with 159 votes against 43 for Bolikango. Lumumba certainly knew, as many Congolese did, that Kasavubu was "lazy, cruel, and cynical," but what he did not know was that, as Antoine Kanza, a former collaborator of Kasavubu's, had tried to warn him, he had just maneuvered to elect a man that "the pressure groups that distrusted [Lumumba] saw as ... a delaying agent, a shrewd politician, a lazy but ambitious man who would have the courage to get rid of him should the need arise."[57] These words of warning proved prophetic.

Peck's *Lumumba* starts with the most bloodcurdling scene of the film, one which the filmmaker has had the greatest trouble coming to terms with as he was researching for the movie. In the middle of a Katangese night, Lumumba's dead body is being cut into pieces and burnt in a barrel of sulfuric acid; afterwards, his skull and bones will be pounded and scattered in the bush. The executors of this macabre assignment are two Belgian brothers commissioned by Belgian authorities to make sure that there remains not a trace of Lumumba and his friends lest Congolese should make the site of their burial a place of pilgrimage and keep their memory and their fight alive. The two brothers, one of whom had gone mad in his later years, were interviewed by an operative of the filmmaker and had given extensive information about the night of their ghoulish mission, which helped Peck recreate the events to their most minute details. What was it that Belgian authorities, and the Western powers, had feared from the young prime minister to the point of reserving him such a horrendous fate? Lumumba's untimely scorching Independence Day speech, a hastily written response to King Baudouin's paternalistic speech, was the catalyst of his insecure rapport with the West.

By design, Lumumba was not scheduled to speak on the occasion of the Congo's independence. Only King Baudouin and President Kasavubu were on the roster of speakers. Kasavubu's speech, which followed King Baudouin's lecture to the Congolese people, was meek, almost submissive. Lumumba was outraged that Kasavubu could remain so passive in the face of what he regarded as insults from the King of the Belgians. So Lumumba wrote what he thought was an appropriate response to Baudouin, just as the Belgian monarch was speaking. After Kasavubu's dreary and repentant intervention, Lumumba stunned the organizers by approaching the microphone. Deconstructing Baudouin speech, Lumumba exposed both the administrations of the Congo Free State and the Belgian Congo for what they were: systems of economic exploitation, military repression, and cultural oppression. Speaking more to the Congolese than to the Belgian guests of the new nation, Lumumba used his speech to vent the *trop plein* of frustration suffered by Congolese under Leopold and the Belgian government. He recalled the times of tears and blood. He insisted that the Belgians keep in mind that they would henceforth be dealing with Congolese as equal partners and no longer as slaves or animals. A phrase he threw at King Baudouin and the Belgian audience was for many critics the catalytic moment of Brussels' inflexibility with the Lumumba government. "We are no longer your monkeys," he said;[58] and although brutal and undiplomatic, Lumumba was only asserting a historical reality. It is true that in the Congo, from Leopold to Baudouin, natives have always been looked upon as apes and treated as such. Culturally, indeed, deeply ingrained in the whites' memory, the Congolese were not humans. They could be captured, beaten, and killed with no real consequences.

In fact, the pre-independence turmoil which, by disturbing the Belgian administration in the Congo, unleashed the colonial brutal military machinery that caused deaths amongst many Congolese fighting for self-determination, has also — and by inadvertently disrupting one of the most cataclysmic scientific experiments ever conducted in Africa — prevented countless casualties among passive, unsuspected Congolese who had put their faiths in the scientific community of the time. In the years preceding 1960, nothing except the Congo's independence was predictable any more, and, in the free-for-all that ensued, thousands of Westerners, from all walks of life, saw themselves packing for their countries. Among them was a polio vaccine researcher, Hilary Koprowski, whose flight, by his own admission, must have spared at least 200,000 Congolese from being fed his Oral Polio Vaccine (OPV), now strongly hypothesized to have introduced the AIDS virus in Africa.[59] Between 1957 and 1960, with the blessing of the Belgian colonial administration,

Koprowski was conducting field trials for a polio vaccine in the Congo during which more than 320,000 Congolese men, women, and children were administered a vaccine of dubious composition. Koprowski's CHAT vaccine was manufactured from chimpanzees' kidney tissue cultures, which many virologists acknowledge today contain the virus that causes AIDS. Although Koprowski's intention was not to infect the thousands of souls that served as guinea pigs during his field trials, the unparalleled carelessness with which he treated the blacks in Central Africa and the scientific community's code of silence that protected him even when it became known that his work had possibly introduced AIDS in Central Africa and imperiled the lives of generations of Africans to come speak to the inconsequential value put on black's lives, and, in this case, on the lives of the Congolese during the Belgian occupation of the Congo. On the day of Congolese independence from Belgium, Lumumba was also ending the Western perception that Congolese were trial monkeys when he declared to Belgium and to the Western world that "we are no longer your monkeys."

On June 30, 1960, in the shocking speech that he delivered at the peril of his life, Lumumba reminded the world that the Congolese holocaust was very much alive in his people's collective memory; which was going to determine independent Congo's political and economic relationships with the white world. For Belgium and its allies Lumumba's intervention was signaling the Congo's capitulation into the camp of those who had never had anything to reproach themselves with in the Congo, that is, Communist Soviet Union. In the days following the independence of the Congo, labeling became a frequent practice, as noted a former minister of the Lumumba government. "We no longer hesitated to describe this or that colleague as reactionary or pro–Belgian; while others were labeled anti-colonialist, socialist, progressive or anti-imperialist — for they were almost always to be seen in company with Guineans, Ghanaians, Egyptians, Czechoslovakians or Russians."[60] Of these labels, Lumumba was tagged with the most lethal, from the Western powers' perspectives; and whether correct or inaccurate, this ideological categorization of Lumumba by Belgium and its partners would thwart their rapports with Lumumba. Obviously, Peck's *Lumumba*, whose clear objective is to conserve for future African generations an image of Lumumba as a prophet and a martyr, a misunderstood African messiah sacrificed on the alter of Western greed does not necessarily strike a fair balance between Lumumba the prophet and Lumumba the confrontational, tentative, and self-contradictory politician. Two hours later, at the reception dinner given in the honor of King Baudouin in the gardens of the *Palais de la Nation*, Lumumba was already regretting his previous outburst and went through all sorts of humiliating contortions to repair the damage he had caused during his earlier speech. Not only did he reiterate Baudouin's paternalistic lecture, but he even went so far as to pledge to Baudouin that "[he] will pray with His majesty by the tombs of the pioneers and the statue of Leopold II, the first sovereign of the independent state of the Congo."[61] This genuflection came too late. The dice were cast. Lumumba's fate was sealed. "It was agreed all over the West the day after Lumumba's speech on June 30: it was the beginning of the end of this man as a politician;" Belgium and its allies believed that Lumumba "would foster Communist infiltration into the Congo. Therefore, they were determined that he be removed from power as soon as possible after June 30, and the Congo restructured on a federal basis, with the cooperation of Kasavubu, Tshombe and Kalonji."[62]

Independence and the Crisis of Confidence

The crisis of confidence between the Western powers and the Congolese government, which Hemelrijck had sought to prevent, had finally reached its breaking point when Brussels decided to trigger the mutiny of the *Force Publique* and the secession of the Katanga. From the time he was appointed as minister to the Congo and Ruanda-Burundi, in November 1958, to the time he resigned from office, in September 1959, Hemelrijck worked at bringing Congolese and Belgians to a happy middle ground; and in all fairness, his decision to exfiltrate Kasavubu and two Abako leaders to Brussels in the aftermath of the *Déclaration* was prompted by his desire for compromise. Paradoxically, Hemelrijck's unorthodox solution, rather than bringing the Congolese political leaders together toward a smooth transition to independence and into a diplomatic relationship between the Congo and Belgium, has contributed to unearthing latent rivalries and complicating Congolese rapports with one another and with the West.

During the three days that the Abako leaders spent in Brussels "for consultation with the Belgian government," Kasavubu had rejected Lumumba's numerous attempts to meet with him. His being flown to Belgium on Belgian military plane and propped up in a luxury hotel on his first trip to the colonist's country had certainly given Kasavubu a sense of entitlement and rendered him incapable of exorcising the ancient ghost of kingly prerogatives that had been haunting him since 1956, when he took over the leadership of Abako. Kasavubu must have already felt like the "King of all the Congolese" consecrated by *Bwana Kitoko* (Baudouin the beautiful); thus his arrogance. From that point on, Lumumba must have felt left out, and despite his exteriors of amicability toward Kasavubu, he must have regarded the latter, as the man of Belgium, a traitor never to be totally trusted. Lumumba's belief that

Kasavubu was a pawn of Belgium had certainly been reinforced by the *tour de bras* that Brussels had exercised on him to make him break his pledge to Bolikango, the other candidate to the presidential seat, and get Kasavubu elected as president. So, Lumumba silently distrusted Kasavubu as much as Kasavubu quietly loathed Lumumba. This situation presented fertile ground for the destabilization of independent Congo; which Belgium used efficaciously when Lumumba became a nuisance to Brussels.

The rebel in Lumumba, which had been lying in wait since his formal apology to King Baudouin on the afternoon of June 30, 1960, came out of hibernation on July 5, 1960, with the mutiny of the *Force Publique*, instigated by General Emile Janssens. The African soldiers were frustrated that independence had not immediately materialized into better living conditions for them. Only days after the Congo's independence, they had watched their political leaders move their families from the African quarters to the white districts; they had seen the *évolués* occupy palaces and residences of former colonial administrators, and they had observed them parade in big, shining cars. As for them, they were still living in segregated barracks under the orders of contemptuous white officers; and their demands for change had only met the disdain of their Belgium Commander, General Jenssens, who had inscribed on a blackboard that as far as he was concerned, *after independence=before independence*; and that soldiers of the *Force Publique* should not be expecting any change in their status as long as he was in charge. General Jessens's intent was to incite a revolt of the African soldiers that would topple the Lumumba government. The reaction his words provoked was not exactly the one he expected, however. The African soldiers revolted indeed, but they also took their frustration on their white officers and the white populations. The African soldiers took hostage some of their white officers, molested them, and dragged them to Lumumba's office, threatening to do them harm if their demands for promotion and reforms of the army were not satisfied. They insisted that General Janssens be replaced by a black officer. Other soldiers took to the streets, looting residences and businesses and assaulting whites at random. Cases of rapes of white women were reported.

In response to the crisis Lumumba convened an emergency meeting with his ministers at Camp Leopold; which resulted in a number of provisions addressing the grievances of the black soldiers. Nevertheless, events developed at such a speedy pace that the Congolese government's measures seemed to come too late. Many of the white residents of the Congo had already fled to neighboring countries; the word was out that the Congo had fallen into chaos and that Lumumba had sold the country to the Communists. During the Brussels Roundtable, Tshombe, who was until then practically unknown on the political scene, had delivered a speech that had captured the attention of Belgians nostalgic of the colonial era. "We are fully conscious," he declared, "of the risk that independent Congo may lose the benefit of the social and economic progress bestowed on it by Belgium, and may even fall behind unless it continues to benefit from Belgian financial and technical assistance, and also unless new capital investments are forthcoming."[63] The rich white settlers and the mining interests of the province of Katanga, who had always dreamt of having a separate, rich Katanga, had been observing Tshombe since independence and knew that they could always count on the ambitious Conakat leader to counterbalance Lumumba's influence should the need arise. On July 10, 1960, the Belgian minister of foreign Affairs, Pierre Wigny, and the Belgian minister of defense, Gibson, ordered Belgians troops to land in Elisabethville, under the pretext of protecting Western settlers and businesses. One day later, Tshombe proclaimed the effective independence of the province of Katanga, accusing Lumumba of systematic disorganization and Communistic leaning, while pathetically begging Belgium to "join us in close economic community ... to continue [its] technical financial and military aid; and also help us in reestablishing public order and security." Once again, Congolese leaders had demonstrated their utter lack of maturity. Tshombe had put too much faith in Belgium, and Brussels was going to use him as a pawn to prove Lumumba worthless, only to dump him like a useless sock once Belgium had reached its goal; and the goal was to establish that the Congo was not ready for independence. Neither Belgium nor its allies ever recognized Katanga as an independent state. In fact, it was the very Belgian officials who inflated the ego of Katangese leaders so as to lead them to secede that "in secret diplomatic messages, recommended all self-respecting states not to lower themselves to recognize a province which, though it called itself independent, had in fact returned to being a colony."[64] If Belgium was only disposed to re-colonize a cohesive Congo and would, consequently, not acknowledge Katanga's independence, neither was Lumumba willing to govern a dismembered country. So, in the hope of appeasing the Congolese populations and reuniting the country, Lumumba and Kasavubu flew to renegade Katanga. Their Belgian pilot was refused access to Elisabethville Airport's landing strip by Tshombe, and Lumumba's plane was forced to land in a remote area of Katanga. Affected by Tshombe's humiliation and the Belgians' patent desire to re-colonize the Congo by using the Katangese separatists as pawns, Lumumba and Kasavubu — but obviously Lumumba more than Kasavubu — sent multiple contradictory appeals for help and panicky threats to Leopoldville, where in their absence, the deputy prime minister, Gizenga, was trying as best as his limited experience permitted him to keep government running.

In fact, while Lumumba and Kasavubu were in the Katanga, Gizenga had convened councils of ministers to which he had, in a reckless move, invited Belgian ministers de Schrijver and van der Meersch, Belgian ambassador van den Bosch, and American ambassador Timberlake. At one of these very meetings, and in front of the Belgian officials, Gizenga transmitted to Timberlake Lumumba's request for American military aid and discussed the strategic deployment of Congolese troops in the country. Those Congolese ministers, like Thomas Kanza, Delvaux, Bomboko, and Mandi, who thought that Gizenga's decision to discuss the Congo's sensitive issues in front of foreign officials was unwise, knew that Lumumba's demand would never meet with a positive answer and that "from that time on, the Congo could count only on her true friends for aid and assistance, and those true friends would not be found among those countries which had military alliances with Belgium."[65] Having little faith in any American intervention, Lumumba also sent a request to the United Nations to stop the aggressive Belgian military intrusion in the Congo, to formally reject the Katangese secession, and to have technical assistance through the UN member states sent to Leopoldville. However, before the UN Security Council could meet to discuss a resolution regarding the Congo crisis, Lumumba, upon the advice of radical Congolese nationalists, officially broke diplomatic ties with Belgium, asked Ghana for military support, and intimated to the Soviet Union that the Congo stood ready to call for Moscow's help. All these paradoxical and inexpert decisions by Lumumba's government reinforced Lumumba's detractors' conviction that the Congolese prime minister was an unstable man, and these assessments did little to bring Lumumba any sympathy in the auditorium of the United Nations, where despite the great diplomatic efforts undertaken by the Congolese minister-delegate to the UN, Thomas Kanza, discussions of the Congo crisis by the United Nations Security Council fell into the cauldron of Cold War politics and UN cumbersomeness.

In the hope of making a more convincing case for his government and speeding up a United Nations resolution about the Congo, Lumumba led a Congolese delegation to New York on July 24, 1960. In the United States, Lumumba's impulsiveness and impatience got ahead of him, and he made a number of blunders; which, in the context of the Cold War, proved devastating for the future of his country. Lumumba's confrontational style clashed with Dag Hammarskjöld's stubbornness on several points. Lumumba thought that the UN secretary general was insincere and partial, and Hammarskjöld thought that Lumumba was an unsteady extremist. Furthermore, miscalculating that an open conflict between the Western and the Eastern blocs would benefit his cause, Lumumba had a number of private meetings with the Soviet deputy foreign minister, Vasily Kuznetzov, and even accepted an invitation from the latter to visit Moscow, hours before he was scheduled to meet with

President Eisenhower. This strategy proved damaging. The White House cancelled Lumumba's meeting with the American president, and the Congolese
prime minister lost an infrequent opportunity to directly present his case to
the leader of the free world, and, according to Hammarskjöld, "the only ally
the central Congolese government [could] count on, the only one that sin-
cerely [supported] what the UN [was] doing in the Congo."[66] Having alienated political decision makers from the Congolese cause, Lumumba then
worked at scaring away potential investors in the Congo, by giving hints of
total overhaul of pre-independence economic conventions signed between the
Belgians and American investors, thus adding further credence to America's
suspicion that investments in the Congo were susceptible to nationalization
under his leadership. Indeed, for powerful financial interests, such as the Rockefeller group and the Guggenheim group, who had several opportunities to
observe that Lumumba's words were not mere rhetoric but could rather be
easily converted into actions, the declaration by the Congolese prime minister that every financial contract signed before the Congo's independence would
be on the table for review augured very somber days to come. Lumumba was
known to have followed up on his promises of Africanizing the army, raising
the black soldiers' ranks by one position, and augmenting their salaries by 30
percent. Even in the best possible scenario, this last measure could be dele-
terious and thus disadvantageous for American businesses in the Congo. Were
black workers to follow the precedent set by the *Force Publique* and go on
strike for better wages, Western businesses in the Congo could see their dividends drastically slashed. Lumumba's economic vision won him no friends
among American bankers. In the end, Lumumba's New York trip yielded no
positive results. All he obtained were vague, hardly enthusiastic promises of
technical aid by Hammarskjöld.

Despite the undiplomatic ways in which he expressed them, Lumumba's
misgivings about the UN secretary-general were right. Notwithstanding Hammarskjöld's pledge to Congolese leaders that he was working for a positive
resolution of the Congo crisis, the secretary-general was actually trying to realize Baudouin's dream of re-conquering his lost colony. Since Lumumba's
eventful speech of June 30, 1960, and particularly with the violent rioting of
the Congolese army and the ensuing massive exodus of Belgians, Brussels,
through its ambassador in the Congo, Jean van den Bosch, had been exploring the possibility of finding a substitute to Lumumba. Justin Bomboko who,
"throughout the Congo crisis ... [had] kept in touch with Belgian emissaries,"
was slated for this post. Brussels hoped that Bomboko, foreign minister in
Lumumba's government and one of the moderate leaders ready to accept Belgium's protection, would be one of its puppet leaders for a confederated Congo
rallied around Tshombe's Katanga. Belgium's crusade for federating the Congo

was so well managed that it became a rallying cry for Belgians of all trades (politicians, journalists, missionaries) as well as non–Belgian Westerners with colonialist bent. When, after much delay, the UN Security Council finally passed a resolution demanding the withdrawal of Belgian troops, it was in Leopoldville that the withdrawal actually took place. In Katanga, the Belgian troops remained in place. "The UN acted as a political but also military buffer between the Congolese government and Tshombe. Moreover, contemptuous of Leopoldville's sovereignty, UN leaders condoned the fact that Belgian administrators and advisers were staying on to build Tshombe's state. Belgian soldiers also had the right to stay: Changing into African uniforms, they could create a Katangese army."[67] This arrangement was wanted by Baudouin and Tshombe, and Hammarskjöld hinted that he supported it. Through a report of August 6, 1960, which he sent to King Baudouin, the UN secretary-general stated that the presence of UN troops in the Katanga should by no means be construed as prompted by Tshombe's intent to secede from the Republic of Congo.[68] In fact, the decision to position UN troops in Katanga had first to gain Tshombe's approval, and when on August 10, 1960, the UN Blue Berets finally entered Katanga, Belgium breathed an air of optimism; it was henceforth evident, as Belgian minister of African Affairs, Count Harold d'Aspremont Lynden had expressed in a telegram to the King of the Belgians that "Katangese structures will be protected by UN troops and, in not too distant future, by Katangese troops under command of Belgian officers."[69] The reality on the ground confirmed the scheme of collusion between Brussels and the UN. While the UN was propping up Tshombe's renegade regime, the democratically elected government of Lumumba was being financially constricted. Hammarskjöld insisted that any financial and technical assistance offered to Lumumba's government by any country should go through the United Nations and approved by him, as chairman of a consultative committee he formed, and which was composed of representatives at the United Nations of the countries that had contributed assistance to UN operation in the Congo, that is, Canada, Ethiopia, Ghana, Guinea, India, Indonesia, Ireland, Liberia, Mali, Morocco, Pakistan, the Sudan, Sweden, Tunisia, and the UAR (the United Arab Republic). This consultative committee under the auspices of Hammarskjöld had far-reaching authority; it was, in effect, a committee formed to "direct [the Congolese government] along the path it thought best for economic political and social life of the country and its people."[70] Clearly, Hammarskjöld was taking his orders from Belgium as a neocolonial power and from Washington as the leader of the Western powers and guarantor of American financial interests in the Congo. It is not clear whether Hammarskjöld had hardened and radicalized his position after bad treatments he received from Lumumba and his ministers or whether it had all along been his plan to play Brussels and Washington's game. One can only give Hammarskjöld the benefit of the doubt, and surmise that the secretary-general of the United Nations, this most prestigious institution, should be too rational a politician with too hard a shell to have international policy dictated to him by his mood. One should give Hammarskjöld the *benefit of level-headedness* and, thus, presume that his design for the resolution of the Congo crisis, however unfair and diabolical it might have been, was well examined, though skillfully concealed to even those who, like Thomas Kanza, the young Congolese minister delegate to the United Nations, had come to trust him at the peril of their lives. If Lumumba was awkward and politically inexperienced, Hammarskjöld, as for him, was in fact a coherent crooked.

Indeed, in July 1960, the radical fringe of Lumumba's government had very strong suspicions as to where Hammarskjöld dilatory method was taking the Congo. It was taking the Congo to balkanization. Exceeded, Lumumba's closest collaborators, led by vice prime minister, Gizenga, certainly receiving his orders from Lumumba who was still in North America, decided to act; however, they responded, once again, in a manner that was totally unbecoming of national leaders supposed to privilege diplomatic outcomes to their country's dilemma. The Congolese leaders elected to use Lumumba's signature strategy, the one he had employed against King Baudouin on Independence Day; they decided to publicly humiliate the United Nations secretary-general. On July 30, 1960, at a dinner that was given in honor of Hammarskjöld, who had arrived days earlier in the Congo to appraise the conditions of any UN intervention, Gizenga, without prior notice, relayed on radio a surprise speech in which he questioned the integrity of the United Nations secretary-general and expressed his disillusion with the institution. Was that the move that tipped the balance against the people of the Congo and caused the UN to work in the corner of Belgium and the United States? As suggested earlier, one has to give the secretary-general the benefit of rationality and conclude that he had only been paying lip service to Leopoldville's exigencies while secretly protecting Belgian and American financial interests. Protecting these interests supposed that Lumumba should be eliminated, especially in light of his increasing radicalization and unyieldingness, and sometimes, in light of his illogical behavior since his return to the Congo from a globetrotting tour that took him to the capitals of some of the most vehement critics of colonialism.

In effect, before returning to the Congo from his failed New York trip, Lumumba had traveled to Montreal, and then to London, where he had met with the ambassadors of Tunisia, Ghana, Morocco, and Ethiopia. He then went to the nations of Algeria, Morocco, and Guinea, whence he arrived in the Congo "completely hypnotized" by the unmitigated anti-imperialist rhetoric his guest served him. Upon his return to the Congo, Lumumba found a country almost on its knees, in a more distressing state than he had left it two weeks before; a country that needed a strong leader with superlative abilities for negotiation. Unfortunately, negotiation skills were what Lumumba lacked most. On the other hand, the prime minister was not deficient in confrontational talent; and to prove it, he made a series of problematic decisions. On August 8, 1960, Lumumba gave a speech that indicated in no ambiguous terms that the United Nations, its secretary-general, the United States, and the Western powers were all corrupt entities; and without either consulting a delegation that he had earlier sent to the UN to make a case for his government, Lumumba declared a state of emergency, ordered the Belgian embassy to close and its staff to go back to Belgium, ordered Congolese students in Belgium to return to the Congo, and announced an independent African states summit to take place in the Congo on August 25. On August 15, Lumumba cancelled a *tête-à-tête* he was to have with Hammarskjöld, just three hours before the scheduled meeting, and from then on, would only communicate with the secretary-general of the United Nations through an exchange of fault-finding letters; which did nothing to improve his rapport with those who, unfortunately, had real decision power over the future of the Congo. On August 17, Lumumba called a press conference in which he contradictorily denounced the incompetence of the United Nations, dismissed the institution as irrelevant, and yet asked for its help in solving the Congo crisis. Finally, on August 27, Lumumba put his threat of requesting help from the Soviets into effect. In preparation for the invasion of the renegade provinces of Katanga and Kasai and the unification of the Congo, Lumumba received aid from the Soviet Union in the form of military technical assistance, over 100 Soviet military trucks, and 16 Ilyushin transport planes. Belgium, who "had done her best to make the West permanently uneasy at seeing Lumumba at the head of the Congolese government," and who had proclaimed all along that "Lumumba was a Communist, an anti-white, and an anti–Westerner," could now feel justified in her belief in the eyes of the Western alliance. The Russian presence in the Congo convinced public opinion in the Western community that "the Congo as governed by Lumumba was already more than half-way to being a Communist and anti–Western power"[71]; and if Lumumba's troops, which had started a successful invasion of Kasai and Katanga on August 31, 1960, were left to finish their operation of forced reunification, the whole Congo, and with it the Western financial interests, could be irremediably controlled by Moscow. To prevent this from happening, a coalition of Belgian envoys, American diplomats, and unprincipled Congolese politicians prepared to stage a constitutional crisis that would topple Lumumba, even eliminate him. American ambassador Clare Timberlake was working as liaison with the American financial interests to provide funds in support of Kasavubu. General Ben Kettani, the deputy to Carl von Horn, the UN force commander, in his quality of UN military assistant, was conditioning the Congolese National Army to be more committed to Mobutu, who was under CIA influence, than to Commander-in-Chief of the armed forces, Victor Lundula, who was appointed by Lumumba, and also very close to him. Inside Lumumba's government, Albert Delvaux and Bomboko had been persuaded to defect. Also, Lumumba's military campaign in South Kasai would be used against him. Though strategically successful, the campaign against Kalonji was a humanitarian disaster, as it had caused the deaths of many civilians, especially in the regions of Mbuj-Mayi and Kasengulu. On September 5, in a bold and unpredicted move, using as his pretext the Kasai massacre, which Hammarskjöld had conveniently overstated as a genocide, Kasavubu announced the dismissal of Lumumba on Congolese National Radio. A few minutes after Kasavubu's declaration, Lumumba also went on national radio to dismiss Kasavubu as head of state. Two of Lumumba's ministers who countersigned Kasavubu's order of dismissal of the prime minister, as required by the Congolese constitution or *Loi Fondamentale* were, as expected, Bomboko and Delvaux. Neither Kasavubu's order nor Lumumba's ever took effect, for the Congolese parliament annulled them and tried, with the help of the new special representative to Hammarskjöld, the Indian Rajeshwar Dayal, to resolve the crisis between the two leaders amicably. This was to no avail, for too much work was already undertaken by those whose interests lay in the permanence of the Congo crisis.

Before Rajeshwar Dayal, who had replaced Ralph Bunche, arrived in the Congo, the American Andrew Cordier, acting as special secretary to the United Nations secretary-general/chairman of the consultative committee actually governing the Congo, had successfully managed to steer the affairs of the Congolese government in such a way as to strip Lumumba of any power and favorably position the Western coalition and their corrupt local informants (Tshombe, Kalonji, Kasavubu, Delvaux, and Bomboko). Cordier provided Kasavubu with Moroccan bodyguards; he disabled the Congolese National Radio by removing a key piece from the broadcasting equipment; and he ordered the closure of all Congolese airports except the ones in Katanga "where the Belgians were making the rules." Consequently, Congolese could only receive propagandist news from Radio Elisabethville and Radio-Makala, which were in the service of the Belgians, the white mercenaries, and the Kasavubu-Kalonji-Tshombe alliance. On September 12, 1960, the constitutional crisis was effective, as two Congolese delegations were sent to the UN Security Council to discuss the Congo crisis: a delegation led by Thomas Kanza, representing the Lumumba government, and another one, conducted by Justin Bomboko, representing Kasavubu. Confusion in the Congo intensified, as it became difficult for the populations to figure out which of Lumumba's government and Kasavubu's was actually running the country. This planned confusion by the Western coalition provided them the occasion to implement the coup that would finally rid them of Lumumba. Tshombe, his Belgian advisers, and General Kettani had already won the cause of the Congolese National Army soldiers by bribing them heavily. The soldiers had not been paid since the beginning of the crisis and, by then, their only allegiance was to their growling stomachs. On September 14, the Congolese National Radio, until then disabled by Cordier, went on air to allow Joseph-Désiré Mobutu to announce to the world that for the sake of the Congolese people, he had decided to "temporarily neutralize" both Lumumba and Kasavubu, until such time as the two leaders could come to their senses and decide to work for the good of the country and not for themselves. This was "not a military *coup d'état,*" Mobutu insisted, "but merely a peaceful revolution; no soldier will be in power." Instead, the country would be run by a college of commissioners composed of university graduates and students. That college of commissioners was, curiously, to be led by Bomboko; and while Lumumba was confined in house arrest, "the apparently 'neutralized' Kasavubu presided over the swearing-in ceremony for the young commissioners, and continued to discharge his official functions such as receiving foreign envoys."[72] This is because Kasavubu, owing to his reputation of a coward and opportunist, had been doing what the Americans wanted him to do, while Lumumba had openly defied Mobutu's demand that he rally Washington. Indeed, as Kanza noted, "from 14 September, the Congo openly became a satellite country of the Western bloc. Following Mobutu's "peaceful revolution," The Congolese National Radio opened for good; airports reopened under the auspices of the United Nations; Russian diplomats and technicians were summoned to leave the Congo, and the military operations against Kasai and Katanga were stopped. From then on, "any representatives of other countries wanting to intervene there must first make sure they had the written or understood approval of Washington." The United States had started a progressive debelgianization and a slow Americanization of the Congo. Over time, the Belgians came to realize that they were no longer the masters in the Congo. A new sheriff was in town, America. The Belgians were thenceforth mere go-betweens that Washington still needed in its colonizing enterprise.[73] The Americans, in their colonization of the Congo, had decided to proceed more carefully, however. For Washington, it was more prudent to work from behind the scene, pulling the strings on known Congolese leaders with established constituencies that would just act as facades, than to be on the forefront. Of the two Congolese leaders needed for the American colonization of the Congo, Kasavubu was malleable; Lumumba was inflexible and showed not the slightest hint of ever being bought. The former could stay; the latter had to be disposed of. The American decision to directly get involved in the possible elimination of Lumumba came on August 26, 1960, in the form of a telegram that Allen Dulles, the Head of the CIA, sent to the CIA station chief in Leopoldville, Laurence Devlin, and which read "We conclude that [Lumumba's] removal must be an urgent and prime objective and that under existing conditions this should be a high priority of our covert action;" a decision for which Richard Bissell, the CIA Deputy Director for plans, would later provide more precisions: "[The CIA] had put a top priority ... on a range of different methods of getting rid of Lumumba in the sense of either destroying him physically, incapacitating him, or eliminating his political influence."[74] A CIA scientist, Sydney Gotlieb, was consequently ordered by his superiors to prepare a chemical composition that would be used against Lumumba. This plan would not be carried out. Lumumba himself would facilitate his own death. On November 27, 1960, refusing to take his friends' advice that leaving his official residence and the protection of the UN force could be suicidal, Lumumba eluded the UN guards and escaped from his residence in an attempt to rally his hardcore supporters in Stanleyville, where Gizenga had established the nationalist government. Captured by the Congolese army on the bank of the Sankuru River, with two of his collaborators, Mpolo (Minister of youth and sport) and Okito (Vice Presidence of the Senate), Lumumba was "beaten like a dog," taken back to Leopoldville, and paraded as a disgraceful and vulgar criminal by self appointed "Major" Gilbert Pongo, a politician whose "hatred for Lumumba and Lumumbists verged on the paranoiac," before being incarcerated in Thysville. Some of Lumumba's prison guards in Thysville were sympathetic to him. In fact, they had even threatened to set Lumumba free. So, Lumumba's political opponents in Leopoldville, precisely Kasavubu, Mobutu, and Bomboko, decided that it would be wiser to transfer Lumumba to a "safer" location. Initially, Kalonji wanted the honor of having Lumumba sent to him at Bakwanga. Bakwanga was reputed as the slaughter house of political opponents, and Kalonji wanted to kill Lumumba there on a public esplanade, cut his body in pieces, and feed it to the families of the victims of Lumumba's anti-cessessionist campaign in Kasai. However, Munongo, Tshombe's strongman, wanted this honor to be reserved to the Katangese.[75] In any case, because UN troops were stationed in Bakwanga, transferring Lumumba there could not be inconspicuously. So, on January 17, 1961, Lumumba and his companions were transferred to Elisabethville in Katanga and delivered to his fiercest Congolese enemies, Moïse Tshombe and Godefroid Munongo, who tortured him in an inhabited house, the Villa Brouwez, before delivering him to the blows of Belgian and Katangese soldiers, who executed him and buried him in a shallow grave whence his body was removed one night and dismembered and burnt in sulfuric acid. Lumumba had to be eliminated before the January 20, 1960, swearing in ceremony of President Kennedy, as Kennedy was likely to seek another resolution to the Congo crisis. Since Lumumba's death all the actors of the Congo crisis have been involved in a comic contorsion to prove their innocence. In a way, Lumumba's fate is like that of the Congo. Lumumba's body, like the body of his country, has been the theater of competing western as well as African interests that have ultimately caused him to be cut into pieces. In this theater, Lumumba's crime is to have trusted the good faith of humanity and to have been an idealist of independence, often to the point of utter *naïveté*, to the point of inflexibility. Naivety, inflexibility, and political ineptitude are no crimes comparable to the genocidal impulses of King Leopold II and Hitler. Those who have sought to analogize Lumumba's fight for freedom and dignity to Hitler's urge to purge the world of one race of human beings were obviously blinded by their own racism.

Conclusion

I hope to have offered scholars of culture studies, history, contemporary literary theory, and visual arts a book that connects these disciplines in ways that are both instructive and straightforward. Contemporary literary theory, which constitutes a fundamental element of college students' training in critical and comparative thinking, can sometimes appear excessively conceptual and nebulous. Deleuze's notion of the Rhizome, Derrida's concept of archetrace, Lacan's mirror stage or Althusser's idea of the Ideological State Apparatus, for instance, have this in common that they all deal with the question of subject constitution. However, a treatment of these notions in isolation could seem far removed from the real for most undergraduate students as much as it is often daunting for many graduate students. By elucidating these concepts through Francophone cinema, however, the book fulfills, in its first section, the double promise of, on the one hand, setting the stage for a transcultural engagement between Francophone filmmakers, theoreticians in their own right, and European Continental theorists, and, on the other hand, clarifying, through images of thought, what these concepts mean in the real, how they persist in the day by day lived experiences.

In this perspective, I have reactivated the untimely debate between Hegel and Fanon by way of Ba Kobhio's film about the contribution of Schweitzer in Lambaréné, Gabon. The analysis of the film has provided opportunity for giving form to the abstract terms of Hegel's tale of recognition, to linking what happens in the real world to the language of the *Phenomenology of the Spirit*, and to assessing Fanon's rejoinder of Hegel's dialectic. The result is a first chapter that shows the application of Ba Kobhio's *the Great White Man of Lambaréné* to existential questions and ascertains the importance of Fanon's discourse, today again. In this age of general euphoria about *globalization*, Fanon gives us cause to be watchful and to globalize with caution. The particular Francophone African brand of governance has been indicted as structuralist in a second chapter that, by way of Kanyinda's *Le damier* and Sissoko's *Guimba the Tyrant*, analogized the locus of the body politic's discourse to a

224

chess board and associated political praxis to a game of chess or a game of checkers where no positioning is legitimate outside the imposed Grand-Narrative of a dictatorial Grand-Narrator. What differs the Francophone political Grand-Narrative from the thousands of Grand-Narratives that govern the lives of most human societies and which are known as ideologies is that the former is not even ideological in the proper sense of the term. It is not rooted in reason but in political irrationality. It is rooted in the illogical whims of the kind of absolutist autocrats who, like Mobutu of former Zaire, have made a mockery of the so painfully acquired African independences. Ideology per se, the sum total of dogmas that pull individual members of a community into an alliance of likeminded people, functions, according to Althusser, as a well-oiled machine of structuration. It has several components, familial, religious, legal, and political, each with a defined purpose. Some components of ideological machines are violent and seek to convince by force, like the legal component and its system of army, police, and prison; and some component are friendlier and seek to indoctrinate by persuasion, like culture and its system of praises, handshakes, and smiles or like school and religion and their systems of reward and promise. Three chapters made this case tangible. Chapter three showed that in states where political and religious wills-to-power conflate, such as Algeria, the lines between violent and soft ideological apparatuses tend to blur, too. Chapter four showed that in some societies, such as the Bambara of West Africa, ideological indoctrination is too often unambiguously scarrifying. Clitoridectomy is an ideological gesture that contributes to policing gender roles and boundaries. Chapter six demonstrated that though language usually appears as the ultimate Ideological State Apparatus, it is in fact movement that occupies this place. Control of movement is the most decisive ideological gesture as Nouri Bouzid's *Bent Familia* and Moufida Tlatli's *The Silences of the Palace* have helped demonstrate.

The second section of this book has adopted the more traditional thematic analysis, however with an interdisciplinary tweak. Chapter seven has integrated the findings of history, anthropology, archeology, ethnography, and linguistics to Burkinabé Dani Kouyaté's filmic pronouncements in *Keita: The Heritage of the Griot* in order to present as complete an organizational map as possible of the Old Mali Empire in particular, and Ancient Africa in general. The result is a text that reveals a great spirit of innovation and inventiveness in pre-colonial Africa despite the oft-iterated assumption in Western discourses that Africa created nothing. Chapter eight denounced the predatory impulses of France in Francophone Africa; which, after the abolition of slavery, sustained the open exploitation of the continent during the colonial era and is now continuing under the guise of this artifice that is so pompously referred to as globalization. The French brand of globalization is too often a ruthless bludgeon against African political and economic independence. In Côte d'Ivoire, globalization *à la française* has occasioned the collapse of democracy, the seizure, under the pretense of privatization, of statal and parastatal companies by French capitalists conspiring with corrupt local informants, and the execution of the resisting Ivorian youth by the French military sent in by French politicians to protect French dividends. Likewise, chapter 9 denounced the Belgian brand of globalization; which in the Congo, from Leopold II to Baudouin, slaughtered more than ten million Congolese, pillaged the country's natural resources, and with the help of the Western coalition and a few corrupt Congolese "leaders," eliminated freedom fighters, appointed handpicked kleptocrats who left the country in political and economic shamble. I have wanted the language of this book to be accessible to undergraduate and graduate students in culture studies and visual arts. I hope to have reached this goal without chipping away at the substance of the discussions.

Appendix A

King Leopold's Mandate to His Missionaries on Their Way to the Congo Free State[1]

This note, which has been widely circulated as King Leopold II's mandate to his missionaries is extremely instructive as regards the collusion existing between the church and the King of the Belgians in the exploitation of the natives of the Congo. Notwithstanding its disputed authenticity, the letter is edifying by its mere confirmation of the situation that contemporaneous travelers in Central Africa have observed in the Congo.

Reverends, Fathers, and Dear Compatriots:

The task that is given to fulfill is very delicate and requires much tact. You will go certainly to evangelize, but your evangelization must inspire above all Belgium's interests. Your principal objective in our mission in the Congo is never to teach the niggers to know God, this they know already. They speak and submit to a Mungu, one Nzambi, one Nzakomba, and what else I don't know. They know that to kill, to sleep with someone else's wife, to lie and to insult is bad. Have courage to admit it; you are not going to teach them what they know already. Your essential role is to facilitate the task of administrators and industrials, which means you will go to interpret the gospel in the way it will be the best to protect your interests in that part of the world. For these things, you have to keep watch on disinteresting our savages from the richness that is plenty [in their underground. To avoid that they get interested in it, and make you murderous] competition and dream one day to overthrow you. Your knowledge of the gospel will allow you to find texts ordering, and encouraging your followers to love poverty, like "Happier are the poor because they will inherit the heaven" and, "It's very difficult for the rich to enter the kingdom of God." You have to detach from them and make them disrespect everything which gives courage to affront us. I make reference to their Mystic System and their war fetish — warfare protection — which they pretend not to want to abandon, and you must do everything in your power to make it disappear. Your action will be directed essentially to the younger ones, for they won't revolt when the recommendation of the priest is contradictory to their parent's teachings. The children have to learn to obey what the missionary recommends, who is the father of their soul. You must singularly insist on their total submission and obedience, avoid developing the spirit in the schools, teach

227

students to read and not to reason. There, dear patriots, are some of the principles that you must apply. You will find many other books, which will be given to you at the end of this conference. Evangelize the niggers so that they stay forever in submission to the white colonialists, so they never revolt against the restraints they are undergoing. Recite every day — "Happy are those who are weeping because the kingdom of God is for them." Convert always the blacks by using the whip. Keep their women in nine months of submission to work freely for us. Force them to pay you in sign of recognition — goats, chicken or eggs — every time you visit their villages. And make sure that niggers never become rich. Sing every day that it's impossible for the rich to enter heaven. Make them pay tax each week at Sunday mass. Use the money supposed for the poor, to build flourishing business centers. Institute a confessional system, which allows you to be good detectives denouncing any black that has a different consciousness contrary to that of the decision-maker. Teach the niggers to forget their heroes and to adore only ours. Never present a chair to a black that comes to visit you. Don't give him more than one cigarette. Never invite him for dinner even if he gives you a chicken every time you arrive at his house.

Appendix B

*Speech of Baudouin I, King of the Belgians,
on the Occasion of the Independence of the
Republic of the Congo, June 30, 1960*

Mr. President,
Gentlemen,

The independence of Congo represents the end result of the work conceived by the genius of King Leopold II, undertaken by him with tenacious courage and continued with the perseverance of Belgium. It marks a decisive hour in the destinies, not only of the Congo itself, but, I say it without hesitation, of the entire African continent.

For eighty years, Belgium sent the best of its sons to your soil, first to free the Congo basin from the odious slave trade that decimated its population, then to unite the previously rival ethnic groups that are now ready to build together the largest independent state of Africa; finally to invite the diverse regions of the Congo that you represent here in a united parliament to a happier life. In this historical moment, we should all remember the pioneers of African emancipation and those who, following their footsteps, have made the Congo what it is today. They deserve both our admiration and your thanks, for it is they who, by dedicating all their efforts and even their lives to a grand ideal, brought you peace and enriched your moral and material assets. They must never be forgotten by Belgium or by the Congo.

When Leopold II undertook the grand oeuvre whose success is being celebrated today, he did not come to you as a conqueror but rather as a champion of civilization.

The Congo, from the moment of its creation, opened its borders to international trade; Belgium never instituted a monopoly in the Congo to its exclusive interests.

The Congo has been equipped with railways, roads, maritime traffics and air traffics which, by connecting your populations, have facilitated their unity and opened the country to the rest of the world.

A health service, whose establishment required decades of effort, has been patiently organized and has delivered you from very devastating diseases. Numerous well-resourced hospitals have been built. Agriculture has been improved and mod-

229

ernized. Large cities have been erected and, throughout the country, living conditions and health conditions show impressive developments. Industrial companies have developed the natural resources of the soil. The considerable expansion of economic activities increased the well-being of your populations, thus outfitting the country with a specialized workforce indispensable for its development.

Thank to missionary schools, as well as schools that the government built, basic education has reached an enviable expansion: an intellectual elite is being constituted, which your universities will rapidly increase.

More and more skilled workers in agriculture, industry, craftsmanship, trade, and administration introduced into all the classes of the population individual emancipation, which is the true basis of any civilization. We are delighted to have given to the Congo, in spite of the greatest difficulties, the elements indispensable to the armature of a country on its way to development.

The big wave of independence that is sweeping the entire continent of Africa has found the greatest understanding among the Belgian ruling class. Faced with the unanimous desire of your populations, we have not hesitated to grant you, from this day, your independence.

Now, gentlemen, it behooves you to prove that we were right to trust you.

From now on, Belgium and the Congo are standing side by side, as two sovereign states, but linked by friendship and determined to help one another. So, today we entrust you with all the administrative, economic, technical, and social services, as well as the judicial organization without which no modern State can survive. The Belgian agents are ready to offer you a loyal and enlightened assistance.

Your task is immense, and you are the first to admit it. The main perils that threaten you are the inability of the populations to govern themselves, the tribal wars that in the past have caused so much desolation, and which should not be allowed to return, and the temptations that some foreign powers ready to take advantage of the slightest weakness can create in certain regions.

Your leader will experience the difficult task of governing. Despite the party to which they belong, they will have to think first about the general interests of the country. They will have to teach the Congolese people that independence is not realized through the immediate satisfaction of simple desires, but rather through work, through the respect of the freedom of others and the rights of the minority, through tolerance and through discipline, without which not a single democratic regime can survive.

I would like to particularly commend the Force Publique which has accomplished its difficult mission with flawless courage and dedication.

Independence will require from everyone efforts and sacrifices. You will need to adapt the institutions to your understanding and to your needs, so as to make them stable and objective. You must also educate qualified administrative leaders, intensify the intellectual and moral education of the people, maintain the stability of the currency, and preserve your economic, social, and financial organizations.

Do not compromise your future with hasty reforms and do not replace the institutions that Belgium is handing you unless you are certain of replacing them with better ones.

Maintain the activity of health services with vigilance, for their interruption will have disastrous consequences and will bring back diseases that we have successfully eradicated. Take also good care of the scientific work, which is for you a priceless intellectual heritage. Do not forget that a serene and independent justice is a factor of social peace: insuring the respect of every person's right confers to a State great moral authority in the international arena.

Do not be afraid to ask for our help. We are ready to be by your side to help you with our wisdom in order to train with you the technicians and civil servants that you will need.

Africa and Europe complement each other mutually and are destined, through cooperation, to the most brilliant development. The Congo and Belgium can play a role of utmost magnitude, through a constructive and fecund collaboration, in the reciprocal trust.

Gentlemen,

The entire world is watching you. On the day when the Congo is autonomously choosing its style of life, I wish that the Congolese people keep and develop the heritage of spiritual, moral, and religious values that is common to us and which transcends political vicissitudes and differences of race and boundary.

Remain unified and you will deserve the great role that you are destined to play in the history of Africa.

People of the Congo, my country and I acknowledge with joy and emotion that, on this day of June 30, 1960, in full agreement and friendship with Belgium, the Congo is acceding to independence and to international sovereignty.

May God protect the Congo!

Baudouin I, King of the Belgians

Appendix C

Speech of Prime Minister
Patrice Emery Lumumba on the
Occasion of the Independence of the
Republic of the Congo, June 30, 1960

For most observers, it is Lumumba's rejoinder of King Baudouin's paternalistic speech on the occasion of the Congo's independence, on June 30, 1960, that ultimately branded Lumumba as a rebel, and anti–Westerner, and anti-white, and which sealed his fate and that of Independent Congo.

Brothers and Sisters of the Congo
Fighters of Independence, today victorious

I greet you in the name of the Congolese government

To all of you, my friends, who have relentlessly fought beside us, may this day of June 30, 1960 be forever inscribed in your hearts; may it be a date whose significance you proudly teach your children, so that they, too, may teach their children and their grand-children the glorious story of our struggle for freedom.

For, this independence of the Congo, although it is celebrated today in harmony with Belgium, a friendly nation, with which we deal as equal partner, was conquered, as every good Congolese will always remember, through a struggle [applause], a daily struggle, a passionate and idealist struggle, a struggle in which we spared neither our strength and sacrifice nor our suffering and blood.

This struggle of tears, of fire, and of blood, we are proud of it to the depths of our souls, for it was a noble and just struggle, an indispensable struggle waged to put an end to the humiliating slavery that was forced upon us.

This was our burden in eighty years of colonialist regime; and our wounds are still too fresh and too painful for us to erase that burden from our memories. We have known oppressive labor required of us in exchange for salaries that could not feed us properly, nor dress us, nor shelter us decently, nor allow us raise our children as loving parents would their dear offspring.

We have endured, day and night, ironies, abuses, and blows because we were

232

Negroes. Who will ever forget that to a black it was acceptable to say "tu," not as a friend, but rather, because the honorable "vous" was only reserved to whites?

We have witnessed the occupation of our lands in the name of supposed legal texts that only legitimized the rule of the strongest.

We have seen how the same law had different applications for whites and for blacks: helpful to some, cruel and inhumane to others.

We have known the atrocious sufferings of those whose political opinions or religious beliefs were unacceptable; exiled in their own country, their fate was worse than death itself.

We have seen in the towns, magnificent dwellings for whites and crumbling sheds for blacks. A black was not allowed in the so-called European theaters, restaurants or stores. A black travelled in the hold, at the feet of the white in his luxurious cabin.

Who will ever forget the guns that killed so many of our brothers, the cells in which those who would no longer accept the regime of oppression and exploitation were brutally thrown [applause]?

All this, my brothers, we have suffered greatly.

However, we, whom have been chosen by the your elected representatives to lead our dear country, we, who have suffered the colonialist oppression in our bodies and in our hearts, say it to you loudly, all this is henceforth finished.

The Republic of the Congo has been proclaimed, and our country is now in the hands of its own children.

Together, my brothers and sisters, we will start a new struggle, an uplifting struggle that will lead our country to peace, to prosperity, and to greatness.

Together, we will establish social justice and insure that each person receives fair compensation for his work [applause].

We will show the world what the black man can do when he works in freedom, and we will make the Congo the symbol of hope of all Africa. We will insure that the lands of our country really benefit its children. We will review all the old laws and make new fair and noble laws.

We will put an end to the oppression of free thinking and make sure that all the citizens are able to fully enjoy the fundamental liberties guaranteed by the Declaration of the Rights of Man [applause].

We will efficaciously do away with any sort of discrimination, and we will give each person the just position that human dignity, work, and dedication entitle him.

We will institute peace, not with guns and bayonets, but with hearts and good will.

And for all this, fellow countrymen, be assured that we can count on our enormous strengths and immense riches, but also on the support of many foreign countries whose collaboration we will welcome as long as it is loyal and does not seek to impose any particular politics upon us [applause].

In this domain, Belgium, which has finally understood the direction of history and has not attempted to stop our independence, is ready to bring us its help and friendship, and a treaty has just been signed in this regard between our two equal and independent countries. This cooperation, I am convinced, will be beneficial to our two countries. As far as we are concerned, while remaining vigilant, we will respect the obligations to which we freely committed.

Thus, both within and without, the new Congo, our dear Republic, which my government will create, will be a rich, free, and prosperous country. However, for us to reach out to our goal with no delay, all of you, Congolese lawmakers and citizens, I ask that you help me with all your might.

I ask you to turn your back to the tribal wars that exhaust us and risk making us despised abroad. I ask the parliamentary minority to help my government with a constructive opposition and to remain strictly within the legality of democracy.

I ask that none of you shies away from any sacrifice in order to insure the success of our grandiose undertaking.

Finally, I ask that you unconditionally respect the lives and the properties of your fellow countrymen and of the foreigners living in our country. If the behavior of these foreigners is improper, our justice will not hesitate to expel them from the territory of the Republic; if, on the other hand, their behavior is good, they should be left in peace, for, they, too, work for the prosperity of our country.

The Congo's independence marks a decisive step toward the liberation of the entire African continent [applause].

Here is, Sire, Excellencies, Ladies, Gentlemen, my dear fellow countrymen, my race brothers, my bothers in arms, what I wanted to say to you in the name of the government, on this magnificent day of our complete and sovereign independence [applause].

Our government strong, national, popular will be the force of this people.

Glory to the fighters of national freedom!

Long live Independence and National Unity!

Long live the Independent and sovereign Congo [prolonged applause]!

Patrice Emery Lumumba, Prime Minister

Notes

Introduction

1. See "Decolonizing Film in Africa: Contesting the Dream Factory. *http://www. und.ac.za/und/ccms/articles/decolflm.htm*. Accessed on 12/8/2000.

2. Med Hondo, "What is Cinema to Us?" *African Experience of Cinema,* eds. Imruh Bakari, and Mbye Cham (British Film Institute, 1996), 39–41.

3. Manthia Diawara, *African Cinema, Politics and Culture* (Indianapolis: Indiana University Press, 1992), 42.

4. Quoted in Martin Mhando, "Approaches to African Cinema Study," http:// www.sensesofcinema.com/contents/00/8/af rican.html Accessed on 12/8/20003, 170.

5. Mhando, 6.

6. See Martin Mhando, "Approaches to African Cinema Study," *http://www.sensesof cinema.com/contents/00/8/african.html*. Accessed on 12/8/2003, and Keyan G. Tomaselli, "Decolonizing Film in Africa: Contesting the Dream Factory," http://www.und. ac.za/und/ccms/articles/decolflm.htm. Accessed on 12/8/2000.

7. See K. Martial Frindéthié, *The Black Renaissance in Francophone African and Caribbean Literatures* (Jefferson: McFarland, 2008), 108–111.

8. James Monaco, whose approach to film is primarily semiological, while deploring that "[T]he earliest film texts — even many published recently — pursue with short-sighted ardor the crude comparison of film and written/spoken language," at the same time, has no problem arguing that " a film shot is something like a sentence, since it makes a statement and is sufficient in it-self." See *How to Read a Film: The Art, Technology, Language, History and Theory of Film and Media* (New York: Oxford University Press, 1977), 128.

9. See Noël Carroll, *Interpreting the Moving Image* (Cambridge: Cambridge University Press, 1998), 6.

Chapter 1

1. See Frantz Fanon, *Les Damnés de la terre* (Paris: François Maspéro, 1961), translated by Constance Farrington as *The Wretched of the Earth* (New York: Grove Press, 1963).

2. See Bassek Ba Kobhio, director, *The Great White Man of Lambaréné*, Cameroon/ France, 1995.

3. Most of the biographical information on Albert Schweitzer has been inspired by James Brabazon's *Albert Schweitzer: A Bibliography* (New York: G.P. Putnam's Sons, 1975).

4. I am using the signifier "East" in the sense that Edward Said would use it, that is, the East as all that of which the West speaks. See Edward Said, *Orientalism* (New York: Pantheon Books, 1978), 4–7.

5. Friedrich Hegel, *The Phenomenology of Spirit,* trans. J.B. Baillie (London: Allen and Unwin, 1910), 231.

6. *Ibid.*, 233.

7. *Ibid.*, 231.

8. *Ibid.*, 233.

9. *Ibid.*, 61.

10. According to LeBon, "It is a childish chimera to believe that governments and

constitutions count for anything in the destinies of a people. The destiny of a people
lies in itself and not in exterior circumstances. All that can be asked of a government is that it shall be the expression of the
sentiments and ideas of the people it is called
on to govern, and by the mere fact that it exists, it is the image of that people. There are
no governments or constitutions of which it
can be said that they are absolutely good or
absolutely bad. The government of the king
of Dahomey was probably an excellent government for the people it was called on to
rule over, and the most ingenious European
constitution would have been inferior for
his people. This truth is unfortunately ignored by statesmen who imagine that a
mode of government can be exported, and
that colonies can be governed with the institutions of the metropolis. It would be as
futile to wish to persuade fish to live in the
air, under the pretext that aerial respiration
is practised by all superior animals." See
Gustave LeBon, *The Psychology of Peoples,*
trans. Lilian A. Clare (New York: G.E.
Stechert, 1912), 136.

11. Fanon, *The Wretched,* 31–33.
12. Frantz Fanon, *Black Skin, White
Masks,* trans. Charles Lam Markmann (New
York: Grove Press, 1967), 222.
13. *Ibid.,* 220.
14. Hegel's *consciousness* could as well be
termed the *unconscious* since the full significance of the process of recognition is not
obvious to the subjects involved in the intersubjective relationship, as if everything
were taking place in spite of them.
15. For the French psychoanalyst Jacques
Lacan, the structure of language is like the
structure of the unconscious. Language is at
the basis of the formation of the "I" and reveals a lot on the subject's psychic state. The
unconscious is not ruled by sick, repressed
desires that one has to overcome so as to
reach out to a perfected adult stage, as Freud
has stated. Instead, Lacan sees the unconscious as governed by language and its inventory of signs, representations, and images. The subject constitution, the "I" is not
a finite moment, but a process of becoming
mediated through the linguistic register. See
Écrits: A Selection, trans. Alan Sheridan
(New York: Norton, 1977).
16. Fanon, *Black Skin,* 17–21.

17. Fanon, *The Wretched,* 220.
18. *Ibid.,* 93–94.
19. *Ibid.,* 94.
20. Fanon, *Black Skin,* 47.
21. In *Je suis martiniquaise,* the female
protagoniste, a black woman from Martinique, is contented with the mere fact that
her lover is white. That her white lover hides
her away when company comes is the least
of her concerns. He is white, and that is sufficient. In *Black Skin, White Masks* Fanon
has derided this posture as the black woman's desire to whiten her race. See Mayotte
Capécia, *Je suis martiniquaise* (Paris: Correa, 1948).
22. Lola Young, "Missing Persons: Fantasising Black Women in *Black Skin, White
Masks.*" In *Fact of Blackness: Frantz Fanon
and Visual Representation,* ed. Alan Read
(Seattle: Bay Press, 1996), 89–90.
23. bell hooks, "Feminism as a Persistent
Critique of History: What's Love Got To
Do with It?" *Fact of Blackness: Frantz Fanon
and Visual Representation,* ed. Alan Read,
76–85 (Seattle: Bay Press, 1996), 81–83.
24. See Kobena Mercer, "Decolonisation
and Disappointment: Reading Fanon's Sexual Politics," *Fact of blackness: Frantz Fanon
and Visual Representation,* ed. Alan Read,
114–31 (London: Institute of Contemporary
Arts, institute of International Visual Arts,
1996).
25. Anne Laure Folly, director, *Femmes
aux yeux ouverts,* Togo, 1994.
26. Fanon, *The Wretched,* 36–37.
27. See chapter 8 in this book.

Chapter 2

1. Blaine Harden, "A Continent's Slow
Suicide: A Compilation" in *Reader's Digest,*
May 1993, 112–13.
2. The situation in Anglophone Africa
is no less tragic. Many would suggest that it
is worse. However, I shall attempt to remain
focused on Francophone Africa, whose
filmic tradition I investigate in this study.
3. On December 24, 1999, Côte
d'Ivoire, the West-African haven since the
1960s, joined the long list of praetorian
regimes in Africa with the military coup of

General Robert Guéi, which ended the Bédié presidency. Guei himself was dethroned on October 24, 2000, by a popular revolt when he attempted to retain power by force, despite the civilian Laurent Gbagbo's victory at the poll in a much reticently organized election. Since September 19, 2002, rebel armies have occupied the northern and western parts of Côte d'Ivoire after a failed bloody coup against the elected president, Laurent Gbagbo.

4. In the 1980s, after the fall of Bokassa, I befriended two young men, who came to the Université d'Abidjan to complete a PhD in sociology. These two Central African students would never have sat together had it not been for the strange political circumstances, which often in Africa, stands the world on its head. Jean Claude Belleka was the young brother of one of Bokassa's numerous wives. He was familiar with palace life and very close to the dictator, whom he continued to visit at the Residence Indénié in Abidjan, where the deposed emperor found political asylum thanks to Houphouët Boigny. Walidou Chahir Modibo, as for him, was the son of a renowned marabout, who died in Bokassa's jails under the suspicion that he was working for the dictator's opponents. Chahir was one of the main instigators of the student revolution, which, in 1976, brought down the emperor. In Côte d'Ivoire, I became the bridge between Chahir's proletarian world and Jean-Claude's bourgeois upbringing. We spent numerous hours in political discussions both on campus and in the many *maquis* (local bars) of Abidjan. Although these discussions were passionate, they never turned violent, and they always ended with both Jean-Claude and Chahir recollecting Bokassa's follies; they were hilarious and chilling at the same time.

5. See Charles Bally, and Albert Sechehaye, *Cours de linguistique générale* (Paris: Payot, 1972). References here are to the English edition of Ferdinand de Saussure, *Course in General Linguistics*, trans. Wade Baskin (New York: New York Philosophical Library, 1959), 88.

6. By contending that all linguistic systems are constituted by a series of differences (a series of differences of sound combined with a series of differences of ideas), and that

any linguistic sign derives its value from its difference from the sign next to it, Saussure takes into account only the signs *in presentia* (114–15).

7. For a more elaborate discussion about State and nomad existences, see Gilles Deleuze and Félix Guattari's chapter on "Treatise on Nomadology — the War Machine," in *A Thousand Plateaus: capitalism and Schizophrenia,* trans. Brian Massumi (Minneapolis: University of Minnesota Press, 1987), 351–422.

8. *Ibid.*, 381.

9. Checkers players know that this *game* is actually a *play*; it respects no established rule of cast, class, age, and decency. It is a play that allows participants to bend socio-cultural rules and to engage one another within a healthy sin of taunting and violation.

10. Sandra W. Meditz, and Tim Merrill, *Zaire: A Country Study,* eds. (Washington, DC: Federal Research Division, 1993), 54.

11. *Ibid.*, 167–68.

12. *Ibid.*, 154.

13. Robert Edgerton, *The Troubled Heart of Africa: A History of the Congo* (New York: St. Martin's Press, 2002), 207.

14. *Ibid.*, 208.

15. Cheick Oumar Sissoko, director, *Guimba the Tyrant,* Mali, 1995.

16. On the role and position of the griot in Africa and the Antilles, see respectively Laye Camara's *Le Maître de la parole* (Paris: Plon, 1978), translated from the French by James Kirkup as *The Guardian of Speech* (New York: Aventura, 1984); Patrick Chamoiseau, and Raphaël Confiant's *Lettres créoles: tracées antillaises et continentales de la littérature* (Paris: Hatier, 1991).

17. It is no secret that even though grandmothers were not officially recognized as griots, their formidable storytelling abilities were known to rival, and even threaten, the authority of their male counterparts.

18. Laye Camara, *The Guardian of Speech,* 27.

19. See *Dark Child,* 38–39.

20. See Jacques Bourgeacq, *L'Enfant noir de Camara Laye: sous le signe de l'éternel retour* (Quebec: Éditions Naaman, 1984).

21. See, for instance, *A Thousand Plateaus,* 245–46.

22. Patrick Chamoiseau, and Raphaël Confiant, *Lettres créoles: tracées antillaises et*

continentales de la littérature (Paris: Hatier, 1991), 61.
23. *Ibid.*, 59.

Chapter 3

1. See Merzak Allouache, director, *Bab-El-Oued*, Algeria, 1994; and Karim Dridi, director, *Bye Bye*, France, 1996.
2. Fencing out is not just a fancy expression. It is not an abuse of language. Both the 1992 and the 1996 American presidential campaigns offered a paradigm of the kind of language that can be generated within an ideology of intolerance. In 1992, amidst the talk of NAFTA (North American Free Trade Agreement), Pat Buchanan, fearing for the contamination of the so-called economic and cultural sovereignty of his country, actually suggested that the United States of America be fenced in from its South American neighbors. It is in the same context that Ross Perot, supporting Buchanan's idea, depicted the Mexican citizen — whose economic culture he sees as a menace to the American worker — in terms short of words one would use to describe the troglodyte who has not yet risen to the most archaic form of technology. Today again, as the debate on immigration is revived, the proponents of a fence along the American/Mexican border, led by CNN's Lou Dobbs, are being increasingly vocal, and their rhetoric seems to meet very little outrage.
3. Jacques Derrida operates this reversal of binary oppositions by arguing that the very opposition speech/writing, which, by proclaiming the primacy of speech over writing, constitutes the foundational ground of Saussurean linguistics, bears at its core the recognition of the weakness of speech. See *Of Grammatology*, trans. Gayatri Chakravorty Spivak (Baltimore: The Johns Hopkins University Press, 1974). Here, Derrida writes, "What is intolerable and fascinating is indeed the intimacy intertwining image [writing] and thing [speech], *graph, i.e.,* and *phonè*, to the point where by a mirroring, inverting, and perverting effect, speech seems in its turn the speculum of writing, which 'manages to usurp the main role" (36). "[This] usurpation necessarily

refers us to a profound possibility of essence. This is without doubt inscribed within speech itself and [Saussure] should have questioned it, perhaps even started from it" (40).
4. Interpellation, Althusser explains, is the Ideological State Apparatus's quintessential method of recruitment of concrete individuals as concrete subjects or of transformation of concrete individuals into concrete ideological subjects. In its most simplistic interpretation, Interpellation could be compared to the mere act of hailing an individual in the street. All works as if the Ideological State Apparatus, like the police man in the street, were hailing somebody ("hey, you there"). The simple fact of responding to the hail, turning around to look in the direction of the hail for instance, presuppose recognition (*reconnaissance*) whereby the respondent acknowledges that the hail was addressed specifically to him/her and not to anyone else, and is, by virtue of that recognition, always already drawn within the ideology and its system of rituals. Althusser argues that the human being is an ideological subject (is always already hailed by an ideology by the mere act of recognizing and reiterating daily societal rituals) who, unless he/she performs a certain scientific distanciation from self, seldom acknowledges his/her own implication in ideology but the other's. It is in this sense that one can say that ideology has no outside (for itself) while being at the same time nothing but outside for science and reality. See Louis Althusser, *Lenin and Philosophy*, trans. Ben Brewster (New York: Monthly Review Press, 1971), 171–76.
5. Jacques Derrida, and Geoffrey Bennington, *Jacques Derrida*, trans. Geoffrey Bennington (Chicago: University of Chicago Press, 1993), 190.
6. See Tom Conley's afterword in Réda Bensmaïa's *The Year of Passages*, trans. Tom Conley (University of Minnesota Press, 1995).
7. See Edouard Glissant, *Caribbean Discourse*, trans. and introd. Michael Dash (Charlottesville: University Press of Virginia, 1989). For Glissant, the letter is a tool of *forced poetics* and the word an instrument of *natural poetics*. The realm of natural poetics, Glissant maintains, is the traditional culture, that is, the place where the means

of expression (language) and the form of expression (the collective attitude toward the language used) "coincide and reveal no deep deficiency" (121). The domain of forced poetics, on the other hand, lies at the intersection of the written and the spoken. This place where "mother tongue" — the word — and "father tongue" — the letter — interlace constitutes the locus of the black French subject's lingering *malaise*, the invasion of its authentic substance by a foreign and ill-intentioned body. Thus, Glissant suggests, the written threatens to render the spoken impotent, to numb it and keep it in *inertia*. Glissant's dichotomies natural poetics/forced poetics and spoken/written mirror the opposition movement/inertia. "To move from the oral to the written," he affirms, "is to immobilize the body to take control (to possess it)" (123). While the written demands no movement — insofar as for writing to take place, the writer's body has to remain still — "the hand wielding the pen (or using the typewriter) does not reflect the movement of the body, but is linked to (an appendage) the page" — the oral cannot be removed from the movement of the body": The utterance depends on posture, and perhaps is limited by it" (122).

8. As writes Althusser, when one starts to inquire about why the representation given to individuals of their (individual) relation to the social relations which govern their conditions of existence and their collective and individual life is necessarily an imaginary (or alienated) relation, and what the nature of this alienation is, "the question explodes the relation by a 'clique,' by a group of individuals (Priests or Despots) who are the authors of the great ideological mystification." See *Lenin and Philosophy*, 165.

9. Edmond Jabès, *A Foreigner Carrying in the Crook of His Arm a Tiny Book,* trans. Rosmarie Waldrop (Hanover: Wesleyan University Press, 1993), 10, 12.

10. See, e.g., *Anti-Oedipus*, 320.

Chapter 4

1. As Althusser writes: "I say: the category of the subject is constitutive of all ide-

ology, but at the same time and immediately I add that *the category of the subject is only constitutive of all ideology insofar as all ideology has the function (which defines it) of 'constituting' concrete individuals as subjects.* In the interaction of this double constitution exists the functioning of all ideology, ideology being nothing but its functioning in the material forms of existence of that functioning ... it is essential to realize that both he who is writing these lines and the reader who reads them are themselves subjects, and therefore ideological subjects." See *Lenin and Philosophy*, 171.

2. See Jacques Lacan, "The Mirror Stage as Formative of the Function of the I," *Écrits: A Selection,* trans. Allan Sheridan (New York: W.W. Norton, 1977) 1–7.

3. See Althusser, *Lenin and Philosophy and Other Essays,* 200–202.

4. See Écrits, 149.

5. Amadou Saalum Seck, director, *Saaraba,* Senegal, 1988.

6. Cheick Oumar Sissoko, *Finzan,* Mali, 1990.

7. Critics who have denounced the hegemony of (Western) theory in black letters and visual arts are, among others, Vumbi Yoka Mudimbé, in *L'Odeur du Père: essai sur les limites de la science et de la vie en Afrique Noire* (Paris: Présence Africaine, 1982); Gwendolyn Mae Henderson, "Speaking in Tongues: Dialogics, Dialectics, and the black Woman Writer's Literary Tradition," in *Reading black, Reading Feminist: A Critical Anthology,* ed. Henri Louis Gates, Jr. (New York: Meridian, 1990), 116–42; Barbara Christian "The Race for Theory," *Contemporary Postcolonial Theory: A Reader,* Padmini Mongia (London: Arnold, 1996) 148–57; Olufemi Taiwo, "Exorcising Hegel's Ghost: Africa's Challenge to Philosophy,"; Keyan G. Tomaselli, "Decolonizing Film in Africa: Contesting the Dream Factory," *http://www.und.ac.za/und/ccms/articles/decolflm.html*

8. See "Approaches to African Cinema Study," available at http://www.sensesofcinema.com/contents/00/8/african.html. Accessed on 12/8/2000.

9. See Fanon, *The Wretched of the Earth,* trans. Constance Farrington (New York: Grove Press, 1965), 148–205.

10. In his attempt to free himself from

his depersonalized self built up by colonial French ideology and to return to what he perceived as the quintessential African nation (Algeria), Fanon was criticized by some Algerian activists for trying to be more Algerian than the Algerian people; thus, exoticizing — from his privileged position of intellectual elite — customs he was hardly familiar with (such as the tradition of the veil), and, in the process, providing a rationale for the ultra-conservative fringe of the Algerian population (see Isaac Julien's movie, *Frantz Fanon: Black Skin, White Masks*).

11. Emphasis is mine. Let us point out that the use of the first person possessive is as deceiving as Fanon's discourse. Several critics have noted Fanon's duplicitous posture in *black Skin, White Mask* whereby he condemns others of a "crime" and absolves himself of the same fault. See for instance, Françoise Vergès's comments in Isaac Julien's documentary *Frantz Fanon: black Skin, White Mask*, or bell hook's "Feminism as a Persistent Critique of History: What's Love Got to Do with It?," in *Fact of blackness: Frantz Fanon and Visual Representation*, ed. Alan Read (Seattle: Bay Press, 1996) 76–85.

12. Frantz Fanon, *Black Skin, White Masks*, trans. Charles Markmann (New York: Grove Press, 1967), 47, 63.

13. In fierce condemnation of Africans criticizing of Negritude, Senghor wrote: "La suprême stupidité, comme on l'a vu faire par certains pourfendeurs de la Négritude, c'est de vouloir expliquer un poème négro-africain avec les arguments de la philosophie et de la politique européenne — si encore c'était ceux de la mathématique, qui est la science du nombre et, partant, du rythme — quand il fallait dire pourquoi et comment nous sommes émus par ce poème ... c'est qu'au fond, trop d'intellectuels négro-africains souffrent du complexe d'infériorité, et ils sont encore à vouloir penser des idées au lieu de sentir, simplement, la beauté dans une intuition fulgurante" (see *Liberté III: Négritude et civilisation de l'universel* [Paris: Seuil, 1977], 428). Is it accidental that Senghor became an eminent member of the French Academy, the first black person to be bestowed such an honor, only to have not a single French official present at his funerals in 2002?

14. For the Zairian/Congolese critic Vumbi Yoka Mudimbé, the underlying presuppositions of the postcolonial African's claims for autonomy can never be divorced from Western thoughts, and especially from Hegelian aprioricities. "Pour l'Afrique, échapper réellement à l'Occident suppose d'apprécier ce qu'il en coûte de se détacher de lui; cela suppose de savoir jusqu'où l'Occident, insidieusement peut-être, s'est approché de nous; cela suppose de savoir dans ce qui nous permet de penser contre l'Occident, ce qui est encore occidental et de mesurer en quoi notre recours contre lui est encore peut-être une ruse qu'il nous oppose et au terme de laquelle il nous attend, immobile et ailleurs." (*L'Odeur du père: essai sur les limites de la science et de la vie en Afrique Noire* [Paris: Présence Africaine, 1982] 13). *(For Africa, to actually escape from the West means to understand what is at stake in being separated from it; it means to understand how close to us the West, insidiously perhaps, has come; it means to know in what allows us to think the West, what is still Western; and to measure how our mutiny against it might be a ruse that it opposes to us and at the end of which it is waiting for us motionless, somewhere else.)*

15. Fanon, *The Wretched*, 42.

16. For an elaborate discussion of the contained individual, see Brian Massumi's chapter on "Habit is the ballast that chains the dog to his vomit," in *A User's Guide to capitalism and Schizophrenia: Deviations from Deleuze and Guattari* (Cambridge: MIT Press, 1992).

17. In the twenty-seventh aphorism of *Beyond Good and Evil*, Nietzsche writes: "It is hard to be understood, especially when one thinks and lives *gangasrotagati*, among men who think and live differently — namely, *kurmagati* (I obviously do everything to be 'hard to understand' myself) — and obviously, one should be cordially grateful for the good will to some subtlety of interpretation."

In the notes to the 1966 edition of *Beyond Good and Evil*, Walter Kauffmann explains these two Nietzschean terms as follows: "*Gati* means gait; *srota,* the current of a river, and *ganga* is the river Ganges. So the word means: as the current of the Ganges river moves. *Kurmagati:* as the tortoise moves. See Friedrich Nietzsche, *Beyond Good and Evil*, trans. Walter Kaufmann (New York: Vintage Books, 1966) 39.

18. See Deleuze and Guattari, *A Thousand Plateaus*, 130.

19. *Ibid.*, 130.

20. Derrida, *Grammatology*, 47.

21. This is what Obioma Nnaemeka points out when she affirms that Bâ's gesture in *So Long a Letter* is analogous to Derrida's in *Of Grammatology* (see "Mariama Bâ: Parallels, Convergence and Interior Space," in *Feminist Issues* 10.1, 1990, 13–35).

22. For a discussion of this enigma in Keïta's and Yaou's writings, see Frindéthié, 125–48.

23. Derrida, *Grammatology*, 112.

Chapter 5

1. Sembène Ousmane, director, *Faat Kiné*, Senegal, 2000.

2. Ngangura Mweze, director, *La vie est belle*, Zaire, 1987.

3. See Nietzsche, on the origins of scholars, In *The Gay Science,* trans. Walter Kaufmann (New York: Vintage Books, 1974), aphorism 348.

4. As writes Georges Bataille: "eroticism is the sexual activity of man to the extent that it differs from the sexual activity of animal. Human sexual activity is not necessarily erotic but erotic it is whenever it is not rudimentary and purely animal." See *Eroticism Death and Sensation*, trans. Mary Dalwood (San Francisco: City Lights Books, 1986), 29.

Chapter 6

1. *Bent Familia,* directed by Nouri Bouzid, in Arabic with English subtitles, Tunisia, 1997.

2. *The Silences of the Palace,* directed by Moufida Tlatli, Tunisia.

3. Deleuze, and Guattari, *A Thousand Plateaus,* 130.

4. *Ibid.*, 77–90.

5. See John Langshaw Austin, *How to Do Things with Words* (Cambridge: Harvard University Press, 1962).

6. Félix Guattari, "A Liberation of Desire," interview by George Stambolian, *Homosexualities and French Literatures: Cultural Contexts/Critical Texts,* eds. George Stambolian, and Elaine Marks (Ithaca: Cornell University Press, 1979), 58–59.

7. Elizabeth Grosz, for instance, contends that the schizoanalytical metaphor of "becoming-woman" entails a recuperation of the positions and struggles of woman. This appropriation of women's agencies operates through a desexualization and aestheticization of being-woman and the legitimation — as a matter of universal imperative, rather than gendered desire — of man's own reorganization and repositioning to becoming powerful. Grosz also criticizes the becoming-woman metaphor as a notion that submits women to men's canonization and prevents them from exploring alternatives relevant to their specificities. Furthermore, she suggests that Deleuze's Guattari's constant references to the "machine" and to "machinic functioning" reflect their approval of models that have historically denigrated women and (de facto) excluded them.

8. Deleuze and Guattari, *Anti-Oedipus,* 75.

9. See *Anti-Oedipus,* 77. In fairness to Grosz, however, I should point out that she clearly understands and emphasizes Deleuze's position that becoming-woman is neither a mere identification with nor a simple imitation of woman by man; for woman, too, like man, must become woman. This, to me, makes of her criticism of Deleuze and Guattari an even thicker simulacrum. See "A Thousand Tiny Sexes: Feminism and Rhizomatics," *Gilles Deleuze and the Theater of Philosophy,* eds. Constantin V. Boundas, and Dorothea Olkowski (New York: Routledge, 1994), 187–210.

10. For Deleuze and Guattari, there are two possible explanations to the sadomasochist act. the clinical or psychoanalytical one perceives sadomasochism as a perverted act whereby the deranged subject seeks pleasure through suffering. This interpretation presupposes that the subject desire is pleasure, which he seeks anywhere but at its locus (the penis). The second explanation, the schizoanalytical one, is that sadomasochism is a detour to circumvent the semiotization of the body. See *A Thousand*

Plateaus: Capitalism and Schizophrenia, trans. Brian Massumi (Minneapolis: University of Minnesota Press, 1987), 155–57.
11. *Anti-Oedipus,* 346.
12. *A Thousand Plateaus,* 7.
13. *The Silences of the Palace* takes place in the pre–Tunisian nation-state; but language-strata, that is language as the act that sutures free flowing intensities, does not have to wait for the formation of the nation-state to be at its service. In fact, it usually pre-exists it as that which formulates the conditions of the nation's existence — if only to be sustained by the nation that it invents.
14. *A Thousand Plateaus,* 281.
15. See *The Seminar of Jacques Lacan: The Ego in Freud's Theory and in the Technique of Psychoanalysis 1954–1955,* ed. Jacques-Alain Miller, trans. Sylvana Tomaselli (New York: W.W. Norton, 1991), 223.
16. See *A Thousand Plateaus,* 25.
17. For an elaborate discussion on the stratum, see Deleuze and Guattari's chapter "10,000 B.C.: The Geology of Morals (Who Does the Earth Think It Is?)," in *A Thousand Plateaus,* 40–74.

Chapter 7

1. *Keita: The Heritage of the Griot* (Burkina Faso, 1995).
2. See K. Martial Frindéthié, *The Black Renaissance in Francophone African and Caribbean Literatures* (Jefferson: McFarland, 2008), 38–57.
3. One mithqual was worth ⅛ ounces of gold.
4. Said Hamdun, and Noël King, *Ibn Battuta in Black Africa,* with a new foreword by Ross E. Dunn (Princeton: Markus Wiener Publishers), 1994, 30.
5. Margaret Shinnie, *Ancient African Kingdoms* (London: Edward Arnold, 1965), 45.
6. Hamdun, and King, 38–39.
7. Shinnie, 50–51.
8. See, e.g., Joseph Conrad, *Heart of Darkness: A Case Study in Contemporary Criticism.* Edited by Ross C. Murphy (New York: St. Martin's Press, 1989); Lucien Levy-Brhul, *La Mentalité primitive* (Paris: Alcan, 1922).
9. Hamdun, and King, 44–46.

10. In Niane's version, the iron rod bends like a bow, but it does not break. See Djibril Tamsir Niane, *Sundiata: An Epic of Old Mali* trans. G.D. Pickett. (Edinburgh: Longman, 1994), 21.
11. Candice L. Goucher, and Eugenia W. Herbert, "The Blooms of Banjeli: Technology and Gender in West African Iron Making," in *The Culture and Technology of African Iron Production,* edited by Peter R. Schmidt (Gainsville: University Press of Florida, 1996), 40.
12. See Terry Childs, and William J. Dewey, "Forging Symbolic Meaning in Zaire and Zimbabwe," in *The Culture and Technology of African Iron Production,* ed. Peter R. Schmidt (Gainsville: University Press of Florida, 1996), 145–71.
13. See Jacques Nenquin, *Excavations at Sanga, 1958. The Prehistoric Necropolis.* Annales, Musée Royal de l'Afrique Centrale, Sciences Humaines, No. 45 (Tervuren, Belgium, 1963); J. Hiernaux, E. de Longress, and J. de Buyst, *Fouilles Archéologiques dans la Vallée du Haut Lualaba. I. Sanga, 1958.* Annales, Musée Royal de l'Afrique Centrale, Sciences Humaines, No. 73 (Tervuren, Belgium, 1971); Pierre de Maret, *Fouilles Archéologiques dans la Vallée du Haut Lualaba, Zaire. Sanga et Katongo, 1974.* 2 vols. Annales, Musée Royal de l'Afrique Centrale, Sciences Humaines, No. 120 (Tervuren, Belgium, 1985); see also, *Fouilles Archéologiques dans la Vallée du Haut Lualaba, Zaire. III. Kamilamba, Kikulu, et Malemba-Nkulu, 1977,* Annales, Musée Royal de l'Afrique Centrale, Sciences Humaines, No. 131 (Tervuren, Belgium, 1992).
14. Candice L. Goucher, and Eugenia W. Herbert, "The Blooms of Banjeli: Technology and Gender in West African Iron Making," in *The Culture and Technology of African Iron Production,* ed. by Peter R. Schmidt (Gainsville: University Press of Florida, 1996), 40–57.
15. Peter R. Schmidt, and Donald H. Avery, "Complex Iron Smelting and Prehistoric Culture in Tanzania," in *The Culture and Technology of African Iron Production,* ed. Peter R. Schmidt (Gainsville: University Press of Florida, 1996), 172–85.
16. David Kellick, "On claims For 'Advanced' Ironworking Technology in Precolonial Africa," in *The Culture and Technol-*

ogy of African Iron Production, ed. Peter R. Schmidt (Gainsville: University Press of Florida, 1996), 257.

17. Pierre de Maret, and G. Thiry, "How Old Is the Iron Age in Central Africa?" in *The Culture and Technology of African Iron Production*, ed. Peter R. Schmidt (Gainsville: University Press of Florida, 1996), 29–39.

18. Peter R. Schmidt, "Cultural Representation of African Iron Production," in *The Culture and Technology of African Iron Production*, ed. Peter R. Schmidt (Gainsville: University Press of Florida, 1996), 9–10.

19. *Ibid.*

20. Schmidt and Avery, 180.

21. J. E. Rehder, "Use of Preheated Air in Primitive Furnaces: Comment on Views of Avery and Schmidt," *The Culture and Technology of African Iron Production*, ed. Peter R. Schmidt (Gainsville: University Press of Florida, 1996), 234–39.

22. Peter R. Schmidt, *Iron Technology in East Africa: Symbolism, Science and Archeology* (Bloomington/Indianapolis: Indiana University Press, 1997), 119.

23. David Kellick, "On Claims," 247.

24. *Ibid.*, 255.

25. *Ibid.*, 258. Emphasis is mine.

26. *Ibid.* Emphasis is mine.

27. Niane, 20.

28. Christopher Ehret, *The Civilizations of Africa: A History to 1800* (Charlottesville: University Press of Virginia, 2002), 229.

29. *Ibid.*, 228.

30. *Ibid.*, 142.

31. Gregory H. Maddox, *Sub-Saharan Africa: An Environmental History* (Santa Barbara: ABC-CLIO, 2006), 50.

32. Goucher, and Herbert, 40–48.

33. *Ibid.*, 46.

34. Camara Laye, *The Dark Child*, trans. by James Kirkup, and Ernest Jones (New York: Hill and Wang, 1992), 37.

35. *Ibid.*, 39.

36. See *The Future of Mud: A Tale of Houses and Lives in Djenné*, a film by Susan Vogel, Mali, 2006.

37. Certainly the Sankarani River

38. Hamdun, and King, 39, 43, 61.

39. *Ibid.*, 56.

40. Justice in Agadez.

41. Frindéthié, 50–51.

42. J. D. Fage, *A History of Africa* (London: Routledge, 1995), 74.

43. Maddox, 54.

44. Ehret, 229.

45. Hamdun, and King, 29–75.

46. See John O. Hunwick, *Timbuktu and the Songhay Empire: Al-Sa'di's Ta'rikh al-sudan down to 1613 and other Contemporary Documents* (Leiden: Brill, 1999).

47. Goucher, and Herbert, 50.

48. Schmidt, *Iron Technology in East Africa*, 274.

49. Adama Doumbia, and Naomi Doumbia, *The Way of the Elders: West African Spirituality and Tradition* (Llewellyn Worldwide, 2004), 91, 53.

50. *Ibid.*, 55–57.

51. Hamdun, and King, 39.

Chapter 8

1. Sidiki Bakaba, director, *Bare Hands Victory* (Abidjan: Kepri Creations, 2005).

2. *The Washington Times*, Special International Report Prepared by *The Washington Times* Advertising Department, July 2, 1999.

3. Olaudah Equiano, *The Interesting Narrative of the Life of Olaudah Equiano, or Gustavus Vassa the African* (New York: Modern Library, 2004).

4. Fage, 334.

5. *Ibid.*, 327.

6. *Ibid.*, 329.

7. Jules Ferry, "Les fondements de la politique coloniale," discours prononcé à la Chambre des députés: le 28 juillet 1885.

8. *Réponse de Georges Clémenceau à Jules Ferry. Débat à la chambre des députés* (le 30 juillet 1885).

9. H. L. Wesseling, *Divide and Rule: The Partition of Africa, 1880–1914*, trans. Arnold J. Pomerans (Westport: Praeger, 1996), 200–203.

10. Fage, 333.

11. See, e.g., Frindéthié, 5–6.

12. *Ibid.*, 28–32.

13. Much of the discussion here is inspired by D. K. Fieldhouse's *The West and the Third World* (Oxford: Blackwell Publishing, 1999), 99–105.

14. Actually, as Fieldhouse notes, evidence points to the contrary. All of black Africa within the European Community's preferential economic system in the 1980s had a lower per capita growth rate than South Asian countries which were not part of the system (see page 105).

15. *Ibid.*

16. Richard Falk, *Predatory Globalization: A Critique* (Malden: Polity Press, 1999), 131.

17. James Petras, and Henry Veltmeyer, "World Development: Globalization or Imperialism?" in *Globalization and Antiglobalization: Dynamics of Change in the New World Order*, ed. Henry Veltmeyer (Burlington: Ashgate, 2004), 18.

18. Steven Hiatt, ed., "Global Empire: The Web of Control," in *A Game as Old as Empire: The Secret World of Economic Hit Men and the Web of Global Corruption* (San Francisco: Berret-Koehler, 2007), 12–29.

19. See *htmlhttp://tempsreel.nouvelobs. com/speciales/elysee_2007/20070504.OBS55 97/segolene_royal_denonce_les_liensentre_sar kozy_bouygues.html* (accessed on 12/9/2007)

20. Xavier Harel, Interview with Ahmadou Kourouma, in *Politique Internationale,* Issue 98 (Winter, 2003), *http://www.politi queinternationale.com/revue/read2.php?id_rev ue=13&id=223&content=texte&search=* (accessed on January 19, 2008).

21. *http://ecbci.frblogs.net/ECB-b1/Avant-et-Apres-1999-b1-p8.htm* (accessed January 19, 2008).

22. Alemayehu Geda, and Abebe Shimeles, "Openness, Trade Liberalization, Inequality and Poverty in Africa," in *Flat World, Big Gaps: Economic Liberalization, Globalization, Poverty & Inequality*, eds. K.S. Jomo and Jacques Baudot, (London: Zed Books, 2007), 304.

23. Assié-Lumumba, and Lumumba-Kasongo, "Côte d'Ivoire (Ivory Coast) in the French and Global Capitalist System," in *Africa Update*, vol. X, Issue 4 (Fall 2003).

24. Alemayehu, and Geda, 305.

25. Had not Sarkozy, as French minister of finance and industry, reassured EDF and GDF union members worried about privatization prospects in the following terms on April 4, 2004? "EDF et Gaz de France ne seront pas privatisées. Pourquoi? Parce que EDF et Gaz de France ne seront pas et ne seront jamais des entreprises tout à fait comme les autres ... du fait de leur importance pour l'indépendance nationale, de leur rôle dans le service public de l'électricité et du gaz." *(EDF and GDF will never be privatized. Why? Because EDF and GDF will not be and will never be ordinary companies ... given their importance for national independence, given their roles in public distribution of electricity and gas.)* See *http://sarkozyblog. free.fr/index.php?2004/04/04/108-rencontre-avec-les-syndicats-edf*

26. See Assié-Lumumba, and Lumumba-Kasongo.

27. James Ferguson, *Global Shadows: Africa in the Neoliberal World Order* (Durham: Duke University Press, 2006), 39.

28. The review concluded as follows: "Members congratulated Côte d'Ivoire on its pursuit of macroeconomic stabilization and trade liberalization, and noted the positive effects registered to date. They nonetheless encouraged Côte d'Ivoire to make additional commitments and bind more tariffs so as to ensure that current reforms continue. Participants expressed their conviction that the consolidation of reforms in the goods and services sectors would attract new investment and ensure sustained economic growth." See World Trade Organization, "Trade Policy Reviews: Second Press Release and Chairperson's Conclusions Côte d' Ivoire: July, 1995, *http://www.wto.org/en glish/tratop_e/tpr_e/tp9_e.htm*

29. In a letter to his family, Frantz Fanon expressed his regrets of choosing to fight for France during World War II, complaining that he was wrong to enroll to fight for the freedom of French people while French farmers themselves were not ready to fight for their liberty. See Raoul Peck, director, *Black Skin, White Masks* (videorecording).

30. Martial Frindéthié, "Francopholie," unpublished poem.

32. *Jeune Afrique*, issue 1231 (August 8, 1984), 21.

32. H. K. Bédié, *Les chemins de ma vie: Entretiens avec Eric Laurent* (Plon: Paris, 1999), 50.

33. François Soudan, "Ouattara est-il ivoirien?" (13 juin, 2000), *http://www.jeu neafrique.com/jeune_afrique/article_jeune_af rique.asp?art_cle=LIN13063ouattneirio0* (accessed on January 18, 2008).

34. Bédié, 50.
35. *Ibid.*, 44.
36. Vincent Hugeux, "Quand la Côte d'Ivoire joue avec le feu," *http://www.lex press.fr/info/monde/dossier/cotedivoire/dossier.a sp?ida=418738&p=2* (accessed on January 18, 2008).
37. Jérôme Dupuis, and Jean-Marie Pontaut, "Mains basses sur l'aide européenne," April 6, 2000, *http://www.lexpress.fr/info/ monde/dossier/cotedivoire/dossier.asp?ida=418 736* (accessed on January 18, 2008).
38. *Ibid.*
39. See Bare Hands Victory,
40. Fieldhouse, 72.
41. Mamadou Koulibaly, *La guerre de la France contre la Côte d'Ivoire* (Abidjan: La Refondation, 2003), 4.
42. Interview by Abdou Salam Diop, in "L'Harmattan" No 854-9056, January 2, 2005, *www.midici.com/* (accessed on January 17, 2008).
43. *Ibid.*
44. This amateur video was featured in *Bare Hands Victory.*
45. *La guerre de la France,* 11–14.
46. *http://delugio.blogs.nouvelobs.com/ archive/2004/12/13/du-concept-d%E2% 80%99-ivoirite.html*
47. "Ahmadou Kourouma en crise d'ivoirite," *http://www.afrik.com/article5287. html,* November 20, 2002 (accessed on 1/ 19/2008).
48. Jean-François Bayart, "L'*Ivoirité* vient de loin," interview by Pierre Ganz (RFI), and Vincent Hugeux, November 15, 2005, *http://www.lexpress.fr/info/monde/dossier/cote divoire/dossier.asp?ida=430432* (accessed 1/ 18/2008).
49. Gene M. Grossman, and Elhanan Helpman, *Interest Groups and Trade Policy,* (Princeton: Princeton University Press, 2002), 235.
50. *Ibid.*
51. Bare Hands Victory,
52. Fage, 335.
53. Bare Hands Victory.
54. Much of my discussion here will rely on Glenn Firebaugh's summary of the theories of world stratification as he lay them out in *The New Geography of Global Income Inequality* (Cambridge: Harvard University Press, 2003), 170–84.
55. *Ibid.*, 170.

56. See Bare Hands Victory.
57. See Henry Louis Gates, Jr., *Wonders of the African World* (video recording).

Chapter 9

1. Adam Hochschild, *King Leopold's Ghost: A Story of Greed, Terror, and Heroism in Colonial Africa* (Boston: Houghton Mifflin Company, 1999), 18.
2. Wesseling's *Divide and Rule: The Partition of Africa, 1880–1914,* translated by Arnold J. Pomerans (Westport: Praeger, 1996), 78–79.
3. *Ibid.*
4. *Ibid.*, 85.
5. E.D. Morel, *The Black Man's Burden* (New York: The Monthly Review Press, 1969), 111.
6. George Martelli, *Leopold to Lumumba: A History of the Belgian Congo: 1877–1960* (London: Chapman & Hall, 1962), 12.
7. For an elaborate discussion on this matter, see Wesseling, 93–100.
8. *Ibid.*, 103.
9. Martelli, 186–87.
10. See Peter Bate, director, *White King, Red Rubber, Black Death* (Great Britain, 2004).
11. E.D. Morel, *History of the Congo Reform Movement*, with critical notes by Wm. Louis, and Jean Stengers (Oxford: Clarendon Press, 1968), 15.
12. Jean Stengers, "Critical Notes," in *History of the Congo Reform Movement,* 258.
13. *Ibid.*, 225.
14. *Ibid.*, 270.
15. E.D. Morel, *The Black Man's Burden,* 116.
16. *Ibid.*, 124
17. *Ibid.*, 122.
18. *Ibid.*, 122–21.
19. *Ibid.*, 124–25.
20. *Ibid.*, 134.
21. Hochschild, 134.
22. Fanon, *The Wretched.*
23. See Appendix A.
24. Morel, *The Black Man's Burden,* 164.
25. *Ibid.*, 5
26. Morel, *History,* 56.
27. *Ibid.*, 161–62.

28. *Ibid.*, 162.

29. The real name under which George Washington Williams served remains a mystery, even to his wife who was unable to ascertain it in order to collect his army pension. It is more likely that he served as Charles Steward, the 1865 deserter than William Steward, who was discharged in 1865.

30. Most of the information on the life of George Washington Williams was inspired by John Hope Franklin's *George Washington Williams: A Biography* (Chicago: The University of Chicago Press, 1985).

31. *Ibid.*, 184.

32. *Ibid.*, 181.

33. For the full text of Williams's *Open Letter,* see Franklin, 243–54.

34. *Ibid.*

35. Morel, *History,* 177.

36. Morel, *History,* 162.

37. Georges Nzongola-Ntalaja, *The Congo from Leopold to Kabila: A People's History* (London: Zed Books, 2002), 29.

38. See, among others, Georges Nzongola-Ntalaja, *The Congo: From Leopold to Kabila: A People's History* (London: Zed Books, 2002); Sandra W. Meditz, and Tim Merrill, eds., *Zaire: A Country Study* (Washington, D.C.: Federal Research Division, 1993); Thomas Kanza, *Conflict in the Congo: The Rise and Fall of Lumumba* (London: Penguin Books, 1972).

39. For an elaborate discussion of the Belgian commercial exploitation of the Congo, see Nzongola-Ntalaja, 27–33.

40. See Baudouin's full speech in Appendix B.

41. Martelli, 224n.1.

42. Maurice N. Hennessy, *The Congo: A Brief History and Appraisal* (New York: Praeger, 1961), 65.

43. *Ibid.*, 67.

44. *Ibid.*, 66, 68.

45. *Ibid.*, 75–76.

46. Martelli, 226.

47. Kanza, 61.

48. See previous chapter.

49. Kanza, 73.

50. Ngonzola-Ntalaja, 83.

51. *Ibid.*, 88.

52. *Ibid.*, 285.

53. *Ibid.*

54. Martelli, 224.

55. Kanza, 119.

56. *Ibid.*, 122–23.

57. *Ibid.*, 123.

58. See Lumumba's full speech in Appendix C.

59. Edward Hooper, *The River: A Journey to the Source of HIV and AIDS* (Boston: Little, Brown, 1999), 191.

60. Kanza, 119.

61. See part of Lumumba's makeup speech in Kanza.

62. Kanza, 181.

63. Hennessy, 83.

64. Kanza, 201.

65. *Ibid.*

66. *Ibid.*, 244.

67. Ludo de Witte, *The Assassination of Lumumba,* trans. Ann Wright, and Renée Fenby (London: Verso, 2001), 13.

68. *Ibid.*, 12.

69. *Ibid.*, 13.

70. Kanza, 271.

71. *Ibid.*, 287.

72. Nzongola-Ntalaja, 109.

73. Kanza, 305.

74. De Witte, 17.

75. Chevalier Jacques Brassine, *Enquête sur la mort de Lumumba,* unpublished doctoral thesis (Brussels: Université Libre de Bruxelles, 1991), 9.

Bibliography

Alessandrini, Anthony C. Ed. *Frantz Fanon: Critical Perspectives.* New York: Routledge, 1999.

Althusser, Louis. *Lenin and Philosophy and Other Essays.* Translated by Ben Brewster. New York: Monthly Review Press, 1971.

Appiah, Kwame Anthony. "Is the Post- in Postmodernism the Post- in Postcolonial?" *Contemporary Postcolonial Theory: A Reader,* edited by Padmini Mongia, 55–71 London: Arnolds, 1996.

Austin, John Langshaw. *How to Do Things with Words.* Cambridge: Harvard University Press, 1962.

Avery, Donald H., and Peter R. Schmidt. "Use of Preheated Air in Ancient and Recent African Smelting Furnaces: A Reply to Rehder." In *The Culture and Technology of African Iron Production,* edited by Peter R. Schmidt, 240–46. Gainsville: University Press of Florida, 1996.

Ba Kobhio, Bassek. Director. *The Great White Man of Lambaréné.* Cameroon/France, 1995.

Bardhan, Pranab, Samuel Bowles, and Michael Wallerstein. *Globalization and Egalitarian Redistribution.* New York: Russell Sage Foundation, 2006.

Bataille, Georges. *Eroticism, Death and Sensation.* Translated by Mary Dalwood. San Francisco: City Lights Books, 1986.

Bédié, Henri Konan. *Les chemins de ma vie: entretiens avec Eric Laurent.* Paris: Plon, 1999.

Benjamin, Bret. *Invested Interests: Capital, Culture, and The World Bank.* Minneapolis: University of Minnesota Press, 2007.

Bensmaia, Réda. *The Year of Passages.* Translated by Tom Conley. Minneapolis: University of Minnesota Press., 1995.

Bhagwati, Jagdish. *In Defense of Globalization.* New York: Oxford University Press, 2004.

Brabazon, James. *Albert Schweitzer: A Biography.* New York: G.P. Putnam's Sons, 1975.

Buira, Ariel. Ed. *Challenges to the World Bank and IMF: Developing Country Perspectives.* London: Anthem Press, 2003.

Camara, Laye. *Le maître de la parole.* Paris: Plon, 1978.

_____. *L'Enfant noir.* Paris: Plon, 1995.

_____. *The Dark Child.* Translated by James Kirkup and Ernest Jones. New York: Farrar, Straus, and Giroux, 1954.

_____. *The Guardian of Speech.* Translated by James Kirkup. New York: Aventura, 1984.

Capécia, Mayotte. *Je suis martiniquaise.* Paris: Correa, 1948.

Carroll, Noël. *Interpreting the Moving Image.* Cambridge: Cambridge University Press, 1998.

Catey, Wilfred, and Martin Kilson. *The Africa Reader: Colonial Africa.* New York: Vintage Books, 1970.

Césaire, Aimé. "Cahier d'un Retour au Pays Natal." In *Anthologie de la nouvelle poésie nègre et malgache*, edited by Léopold Sédar Senghor, 57–61. Paris: PUF, 1948.

Césaire, Suzanne. "Malaise d'une civilisation." In *Tropiques, Vol.* 5, edited by Aimé Césaire, 43–70. Fort-de-France, April 1942. 45.

Chafer, Tony. *The End of Empire in French West Africa: France's Successful Decolonization.* Oxford: Berg, 2002.

Chamoiseau, Patrick, and Raphael Confiant. *Lettres créoles: tracées antillaises et continentales de la littérature.* Paris: Hatier, 1991.

Childs, S. Terry, and William J. Dewey. "Forging Symbolic Meaning in Zaire and Zimbabwe." In *The Culture and Technology of African Iron Production*, edited by Peter R. Schmidt, 145–71. Gainsville: University Press of Florida, 1996.

Christian, Barbara. "The Highs and Lows of Black Feminist Criticism." *Reading Black, Reading Feminist : A Critical Anthology*, edited by Henry Louis Gates, Jr., 44–51. New York: Penguin Books, 1990.

_____. "The Race for Theory." *Contemporary Postcolonial Theory: A Reader*, edited by Padmini Mongia, 148–57. London: Arnolds, 1996.

Collins, Patricia Hill. *Black Feminist Thoughts: Knowledge, Consciousness and the Politics of Empowerment.* London: Harper Collins, 1990.

Conrad, David C. Rec., ed., and trans. Narrated by Djanka Tassey Condé. *Sunjata: A West African Epic of the Mandé People.* Indianapolis: Hackett Publishing, 2004.

Cousins, Norman. *Dr. Schweitzer of Lambaréné.* New York: Harper and Brothers, 1960.

Deleuze, Gilles, and Félix Guattari. *Anti-Oedipus: Capitalism and Schizophrenia.* Translated by Robert Hurley, Mark Seem, and Helen R. Lane. Minneapolis: University of Minnesota Press, 1983.

_____. *A Thousand Plateaus: Capitalism and Schizophrenia.* Translated by Brian Massumi. Minneapolis: University of Minnesota Press, 1987.

_____. *Kafka: pour une littérature mineure.* Paris: Éditions de Minuit, 1975.

Derrida, Jacques. *Of Grammatology.* Translated by Gayatri Chakravorty Spivak. Baltimore: The Johns Hopkins University Press, 1974.

_____. *Writing and Difference.* Translated by Alan Bass. Chicago: University of Chicago Press, 1978.

Derrida, Jacques, and Geoffrey Bennington. *Jacques Derrida.* Translated by Geoffrey Bennington. Chicago: University of Chicago Press, 1993.

Diawara, Manthia. *African Cinema, Politics and Culture.* Indianapolis: Indiana University Press, 1992.

Edgerton, B. Robert. *The Troubled Heart of Africa: A History of the Congo.* New York: St. Martin's Press, 2002.

El-Ojeili, Chamsey, and Patrick Hayden. *Critical Theories of Globalization.* Houndmill: Palgrave Macmillan, 2006.

Erhet, Christopher. *The Civilizations of Africa: A History to 1800.* Charlottesville: University Press of Virginia, 2002.

Fage, J. D. *A History of Africa.* London: Routledge, 1995.

Falk, Richard. *Predatory Globalization: A Critique.* Malden: Polity Press, 1999.

Fanon, Frantz. *Black Skin, White Masks.* Translated by Charles Lam Markmann. New York: Grove Press, 1967.

_____. *Les damnés de la terre.* Paris: François Maspéro, 1961.

_____. *The Wretched of the Earth.* Translated by Constance Farrington. New York: Grove Press, 1963.

Ferguson, James. *Global Shadows: Africa in the Neoliberal World Order.* Durham: Duke University Press, 2006.

Fieldhouse, David Kenneth. *The West and the Third World: Trade, Colonialism, Dependence and Development.* Malden: Blackwell Publishers, 1999.

Firebaugh, Glenn. *The New Geography of Global Income Inequality.* Cambridge: Harvard University Press, 2003.

Franklin, John Hope. *George Washington Williams: A Biography.* Chicago: The University of Chicago Press, 1985.

Frindéthié, K. Martial. *The Black Renaissance in Francophone African and Caribbean Literatures.* Jefferson: McFarland, 2008.

Gates, Jr. Henry Louis, editor. *Reading Black, Reading Feminism: A Critical Anthology.* New York: Meridian, 1990.

Glissant, Edouard. *Caribbean Discourse: Selected Essays.* Translated and with an introduction by Michael Dash. Charlottesville: University Press of Virginia, 1989.

Goucher, Candice L., and Eugenia W. Herbert. "The Blooms of Banjeli: Technology and Gender in West African Iron Making." *The Culture and Technology of African Iron Production,* edited by Peter R. Schmidt, 40–57. Gainsville: University Press of Florida, 1996.

Groosman, Gene M., and Elhanan Helpman. *Interest Groups and Trade Policy.* Princeton: Princeton University Press, 2002.

Grosz, Elizabeth. "A Thousand Tiny Sexes: Feminism and Rhizomatics." *Gilles Deleuze and the Theater of Philosophy,* edited by Constantin V. Boundas and Dorothea Olkowski. 187–210. New York: Routledge, 1994.

Guattari, Félix. "A Liberation of Desire." Interview by George Stambolian in *Homosexualities and French Literatures: Cultural Contexts/Critical Texts,* edited by George Stambolian and Elaine Marks, 56–68. Ithaca: Cornell University Press, 1979.

Hamdun, Said, and Noël King. *Ibn Battuta in Black Africa.* Princeton: Markus Wiener, 1994.

Haugen, David M., ed. *The Third World.* Detroit: Greenhaven Press, 2006.

Henderson, Gwendolyn Mae. "Speaking in Tongues: Dialogics, Dialectics and the Black Woman Writer's Literary Tradition." In *Reading Black, Reading Feminist: A Critical Anthology,* edited by Henry Louis Gates, Jr., 116–42. New York: Meridian, 1990.

Hennessy, Maurice N. *The Congo: A Brief History and Appraisal.* New York: Praeger, 1961.

Hiatt, Steven. Ed. *A Game as Old as Empire: The Secret World of Economic Hit Men and the Web of Global Corruption.* San Francisco: Berret-Koehler, 2007.

Hochschild, Adam. *King Leopold's Ghost: A Story of Greed, Terror, and Heroism in Colonial Africa.* Boston: Houghton Mifflin, 1999.

Hondo, Med. "What is Cinema to Us?" *African Experience of Cinema,* edited by Imruh Bakari and Mbye Cham, 39–41. London: British Film Institute, 1996.

hooks, bell. "Feminism as a Persistent Critique of History: What's Love Got to Do with It?" In *Fact of Blackness: Frantz Fanon and Visual Representation,* edited by Alan Read, 76–85. Seattle: Bay Press, 1996.

Hooper, Edward. *River: A Journey to the Source of HIV and AIDS.* Boston: Little, Brown, 1999.

Hunwick, John O. *Timbuktu and the Songhay Empire: Al-Sa'di's al sudan Ta'rikh Down to the 1613 and Other Contemporary Documents.* Leiden: Brill, 1999.

Irigaray, Luce. *Parler n'est jamais neutre.* Paris: Éditions de Minuit, 1985.

Jabès, Edmond. *A Foreigner Carrying in the Crook of His Arm a Tiny Book.* Translated by Rosmarie Waldrop. Hanover: Wesleyan University Press, 1993.

Jackson, John G. *Introduction to African Civilizations.* New York: University Books, 1970.

Jomo, K. S., and Jacques Baudot. Editors. *Flat World, Big Gap: Economic Liberalization, Globalization, Poverty and Inequality.* London: Zed Books, 2007.

Julien, Isaac. Director. *Frantz Fanon, Black Skin, White Masks.* United Kingdom, 1996.

Kanza, Thomas. *Conflict in the Congo: The Rise and Fall of Lumumba.* Harmondsworth: Penguin Books, 1972.

Kellick, David. "On Claims for 'Advanced' Ironworking Technology in Precolonial Africa." In *The Culture and Technology of African Iron Production* edited by Peter R. Schmidt, 247–66. Gainsville: University Press of Florida, 1996.

Kouyaté, Dani. Director. *Keita: The Heritage of the Griot*, Burkina Faso, 1995.

Lacan, Jacques. *Écrits: A Selection*. Translated by Allan Sheridan. New York: W.W. Norton, 1977.

Laure-Folly, Anne. Director. *Femmes aux yeux ouverts*. Togo, 1994.

LeBon, Gustave. *The Psychology of Peoples*. Translated by Lilian A. Clare. New York: G.E. Stechert, 1912.

Leiner, Jacqueline. *Aimé Césaire: le terreau primordial*. Gunter Narr Verlag : Études Littéraires françaises, 1993.

Lucas, Jr., Robert E. *Lectures on Economic Growth*. Cambridge: Harvard University Press, 2002.

Lumumba, Patrice. *Congo My Country*. New York: Praeger, 1962.

MacGaffey, Janet et al. *The Real Economy of Zaire: The Contribution of Smuggling and Other Unofficial Activities to National Wealth*. Philadelphia: University of Pennsylvania Press, 1991.

Maddox, Gregory H. *Sub-Saharan Africa: An Environmental History*. Santa Barbara: ABC-CLIO, 2006.

Martelli, George. *Leopold to Lumumba: A History of the Belgian Congo 1877–1960*. London: Chapman & Hall, 1962.

Massumi, Brian. *Schizophrenia: Deviations from Deleuze and Guattari*. Cambridge: MIT Press, 1992.

Meditz, W. Sandra, and Tim Merrill. Ed. *Zaire: A Country Study*. Washington, D.C.: Federal Research Division, 1994.

Mercer, Kobena. "Decolonization and Disappointment: Reading Fanon's Sexual Politics." *Fact of Blackness: Frantz Fanon and Visual Representation,* edited by Alan Read, 114–31. Seattle: Bay Press, 1996.

Mhando, Martin. "Approaches to African Cinema Study." *http://www.sensesofcinema.com/contents/00/8/africanhtml.* Accessed on 12/8/2005.

Monaco, James. *How to Read a Film: The Art, Technology, Language, History and Theory of Film and Media*. New York: Oxford University Press, 1977.

Mongia, Padmini. Editor. *Comtemporary Postcolonial Theory: A Reader*. London: Arnold, 1996.

Morel, Edmund Dene. *History of the Congo Reform Movement,* critical notes by Wm. Roger Louis, and Jean Stengers. Oxford: Clarendon Press, 1968.

_____. *The Black Man's Burden: The White Man in Africa from the Fifteenth Century to World War I*. New York: Modern Reader, 1969.

Mudimbé, Vumbi Yoka. *L'odeur du père: essai sur les limites de la science et de la vie en Afrique Noire*. Paris: Présence Africaine, 1982.

_____. *Parables and Fables*. Madison, WI: University of Wisconsin Press, 1991.

Niane, Djibril Tamsir. *Sundiata: An Epic of Old Mali*. Translated by G.D. Pickett. Edinburgh: Longman, 1994.

Nietzsche, Friedrich. *Beyond Good and Evil*. Translated by Walter Kaufmann. New York: Vintage Books, 1966.

_____. *The Gay Science*. Translated by Walter Kaufmann. New York: Vintage Books, 1974.

Nnaemeka, Obioma. "Mariama Bâ: Parrallels, Convergence and Interior Space." In *Feminist Issues*. 10.1. 1990. 13–35.

Nzongola-Ntalaja Georges. *The Congo: From Leopold to Kabila*. London: Zed Books, 2002.

Ogundiran, Akinwumi, and Toyin Falola. Editors. *Archeology of Atlantic Africa and the African Diaspora*. Bloomington and Indianapolis: Indiana University Press, 2007.

Rehder, J. E. "Use of Preheated Air in Primitive Furnaces: Comments on Views of Avery and Schmidt." In *The Culture and Technology of African Iron Production,* edited by Peter R. Schmidt, 234–39. Gainsville: University Press of Florida, 1996.

Rivera-Batiz, Luis A., and Paul M. Romer. "Economic Integration and Endogenous Growth." In *Imperfect Competition and International Trade,* edited by Gene M. Grossman, 346–66. Cambridge: The MIT Press, 1992.

Said, Edward. *Orientalism.* New York: Pantheon Books, 1978.

Saussure (de), Ferdinand. *Course in General Linguistics.* Translated by Wade Baskin. New York: New York Philosophical Library, 1959.

Schmidt, Peter R. *Iron Technology in East Africa: Symbolism, Science, and Archeology.* Bloomington/Indiana: Indiana University Press, 1997.

_____. "Cultural Representation of African Iron Production." In *The Culture and Technology of African Iron Production,* edited by Peter R. Schmidt, 1–28. Gainsville: University Press of Florida, 1996.

_____. *Historical Archeology in Africa: Representation, Social Memory, and Oral Traditions.* Lanham: Altamira Press, 2006.

_____. "Reconfiguring the Barongo: Reproductive Symbolism and Reproduction Among a Work Association of Iron Smelters." In *The Culture and Technology of African Iron Production,* edited by Peter R. Schmidt, 74–127. Gainsville: University Press of Florida, 1996.

_____. Editor. *The Culture and Technology of African Iron Production.* Gainsville: University Press of Florida, 1996.

Schmidt, Peter R., and Donald H. Avery. "Complex Iron Smelting and Prehistoric Culture in Tanzania." In *The Culture and Technology of African Iron Production,* edited by Peter R. Schmidt, 172–85. Gainsville: University Press of Florida, 1996.

Shinnie, Margaret. *Ancient African Kingdoms.* London: Edward Arnold, 1965.

Sissoko, Cheick Oumar. Director. *Guimba the Tyrant.* Mali, 1995.

Senghor, Léopold Sédar. *Liberté 3: Négritude et civilization de l'universel.* Paris: Éditions du Seuil, 1977.

Spivak, Gayatri Chakravorty. *The Postcolonial Reason: Toward a History of the Vanishing Present.* Cambridge: Harvard University Press, 1999.

Stengers, Jean, and Louis Willam Roger. Editors. *History of the Congo Reform Movement.* Oxford: Clarendon Press, 1968.

Taiwo, Olufemi. Exorcising Hegel's Ghost: Africa's Challenge to Philosophy." *http://www. und.ac.za/ccms/articles/decolflm.html*

Tomaselli, Keyan G. "Decolonizing Film in Africa: Contesting the Dream Factory." *http://www.und.ac.za/und/ccms/articles/decolflm.htm* Accessed on 12/8/2000.

Ukadike, Frank Nwachukwu. *Black African Cinema.* Berkeley: University of California Press, 1994.

Veltmeyer, Henry. Editor. *Globalization and Antiglobalization: Dynamics of Change in the New World Oder.* Burlington: Ashgate, 2004.

Vieyra, Paulin Soumanou. *Le cinéma africain des origines à 1973.* Paris: Présence Africaine, 1975.

Wesseling H. L. *Divide and Rule: The Partition of Africa, 1880–1914.* Translated by Arnold J. Pomerans. Westport: Praeger, 1996.

Witte (de), Ludo. *The Assassination of Lumumba.* Translated by Ann Wright and Renée Fenby. London: Verso, 2001.

Young, Crawford, and Thomas Turner. *The Rise and Decline of the Zairian State.* Madison: The University of Wisconsin Press, 1985.

Young, Lola. "Missing Persons: Fantasising Black Women in *Black Skin, White Masks.*" In *Fact of Blackness: Frantz Fanon and Visual Representation,* edited by Alan Read. Seattle: Bay Press, 1996.

Index